Praise for *In Line Behind a Billion People*

"The hardest challenge in making sense of China's potential is balancing an awareness of its strengths and possibilities with an appreciation of the obstacles and pitfalls it confronts. Damien Ma and William Adams have found a wonderful, original, and convincing way to portray this tension between China's strengths and its vulnerabilities. I hope that anyone who plans to do business with, or even think about, China will read their book."

—James Fallows, *The Atlantic Monthly*, author of *China Airborne*

"If you want to know what keeps Chinese President Xi Jinping awake at night, read this book. It describes the daunting economic, environmental, social, and political problems facing China with lively, jargon-free writing and highly informative facts and graphs. A readable, balanced and comprehensive account that I'll recommend to anyone traveling or doing business in China, and to college teachers."

—Susan L. Shirk, Chair, 21st Century China Program, Ho Miu Lam Professor of China and Pacific Relations, School of International Relations and Pacific Studies, UC-San Diego

"Looking at China through the lens of scarcity rather than abundance is like seeing an infrared picture of a familiar landscape; all sorts of unfamiliar features pop out. Ma and Adams offer a comprehensive, absorbing, and richly detailed account of the many problems on China's horizon, without falling into boosterism or prophecies of doom. Above all, they underline time and again how China's scarcities will reshape the global landscape. A valuable read."

—Anne-Marie Slaughter, Bert G. Kerstetter '66 University Professor of Politics and International Affairs, Princeton University; former director of Policy Planning, United States Department of State

"Damien Ma and William Adams provide an important lens for understanding China's realities and its future potential. While most of the world's attention has focused on China's astonishing growth, Ma and Adams concentrate on the various types of scarcity—from physical resources to social capital to values and political institutions—that confront its leaders and citizens alike. The volume paints a realistic and sobering picture of the country's profound challenges; it then concludes by placing the future squarely in the hands of political leaders who can still tap huge unrealized potential if they boldly adopt the right reforms. Overall, a stimulating and provocative analysis."

—Kenneth Lieberthal, Senior Fellow, The Brookings Institution

"If you think of China as a country of unstoppable economic and political might, read this book and reflect again. Plain sailing does not lie ahead for Beijing. Adams and Ma argue convincingly that dealing with resource scarcities, as well as social and environmental problems, will almost inevitably replace maintaining high output growth as Beijing's principal preoccupation. Their picture of social and economic conditions in China today and challenges facing the country is in my view remarkably accurate, comprehensive, and up-to-date. The economic miracle of the past three decades has not only reduced poverty on an unprecedented scale, but also generated social tensions and scarcities of many things, including clean air and water, arable land, many raw materials and public goods such as social justice, social security, food-, drug-, and workplace safety, healthcare and education services. The book explains the paradox of rapidly rising living standards on the one hand and growing social unrest and mistrust on the other. It also points to the international spillover effects of scarcities in China. A very readable and important new book on China."

—**Pieter Bottelier**, Senior adjunct professor, Johns Hopkins University; former chief of World Bank Resident Mission in Beijing

"The authors decipher, in a very crucial way, what will really drive China as it becomes the largest economy in the world. China's pace of growth will not be the issue, but understanding the levers of government, society, and business in China is instrumental for anybody who wants to be part of such an unprecedented growth story. A must read for business executives who are serious about doing business in China in the coming decades."

—**Mark Goyens**, Former Asia President of Bekaert, currently business advisor to multinational corporations on growth strategies for China, based in Shanghai

"This book, which draws on the authors' many years of living in China and their close personal and professional relationships there, is not just another polemic damning or praising China. It instead illuminates the realities and anxieties of a country poorly understood beyond its borders."

—**Zhang Bin**, Senior Fellow, Chinese Academy of Social Sciences; Head, Department of Global Macroeconomics, CASS Institute of World Economics and Politics

In Line Behind a Billion People

How Scarcity Will Define China's Ascent in the Next Decade

Damien Ma and William Adams

Vice President, Publisher: Tim Moore
Associate Publisher and Director of Marketing: Amy Neidlinger
Executive Editor: Jeanne Glasser Levine
Development Editor: Russ Hall
Operations Specialist: Jodi Kemper
Marketing Managers: Megan Graue, Lisa Loftus
Cover Designer: Chuti Prasertsith
Managing Editor: Kristy Hart
Project Editor: Andy Beaster
Copy Editor: Keith Cline
Proofreader: Debbie Williams
Indexer: Lisa Stumpf
Compositor: Nonie Ratcliff
Manufacturing Buyer: Dan Uhrig

FT Press offers excellent discounts on this book when ordered in quantity for bulk
purchases or special sales. For more information, please contact U.S. Corporate
and Government Sales, 1-800-382-3419, corpsales@pearsontechgroup.com.
For sales outside the U.S., please contact International Sales at
international@pearsoned.com.

First Printing September 2013

ISBN-10: 0-13-313389-3
ISBN-13: 978-0-13-313389-9

Pearson Education LTD.
Pearson Education Australia PTY, Limited.
Pearson Education Singapore, Pte. Ltd.
Pearson Education Asia, Ltd.
Pearson Education Canada, Ltd.
Pearson Educación de Mexico, S.A. de C.V.
Pearson Education—Japan
Pearson Education Malaysia, Pte. Ltd.

Library of Congress Control Number: 2013939746

Damien: For Catherine Hagbom Ma

William: For Fei Yang and Eleanor Adams

Contents

Acknowledgments

This book owes a great deal to the teachers and mentors who shaped our intellectual foundation and that of the contemporaries of our generation. Without standing on the shoulders of giants, this book would not have been possible. Wrestling with the complexity and uncertainty of China has always been a full-contact sport, requiring language skills, cultural acumen, patience, and a healthy dose of on-the-ground experience. It also requires a body of inherited knowledge, whether from those in academia, government, media, private industry, or other practitioners, who paved the way for each successive generation to continue the work of understanding the most important rising power of the 21st century.

To all those mentors and teachers (you know who you are), we owe a great debt of gratitude.

In addition, we want to specifically thank, in no particular order, Jim Fallows, Evan Feigenbaum, Tom Orlik, Pieter Bottelier, Ken Lieberthal, Susan Shirk, Anne-Marie Slaughter, Mark Goyens, Zhang Bin, Jeremiah Jenne, Xiao Yuan, Mary Gallagher, David Gordon, and David Wertime for variously providing useful comments, sharpening our analytical frameworks, and for simply being comrades in arms when it comes to the study of China. And to the China-based journalists, who continue to bring today's China to a Western audience, our work would have been worse off without all your hard work. We also want to thank our editor Jeanne Glasser Levine for shepherding this project, our biggest to date, to its finish line.

We also gratefully acknowledge our employers past and present, especially The Paulson Institute, The PNC Financial Services Group, Eurasia Group, and The Conference Board, for the invaluable insights into China that our colleagues, mentors, and clients have shared with us. Bill also gratefully acknowledges the University of Pittsburgh and its University Center for International Studies and Asian Studies Center for graciously allowing him access to the institutions' world-class China library. And of course, this book represents solely the authors' views and not necessarily those of these fine institutions.

Last but not least, we want to thank our wives, Fei and Catherine, who begrudgingly read and commented on some drafts to humor us. Clearly, we talk about China too much.

China is a country that often surprises and defies attempts to pin it down into simple dichotomies or frameworks, which is why we never get tired of dissecting it and "figuring it out." Bringing a sense of complexity and reality to observing today's China is why we decided to write this book. We hope that you enjoy reading it as much as we did writing it.

Damien Ma & William Adams

Chicago, Pittsburgh, April 2013

About the Authors

Damien Ma (Chicago, Illinois) is currently Fellow at The Paulson Institute, where he focuses on investment and policy programs, as well as the Institute's research and think tank activities. Previously, Ma was a lead China analyst at Eurasia Group, a political risk research and advisory firm. He specialized in analyzing the intersection between Chinese policies and markets, with a particular focus on energy and commodities, industrial policy, U.S.-China relations, and social and Internet policies. Before joining Eurasia Group, Ma was a manager of publications at the U.S.-China Business Council in Washington, D.C. He writes regularly for *The Atlantic Monthly Online* and has been published widely, including in *Foreign Affairs, The New Republic, Slate,* and *Foreign Policy*. Ma is a term member of the Council on Foreign Relations.

William Adams (Pittsburgh, Pennsylvania) is currently Senior International Economist for The PNC Financial Group. At PNC, Adams serves as spokesman on global economic issues and is responsible for its forecasts for China, other major emerging markets, and the Eurozone. Formerly resident economist at The Conference Board China Center, Adams has published extensively on China's economic and financial reforms. He is a center associate and advisory board member of the University of Pittsburgh Asia Studies Center and a member of the economics advisory board of the Duquesne University Palumbo Donahue School of Business.

Introduction

One Beijing morning in early November 2012, seven men in dark suits strode onto the stage of the Great Hall of the People. China's newly elected Chinese Communist Party (CCP) Chairman Xi Jinping stood at the center of the ensemble, flanked on each side by three members of the CCP Politburo Standing Committee. It was the outside world's first chance to take stock of the committee that will run China for the next decade—one that will mark many milestones. Under Xi's watch, which is scheduled to last until 2022, China is expected to overtake the United States as the world's largest economy. That moment when it arrives will likely lead many in the West to pontificate about the reshuffling of the global pecking order. Inevitably, they will breathlessly proclaim that having held the world's "gold medal" for largest GDP since around the turn of the 20th century, the United States will have to yield to China, the new "number one."[1]

That Chinese economic growth has been a success is beyond dispute. Since 2005, China has sprinted past Germany and Japan to become the world's second-largest economy. By the end of 2012, with a GDP preliminarily estimated at $8.3 trillion, the gap between China and number-three Japan in terms of economic output is as large as the entire French economy. Little wonder that "an American 20th century yielding to a Chinese 21st century" has become a popular refrain, as a flurry of commentators and authors argue that the world should prepare for the possibility that it will once again be centered on the Middle Kingdom.[2]

The day that China assumes the mantle of world's largest economy will invite both envy and trepidation, and global perceptions could shift rapidly. The approach of this psychological threshold has already led some quarters of the global cognoscenti to declare the irreversible decline of the American idea as the enduring viability of the China model supplants it. Amid the anticipated "declinist" commentary in the United States and elsewhere, however, too few will pause to ask "so what?" Should China's continued rise really inspire such alternating anxiety and cheerleading? Yes, China is almost guaranteed to become the world's leading economic power, but this achievement will paradoxically say less about China's growing strength and influence than conventional wisdom assumes.

That China will eclipse the United States in absolute GDP terms shouldn't be particularly surprising—it is, after all, home to four times the population of the United States. But perhaps the speed with which China has caught up with the rest of the world, a pace that not even China's own leaders anticipated, will be surprising to many. Yet the speed of growth will no longer be the dominant preoccupation of the country. The perennial "bulls and bears" debate on China's prospects, exclusively focused on the state's struggle to maintain rapid growth, overlooks a more fundamental truth.

Either a continuation or an interruption of growth is unlikely to alter the country's sociopolitical core after 30 years of breakneck development. China has, in fact, already weathered several jarring economic cycles since its transition to a market economy, though the country's statistical system obscured the direct effects at the time.[3] If the country were on the verge of economic and political collapse the moment real GDP growth dipped under 8 percent, it would have already collapsed several times by now. In fact, the Chinese economy is more resilient to the business cycle than is typically acknowledged.

Yet in spite of this, the country's economic and political rise will constrain as much as empower it over the next decade. It will be an era in which the country's ability to sustain economic growth becomes less of a concern. What instead will define China is also what has always defined it: scarcity.

The crucial and intersecting challenges of scarcities, both emerging and intensifying, will consume China's custodians over the next decade. Scarcity is the keen lens through which the economic, social, and political constraints that accompany China's rise can be seen most clearly. Economic dimensions of scarcity are perhaps the most obvious and are subject to frequent discussion. China's supplies of natural resources and labor, the critical inputs that have sustained its stellar growth, are increasingly stressed. Resource scarcity is about to force difficult changes in China's growth model, whether the country is prepared or not. Food, too, faces renewed supply constraints as burgeoning Chinese consumption adds a new set of pressures on domestic production. But as previous decades have witnessed, what happens in China can rarely be contained within its borders. These challenges of scarcity will have far-reaching implications for global supplies, global prices, and global politics.

Although they undeservedly receive much less attention from observers outside China, social dimensions of scarcity will pose as much if not more of a constraint on the country as economic scarcity over the next decade. Whether it is healthcare, education, or the social safety net, public goods in China are in short supply even considering the country's level of economic development. Social dimensions of scarcity, more than simple matters of supply and demand, are also symptoms of intensifying Chinese inequality. Over the three decades in which the Chinese government shifted its emphasis from "class struggle" to economic development, the deepening of inequality has coincided with, and in some ways spurred, the emergence of new social classes in China. New categories such as "elite," the "middle class," and the "migrant class" are far cries from the simple bifurcation of proletariat and capitalist during the halcyon days of communism. Most members of all three groups live materially better lives today than at the end of the planned economy in 1978. But unequal distribution of both the burden of paying for public goods and the access to them often overshadows an aggregate improvement in general welfare.

The emergent middle class and migrant class—that is, the two groups that comprise the majority of China's population—find themselves increasingly in competition over access to social welfare services. The country's sheer scale and density virtually guarantees that competition for social goods like healthcare and pensions will be fierce; structural inequality serves to make what is already scarce even scarcer. What's more, rapid changes in China's demographic structure—with retirees multiplying exponentially and the labor pool stagnating—mean that demand for social goods is rising at the same time that future supply remains in limbo, exacerbating anxieties over scarcity.

Migrant and rural grievances center on the scarcity of opportunities for educational advancement and related barriers to their equal membership in urban life. China's public health, education, and retirement systems are designed in part to keep urbanites happy at the expense of rural Chinese; they are biased toward urban areas. These policies ensured urban support of the social and political status quo when city dwellers recognized that the government was prioritizing their privileges over their more easily controlled, isolated, farm-bound country cousins. But today, when "rural" Chinese float itinerantly from city to city and share information instantly over their mobile phones, this old stabilizer has become a political liability.

Urban middle-class anxieties, in contrast, revolve around the indispensable public goods that they cannot simply buy from the private market: principally among them, the guarantee of safe food, clean drinking water, and healthy air to breathe. And even though they stand ahead of rural Chinese in line for college entrance and hospital admission, urban residents, too, feel hard pressed by the scarcity of good job opportunities for a college-educated workforce. More recently, "the good life" they should be able to provide their families has become a moving target as expectations constantly rise one step ahead of reality. This scarcity of public goods is experienced at a micro level, but has profound macro implications. For instance, how can a hamstrung education system generate the human capital to build an innovation economy? How can the "only-child generation" trust their sick or retired parents to the care of a social safety net punctured with holes?

Similarly, political and institutional scarcity will hamper China's global ascent, even as the country marches toward economic leadership. A paucity of individual freedoms, compelling values, and ideological sustenance will constrain the country's progress and undermine its government's amply funded image-building efforts. To be sure, average Chinese people are freer today than ever before to choose their job, their spouse, where they live, the entertainment they enjoy, and the language with which they express discontent with the government—freedoms that make the shrinking body of topics that they *absolutely must not discuss* seem comically anachronistic. Mainstream Chinese do not necessarily believe that a government "by the people" is the optimal option for China. But they do appear to yearn for a government that is "for the people." The issue for most in the Chinese middle class isn't one of better political models but rather one of expectations for transparency, accountability, and legal norms from their rulers. In the age of instant information and constant connectivity, the Chinese public has little tolerance for a dishonest and opaque government.

The Chinese public has up until now accepted the government's grand bargain: staying out of politics in exchange for prosperity. But will they continue to do so when social equality and good governance trump material welfare as their top concerns? As the CCP gropes for a post-economic growth platform for its rule, the scarcity of values, beliefs, ideas, rule of law, and freedoms that are the hallmarks of an open and tolerant political system becomes harder and harder to ignore. Justifying the party's governance will now depend on delivering on middle-class demands for competent, humane, and accountable governance.

The vast majority of Chinese still believe that the state ought to play a strong role in the economy, certainly a stronger one than that played in the United States. But they are no longer content with the outsized role the state played in the past. In various ways, they appear to be demanding that it retreat from the economic and social realms to create more room for individual freedom and the flourishing of innovative and entrepreneurial dynamism—for the modernity to which China aspires. As more and more Chinese people spend time overseas and seeing the country from the outside becomes familiar, the Chinese public is already recognizing that they too have a say in their country and its global image. That is, in fact, how enduring soft power is accumulated.

This book explores the economic, social, and political scarcities that we believe will be China's chief challenges and preoccupations over the next ten years. Each chapter focuses on a priority or theme that will dominate the administration of Xi Jinping and Li Keqiang.

We begin with the most concrete—economic scarcity—and conclude with the more intangible political scarcity.

Economic scarcity

1. Resources: While supplies last

China has pursued an incredibly resource-intensive growth model despite having among the world's lowest per capita supplies of arable land and water. The country's resource scarcity uniquely combines unprecedented intensity of need with massive scale. The transition from an investment- and export-intensive growth model to one focused on domestic consumption will likely sustain economic growth. But the hundreds of millions of Chinese consumers increasingly aspiring to consumption- and energy-intensive lifestyles that would be familiar to any American will impose severe stresses on already strained natural resources. China's scarcity could easily become the world's scarcity over the next decade—and the "China price" may soon refer to expensive natural resources instead of cheap manufactured goods.

2. Food: Malthus on the Yangtze

The Chinese government has strived for decades to preserve food security, impressively achieving the feat of feeding nearly 1.4 billion people. Yet meeting this goal tells only half the story: "food security" as the government defines it omits huge and growing amounts of imported agricultural products that China relies on to keep food, and in particular meat, on dinner tables. Chinese technocrats will turn to better technology and more efficient production to keep food plentiful, but the bar for success may be impossibly high. As demand for meat grows over the next ten years, and China's agricultural land risks shrinking further, its dependence on imports will most likely grow. Food and commodity prices around the world can be expected to rise inexorably as foreign dinner tables become increasingly priced to Chinese scarcity. The mutual recrimination and blame games that rising food prices will likely inspire could make for an era of ugly global politics and diplomacy indeed.

3. Labor: Where did all the migrants go?

Demographics are changing faster than the Chinese government anticipated. The country is on the cusp of a shift from its era of an enormous labor surplus windfall to one in which labor is becoming scarce—from "demographic dividend" to "demographic hangover." This is particularly visible in the migrant workforce, with a younger generation bringing higher demands and aspirations as an older generation exits the workforce. Rising labor costs are pushing manufacturers to replace workers with more machines or to reconsider earlier decisions to relocate production from advanced economies. Within China, the onset of this structural scarcity is helping the economy transition to a more sustainable model of growth. But it is also creating new challenges: rising fiscal obligations, pressure on the national balance sheet, and the potential emergence of a young and unruly migrant-class labor movement.

Social scarcity

4. Welfare: Socialism with Chinese... actually no, not socialism at all

If you think American healthcare is in disrepair, try visiting a Chinese hospital. Rising episodes of hospital violence, including a spate of stabbings, are symptoms of an ailing healthcare system in which corruption and spiraling costs drive patients to extreme action. The horrendous state of the social welfare system is beyond simple demand and supply considerations. A man-made and policy-induced scarcity of reliable, affordable healthcare and an underfunded pension system compound the insecurity of average Chinese people. As demands for a better system grow, the government is struggling to prevent a revolution of rising expectations.

5. Education: Give me equality... but not until after my son gets into Tsinghua

Admission slots in choice schools are scarce in China's intensely competitive educational system. But the very uneven distribution of these scarce opportunities is even more important to understanding education in China, and its role in Chinese society, than is the average degree of scarcity. Beneath the ostensibly meritocratic system of national test-taking lies an educational system that, like much of the country's welfare state, reserves premium opportunities for holders of urban household registrations. One or two generations ago, this was a force for social stability, keeping potentially unruly urbanites invested in the status quo. But today, the educational system's bias toward urban-registered households actually serves to destabilize Chinese city life. That's because of the systematic discrimination against the migrant class, a group that increasingly and perhaps uncomfortably resembles the kind of "proletarian mass" from which orthodox Marxists would expect social revolutions to rise. Something has to give.

6. Housing: Home is where the wallet is

The housing market was a tremendous driver of growth during the first decade of the 20th century. It also served an important role in maintaining social stability: providing wealth to the emerging middle class, job opportunities to the migrant class, and huge fortunes to the elites. It is such a perfect microcosm of everything that makes the Chinese economy tick that economics professors would have to invent it if it didn't already exist. But the tailwinds that made housing an indisputable boon to developers, investors, and tax collectors over the past decade have now turned into headwinds that could hamper economic and social development. Demographic, economic, and political pressures converge to create an impression of chronic scarcity in China's housing market. The threat of a collapsing real estate bubble may preoccupy foreign observers, but it's the pervasive sense of scarcity of affordable housing that remains a pressing concern for the average urban Chinese family.

Political scarcity

7. Ideology: The unbearable lightness of the Yellow River Spirit

Ask any serving Chinese civil servant what the Yellow River Spirit is and your question will likely be met with a dumbfounded look. So it should be unsurprising that tens of thousands of aspiring Chinese civil servants were stumped when they were asked in the final question of the 2011 civil service exam to expound on the meaning of the obscure reference. "Yellow River Spirit" sounds indistinguishable from any number of party slogans—"harmonious society," for example—but in fact means basically nothing. China has begun to select its civil servants in part based on their ability to convincingly defend an ideological cipher, an important skill for members of a political party that no longer knows what it stands for but must still win the hearts and minds of its citizenry. The CCP has for a generation now defined itself through pragmatism, delivering economic growth in exchange for the mandate to govern. But this grand bargain is breaking down, and will become only more fragile over the next decade—drawing increasing attention to the party's ideological scarcity and confusion over what it stands for.

8. Values: What would Confucius do?

Having completely abandoned communism, the political system has to actively recruit members who can convincingly espouse just about any ideology, or none at all. In a country where all moral life is political, the wishy-washy values and fuzzy principles of China's politics translate directly into a level of emptiness in the lives of average Chinese people, who increasingly seek new avenues for spiritual sustenance and collective national renewal. Yearning for deeper meaning in life has fueled one of China's more serious domestic conflicts of the last 20 years—between the government and religious practitioners—which will only intensify as China's last few tottering octogenarian true believers in utopian Marxism pass away. The growth of the middle class and its post-material yearnings creates unprecedented challenges for the Chinese leadership to provide social stabilizers beyond what material prosperity alone can offer.

9. Freedom: Keep on rockin' in the firewalled world

Chinese people indisputably lead much freer personal and political lives today than ever before. But individual political freedoms are still in short supply and unequally distributed. While few seriously champion Western-style democracy in China, many more crave the freedom of expression, of the press, of mobility, and of thought common in almost all developed countries. So far, the state has done a spectacular job at stifling demands for the individual freedoms that it associates with social instability. But society is growing stronger, its demands amplified by new media. The party-state's default impulse to control is increasingly at odds with a middle class that believes more personal freedom *should* be part of the social fabric. Like previous middle-class formations in other countries, the shift from wealth accumulation to rights advocacy is gradually taking place. The government must adapt and respond credibly or risk losing the loyalty of its most important political constituency.

Whatever China has done it has done in a hurry. A decade's time at Chinese speed creates as much change as occurs in other countries over one or two generations. Yet speed, whether it be GDP growth or an aging society, will be counterproductive to the coming era of Chinese development. China can rest assured over the next decade that it will have significantly narrowed the economic gap with the developed world, barring some unforeseen collapse of growth. The gaps that it must now narrow, after much neglect, are social and political. Each one of its challenges is formidable in and of itself. But the convergence of all three—economic, social, and political—will require Beijing to harness all the resolve and ingenuity at its disposal.

The new Chinese leadership faces a stark choice: summon its political will and forge forward boldly, risking destabilizing changes along the way, or keep its finger in the dyke and risk losing itself and the Chinese public to festering, pervasive social discontent. The political system has absorbed discontent and de-escalated seemingly intractable conflicts more than once—whether it can do so again, without significant changes, remains a looming unanswered (and unanswerable) question.

In the meantime, as outside observers expect the world's soon-to-be biggest economy to exert ever more influence globally, and its own population's expectations rise, Beijing's mandarins face an unprecedented post-development narrowing of options and acute pressure to usher in considerable changes to its political economy. It is these intense pressures and the difficulty of managing change that will dictate the country's behavior, ironically making China a very reluctant economic superpower, begrudgingly pulled into the global spotlight.

Ultimately, a balanced and nuanced portrait of today's China is one of a nation of great aspirations, great achievements, and great limitations. China will need to make fundamental changes to its economic and political ecosystems over the next decade to prevent its limitations from overwhelming its aspirations. But the dramatic transformations that have sprouted every ten years or so since the founding of the modern Chinese republic are reasons to believe that changes will come, if not willfully, then by the indomitable force of necessity.

Part I

Economic Scarcity

1

Resources: While supplies last

Tension had been mounting across Beijing for weeks. Rumors of an impending government crackdown flowed freely, made all the more credible by the denials in the official press. Inevitably, violence erupted.

This was on the eve of the car license plate quota system's launch in 2010.

The municipal government had been working for months on a plan to control Beijing's worsening traffic, which threatened to make the city unnavigable. In the final months of the year, rumors began to spread that limits would soon be imposed on the number of new cars registered in the city. Beijingers rushed to buy cars before an unknown new regime made the process exorbitantly expensive or altogether impossible. Inventories dwindled at dealerships across the city. One particularly enterprising Beijing shopper, determined to take home one of the last models at a dealership, smashed one of the car's windows and declared, "This car's broken, let's see if any of you want it now?!"[1] When told there would be a 2,000 yuan ($350) repair fee charged before he could buy the car, he responded, "Fine by me! ... who knows how much a license plate will cost next year?"

Prescient words: Less than two weeks later, the Beijing municipal government announced a quota on new license plates issued in the city, only allowing one-third as many new registrations in 2011 as in 2010. It also imposed new restrictions on the hours during which cars with out-of-town plates would be allowed on Beijing roads. In the post-planned economy era, China's political leaders have mollified average citizens' ire over rising inequality by explaining that to create a prosperous society, some people needed to become wealthy before others. But in Beijing, at least, the rule is now that first-movers could have their own cars. And as for latecomers, they are denied ownership even if they can afford it.

To be sure, Beijing's limits on new car purchases were not unprecedented. In mainland China's most-developed and urbane city Shanghai, which has allocated license plates by auction for almost two decades, the clearing price of a plate now well exceeds an eye-popping $10,000. True to the disparate natures of these two cities, the path to a license plate in each is quite different: Obtaining a license plate in Shanghai requires a pile of cash; securing one in Beijing requires a favorable decision made by a mysterious bureaucrat in a government back room. The end effect, however, is the same.

Beijing's license plate restrictions were a dramatic about-face for a government with a long history of subsidizing the domestic auto industry, as well as related upstream industries like steelmakers. These policies were intensified during the global recession of 2008–2009: sales taxes on small vehicles were cut by half, and rural households were granted 10% subsidies on purchases of cars, light trucks, and minivans during the first quarter of 2009. China first overtook the United States as the world's largest auto market in January 2009, in the depths of the global recession, and has continued growing. Passenger vehicle sales doubled between 2008 and 2010, with sales of trucks and other commercial vehicles not far behind.

As one of China's wealthiest, best educated, and most economically advanced cities, Beijing's experience of China's auto boom is a steroidal microcosm of the country's future as a whole. One in three Beijing households owned a car in 2010; a decade earlier the figure was only 1 in 40. But progress has come at a price. An IBM survey in mid-2010 showed that Beijing had the world's worst traffic, narrowly beating out Mexico City. Los Angeles, the worst-ranked U.S. city, was only number 14 on the list.[2] Since then, the Beijing municipal government has invested huge resources in controlling traffic. In addition to the license plate quota, the capital has built one of the world's largest subway systems in less than a decade and has set the price of a bus ticket at as little as 0.40 yuan ($0.07). These investments in urban transport infrastructure, some of which were galvanized by the Olympics, have kept the city from grinding to a halt. But they have not come close to improving its overcrowding or miserable traffic jams, some of which have lasted for more than ten days.[3]

Two anecdotes from our recent visits to Beijing illustrate the current predicament. Toward the end of a discussion with a Chinese central bank official, one of us offhandedly asked her if she had any plans to visit the United States. She said she might visit Washington (and asked whether that is close to Pittsburgh, where I live). Quite close, the drive there would only take her as long as the drive across town and back (from Haidian district to Yizhuang). Later that day, as I was emerging from a subway station by the well-known St. Regis hotel, what appeared to be a U.S. congressional research junket—an important-looking, middle-aged Caucasian man flanked by a racially diverse squadron of young, tall, attractive, clipboard-wielding aides in serious suits—passed by and entered into the subway tunnel. Gridlock has become Beijing's great equalizer. With the exception of the Chinese president and other high-powered elites who can have the roads shut down for their motorcades, everyone else who wants to make a meeting on time needs to take the subway.

The radical shift from a government that encouraged citizens to buy cars to one that makes it increasingly difficult to do so typifies a pattern of Chinese economic development. Growing incomes may give Chinese households the necessary purchasing power to afford the modern luxuries they see on American sitcoms, but there simply isn't room in China—or in the world for that matter—for so many to consume so much. Despite its many achievements, the Chinese growth engine and middle-class aspirations of a consumption-intensive lifestyle are becoming increasingly constrained by the zero-sum game of natural resources.

Put simply, there is only so much to go around in China, whether the resource is space, energy, water, or food. Some of these constraints are old enough to be ingrained in Chinese culture; others are new. All are large enough that the rest of the world is already feeling their reverberations.

The explosion of Chinese resource demand has drawn attention from investors and commodity analysts to farmers and environmentalists. While their interest in Chinese resource consumption diverges considerably, they can all agree on this simple fact: The Middle

Kingdom's economic rise is the single most important determinant of global resource demand and pricing. It is also a crucial variable in the extent to which the human race depletes or preserves the world's natural endowments.

But this is not the whole truth. China's economic rise over the past three decades has had a broad deflationary effect on labor costs and the price of manufactured goods, bringing benefits to global consumers. In turn, one-seventh of China's industrial output is exported, much of it destined for consumption in advanced economies. To understand how much, just look around and think for a moment about which of the manufactured items in your immediate field of vision were produced using fossil fuels burnt in China. Heavy industries such as aluminum, for example, are disproportionately the largest energy consumers in China, even when compared to other large developing countries (see Table 1.1). Therefore, China's energy crunch is the world's energy conundrum, since so much of the energy-intensive goods consumed globally now originate from China. This existing paradigm has occasionally led to nationalistic charges of advanced economies outsourcing pollution and environmental damage to China, while basking in a sea of cheaper everything.

Table 1.1   Energy consumption by sector, 2011

	China	India	Russia	OECD Europe	Japan	United States
Energy consumption by sector (percent share)						
Industrial	72%	68%	53%	38%	44%	34%
Residential and Commercial	14%	16%	27%	31%	31%	27%
Transport	14%	16%	20%	31%	25%	38%
Total consumption (quadrillion BTUs)						
	78	17	22	59	15	73

Source: U.S. EIA International Energy Outlook 2011 and authors' calculations

But that isn't entirely accurate either. China has deliberately pursued an industrialization and export strategy premised on integrating itself deeply into the global economy. Consequently, it can no more extricate itself from the global economy than the world can be exempt from the negative externalities of Chinese hypergrowth. But those externalities are not reflected in prices, neither domestically in China nor in the end products that line the shelves of Walmart or Home Depot.

If it continues on the current trajectory, China will find itself *constrained* by its resource fate. A more consumption-intensive China will require a changed mix of resources as China rebalances its growth model by de-industrializing, but its resource hunger overall isn't likely to be easily satiated. Even a modestly slowing Chinese economy will not fundamentally alter the resource intensity of development that aims to create the world's largest middle-class society. Ultimately, there are simply not enough resources for all Chinese consumers to ape American lifestyles, not without severe effects on prices and irreversible despoliation of the environment. The global consequences of the gap beginning to close between Chinese and Western standards of living are already vividly apparent. But first things first: To understand how China got here, and where it intends to go, requires an accurate grasp of where it has been.

The Panda Boom

The incredibly successful growth strategy China pursued in the first decade of the 21st century was responsible for the explosion of its natural resource demand. While the recipe for the "China miracle" has been described elsewhere before, it deserves a short recap because of its centrality to the resource predicament Beijing now confronts. Like an adult panda roughly consuming 10-15% of its weight in bamboo daily, the Panda Boom of the past decade gobbled up commodities and energy voraciously. A fairly simple formula made the Panda Boom possible: taming inflation, plus reforms to make state-directed investment more efficient, plus potent pro-savings policies, plus accommodative foreign conditions to absorb newly expanded production.

It's the CPI, stupid

An investment powerhouse like China's is assembled from several base components. First and foremost is one often overlooked by other chroniclers of its economic history: controlling inflation.

Inflation had spun out of control in the early 1990s, when Deng Xiaoping's Southern Tour campaign to revitalize flagging economic liberalization with more investment overheated the economy. Exacerbating the impact of overheating was the ill-timed decision to liberalize prices of most consumer goods that were previously set by fiat in the planned economy, putting further upward pressure on inflation. Beijing's recent experience with the deleterious effect of runaway inflation on political stability—it was one of the key grievances leading to the 1989 student demonstrations—made the government highly sensitive to surging prices. As a result, conservative controls on money supply and investment growth were quickly imposed in the 1990s. They proved effective as inflation progressively dropped to the low single digits.[4] Even today, Governor of the People's Bank of China Zhou Xiaochuan, remaining in his position for another term as the longest serving Chinese central banker, continues to warn about maintaining vigilance over potential inflation.

China's preoccupation with managing inflation is shared by most successful emerging markets. Price stability's paramount importance to emerging markets' growth potential is actually stated most articulately in the creed that the Brazilian central bank includes in every monetary policy statement:

> High inflation rates lead to the increase in risk premia, both for private and public funding, and to the shortening of planning horizons, both for households and companies. Consequently, high inflation rates reduce investment and economic growth potential, in addition to presenting regressive effects on income distribution. In other words, high inflation rates do not originate any lasting results for economic and employment growth; on the contrary, they create permanent damage to these variables in the medium and long terms.[5]

Worry over inflation isn't just confined to the Zhongnanhai policy wonks. It is a wide concern for a public that remains relatively poor. Complaining about the rising cost of living is a favorite Chinese pastime, of both the chattering class and the average Zhou on the street. For most of the Panda Boom era, market prices for housing, healthcare, and many of life's essential services rose faster than average incomes, as rising spending power chased limited goods. But relative to a more typical developing country, China's performance on controlling inflation has been exceptional (see Figure 1.1). It was an achievement born out of necessity, because the government understood that it was the glue holding together the other pieces of the growth machine.

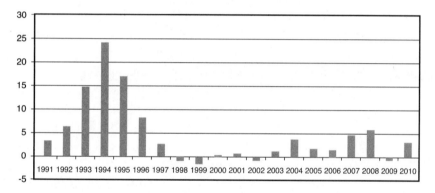

Figure 1.1 Annual CPI inflation, 1991–2010

Source: National Bureau of Statistics

Indeed, taming inflation has played an instrumental role in supporting the Chinese economy's capacity to invest in numerous ways. First, businesses are more confident that investment plans will pay off and not be derailed if input costs grow faster than their product's price. Second, households are encouraged to keep their savings in the banking system, where it can be channeled into investment. Third, price stability supports the foreign exchange value of the currency, making it easier for Chinese businesses to plan for, participate in, and benefit from globalization. Low, stable inflation is one of the most important contributors to growth in developing countries, and China is no exception.

Smashing the iron rice bowl

The Panda Boom's second policy ingredient was fixing the state sector. Liberalization of inefficient state-owned enterprises (SOEs) began in the mid-1990s and accelerated during the 1997–1998 global financial crisis, which originated in Asia. That crisis exposed critical weaknesses of SOEs: Not only were they inefficient, they were also hamstrung by the complex web of price controls on inputs and products.

The endless subsidies doled out to loss-making SOEs had been a chronic drain on central government budgets and weighed down state-owned banks with an unsustainable level of bad loans. Chinese leaders' preferred incremental approach to reforming and opening up the economy wouldn't work for price reform. Allowing one firm to liberalize prices would impose losses on companies downstream, who were prohibited from raising the price of their own products due to the leadership's perennial fear of spiking consumer inflation, even if their inputs had to be purchased at higher market prices. The common folks, or the *laobaixing,* had to be protected, and so state companies tolerated losses and meager margins, as long as they could continue to suckle from the state's coffers. This wasn't sustainable, and everyone knew it. The status quo required an incessant increase in the subsidies keeping inefficient firms afloat and drained resources from more efficient firms—a death by 10,000 transfers, like the one that helped bring down the Soviet Union's economy a decade earlier. A comprehensive solution was urgently needed.

If dramatic price liberalization was off the table, Beijing had to find another way. Such a gambit was distilled into the policy idea of *grasp the large, cast away the small (zhua da fang xiao)*, a consolidation effort on an unprecedented scale. Thousands of small SOEs were restructured, privatized, or just allowed to go bankrupt. As a result, roughly 25 million state employees, who had thought they were promised an iron rice bowl—cradle to grave job protection—faced the trauma of being laid off. Layoffs became so commonplace, especially in urban areas, that a new term *xia gang* was created to describe the situation.

Large state enterprises, those that made up the commanding heights of the economy, were retained as state assets and rolled under the control of a newly created State Assets Supervision and Administration Commission. Firms in strategic industries like energy and telecommunications often expanded in the restructuring process as smaller firms were merged into them or simply exited the market. To help surviving SOEs become more profitable, prices of goods and services produced by the remaining SOEs remained regulated at high levels. The regulatory regime, too, shored up barriers to entry by making competition from new market entrants impossible, boosting the remaining SOEs' profitability and market share. Crucially, the state also absolved SOEs of the responsibility to provide expensive, complex social welfare benefits to their employees.[6] During the heyday of the planned economy, state-owned firms were expected to operate nurseries, elementary and high schools, hospitals, sanitariums, retirement homes, dormitories, guest houses, hotels, and resorts—exclusively serving their own employees at little or no cost, and at a loss to the enterprise.

The role of state banks likewise changed. The Chinese Communist Party (CCP) released them from the obligation to channel deposits into loss-making enterprises and encouraged them to build profitable, self-funded balance sheets. Wiping the slate clean on older bad loans, the banks' nonperforming loans (NPLs) were transferred to government-sponsored "bad banks"—asset management companies back-stopped by the central government. Banks continued to perform some quasi-fiscal roles, such as lending local governments the funds for the ambitious 2008–2010 stimulus program collateralized by government-owned land. In exchange, banks still receive very favorable policy support from the government. However, after the reforms of the late 1990s, banks have also been held to a higher standard for making rational loans that do not go bad. As a result, measured NPLs fell dramatically after the Panda Boom reforms—from 30% of total loans in 2001 to just 1% in 2011—although official statistics likely exaggerate the degree of improvement.

For the state corporations, these reforms were a huge success. Adjusted for inflation, industrial sector profits rose more than seven times between 2000 and 2010, averaging over 20% growth annually. The Chinese corporate sector went from a chronic operating deficit to generating huge streams of surplus cash flow. As a result, China Inc.'s capacity to invest grew exponentially.

The banking sector also had more resources to deploy once it was freed from the shackles of supporting loss-making enterprises. Financial regulators set state-owned bank interest rates at very low levels during the hyper growth era and mandated a large gap between the deposit rates banks paid to savers and the loan rates charged to borrowers. With the economy growing rapidly, deposits yielding less than the inflation rate most years, and loans charging only barely more, it was easy for the banks and the SOEs they financed to be profitable. Money was intentionally kept cheap to fund the massive investments the government believed were necessary for development. And those subsidies had a big impact, particularly on the infrastructure and logistics that reinforced the country's export juggernaut. Relative to its stage of development and national income, China in general has top-notch infrastructure, posing a sharp contrast to the other huge developing Asian economy India.

Under the mattress: Savings gluttony

Yet while state sector liberalization boosted GDP to new heights, it did not translate into an equal improvement in the average household's welfare. SOE reforms were a mixed bag for the employees, to say the least. Urban households raised their precautionary savings as job security deteriorated and SOEs disavowed their responsibilities for providing healthcare, education, and housing to the urban population. The disintegration of the rural healthcare system had the same effect on rural households. And as savings rates rose, the yields paid on bank deposits, the preferred investment of working class Chinese families, fell sharply. The flip side of interest rates kept low to supply cheap funding for infrastructure builders and manufacturers was penurious returns for bank depositors.[7]

Household savers had no choice but to accept the negative "real" (that is, inflation-adjusted) interest rate offered by banks, since regulators effectively prohibited other financial institutions from competing with banks and draining savings out of the official financial system. Households reacted to this policy bias, which favored investment at the expense of savers, by increasing their own precautionary savings to prepare for retirement, reinforcing the liquidity cascading through the financial system. At the end of 2011, the broad money supply (M2, comprising demand and time bank deposits) was 180% of GDP; by comparison, it was 64% in the United States.

But rather than detracting from growth by sapping consumer spending power, sky-high savings rates turbocharged growth. One of the commonalities shared between planned and market economies is that their capacity to invest is basically a function of their savings rate, a relationship well understood by Chinese economic planners.[8]

Ensuring an abundance of savings available to fund investment was the third and related policy component of the Panda Boom.

In addition to compelling households to raise their precautionary savings, China's pro-investment bias also included policies to encourage corporations, and even the government itself, to save to fund an investment-intensive growth model. The state encouraged surviving SOEs to retain and reinvest their growing earnings as they became profitable, rather than paying dividends to the Ministry of Finance, creating a huge pool of retained earnings to invest. Private corporations were encouraged to save, perhaps unintentionally, by the underdeveloped financial system. With no ready access to bank or capital market financing, private corporations needed to retain earnings as a cushion against future cash flow and capital expenditure needs.[9] China's conservative fiscal policy, which kept deficits and public debt small relative to the size of the economy, likewise stimulated abundant financial liquidity by preventing public borrowing from crowding out private borrowers (a common problem in other emerging markets like India in recent years).

Low inflation, a more efficient state sector, and abundant savings unleashed a flood of new investment in productive assets, massively expanding the Chinese economy's potential output and growth rate. The record has been impressive—China over the past decade has nearly quintupled its economy to $8.3 trillion, while averaging a 10% growth rate and obsessively keeping CPI inflation within the 3% to 4% target. But the realization of such enormous growth potential was also predicated on all of the factories with new production capacity securing new sources of final demand for their goods. That demand wasn't to be found at home. Instead, China desperately needed access to markets abroad.

The world ain't so flat, or, good neighbors near and far

Globalization, broadly speaking, was the fourth policy behind the Panda Boom. Playing by the rules of the global status quo has tremendously assisted China's rise, a fact usually only whispered in private in China. The rapprochement and normalization of diplomatic relations with the United States following President Richard Nixon's seminal 1972 trip to China dramatically reduced Beijing's need to expand military capabilities to ward off external threats. Unlike the Soviet Union, China was spared the fiscal and economic burden of an arms race with the United States. Accepting the U.S. geopolitical status quo has maintained peace between China and its 20th century arch-nemesis Japan, as well as uneasy frenemies in Southeast Asia and the Korean peninsula.

A stable regional security environment in the years following the normalization of relations with the United States has allowed Chinese policymakers to overwhelmingly focus on domestic issues. The success and resilience of the bilateral rapprochement can be measured by the relatively low stakes of China's unresolved international disputes—diplomatic "nice to haves" that are more symbolic in nature than core existential "musts," including the disputed status of various barren islands contested by China and its neighbors. Most important of all, Beijing believed the dominant position of the United States in Asia was a stabilizing force. Rather than containing China or balancing against it, as politicians in China and the United States have variously claimed, integration into the U.S.-led international order has been instrumental to China's modernization after the late 1970s.

The Panda Boom era was no exception. China's accession to the World Trade Organization (WTO) in 2001 galvanized global manufacturers, launching a massive migration of labor-intensive links of the global supply chain to Chinese coastal special economic zones (SEZs). Manufacturers had already been attracted to SEZs throughout the 1990s by access to a low-cost and relatively well-educated workforce (nearly all Chinese young people are literate, not true of most poor countries), tax incentives, and often discounted land and utilities. But the holy grail had always been the eventual access to the lucrative 1.4 billion Chinese consumers offered by the WTO deal, an outsized incentive that propelled foreign capital and manufacturing to flood into China.

The mass importation of superior foreign management, technology, and organizational skill significantly boosted the productivity of Chinese manufacturing. Meanwhile, the transfer of foreign firms' experiences and practices rapidly spilled over into the state owned and domestic private sector, as workers adapted to the end of the iron rice bowl by becoming one of the world's most mobile and, complained many managers, least loyal workforces. As a WTO member, China's access to foreign markets, particularly the United States, provided a vital new source of demand for Chinese manufacturers. It also proved timely and important to build stable markets abroad during the disruptive dismantling of the domestic state-owned manufacturing sector.

Similar to previous Asian export powerhouses like Japan, a fixed and undervalued exchange rate tremendously abetted China's globalization. An undervalued exchange rate boosted Chinese competitiveness at the expense of foreign economies. But more importantly, the yuan's peg to the U.S. dollar at a rate much lower than it would have been under more unfettered market conditions kept costs stable for Chinese manufacturers ensconced in global supply chains, allowing them to plan production and pricing in U.S. dollar terms. This would have been impossible under a floating exchange rate regime, because emerging market currencies' exchange rates tend to be volatile, and the primitive Chinese financial system would have been unable to offer adequate tools for Chinese firms to manage foreign exchange rate risks the way manufacturers in advanced economies do. In fact, the yuan's dollar peg played recurring roles in bolstering confidence in the Chinese economy, during the global financial crises of both 1998 and 2008.

In a nutshell, the Panda Boom better situated SOEs to invest, increased the savings available to be invested, and capitalized on foreign markets' capacity to absorb the rapid increase in Chinese output. It was a deliberate process that combined improved efficiency, which economists call intensive growth, and increasing the amount of capital, labor, and natural resources used in production, or extensive growth. The exact share of growth attributable to extensive versus intensive factors is the subject of a longstanding debate among economists that is as passionate as it is obscure.[10] Opinion ranges from the pessimists, who see Chinese growth almost entirely as a result of extensive factors, with little improvement in efficiency possible in a state-dominated economy, to the optimists, who argue that intensive efficiency improvements have been substantial and explain how China sustained double-digit growth so much longer than other emerging markets. Within these range of possibilities, there is a broad consensus that extensive factors account for the majority of Chinese economic growth since the launch of the market economy, and will likely continue to do so for the next decade, albeit with some alterations.

Bamboo consumption continued...

By 2012, signs emerged that the curtains were closing on the Panda Boom era. Indeed, Chinese GDP growth began descending into the single digits in 2011 and even dipped under the symbolically important 8% threshold in 2012, a consequence of both domestic and external factors. Externally, advanced economies were, and will continue to be, mired in a long, slow process of deleveraging for many years, sapping demand for Chinese exports. Domestically, Beijing's efforts to slow housing price appreciation slowed construction and investment activity. A less-bustling Chinese economy translated into softer demand in global resource markets: Oil and iron ore prices were both more than 20% off of their peaks during the first half of 2012.

But those expecting a sustained correction in Chinese resource demand will likely be disappointed. Even as China's growth comes off its heights, there are many reasons to expect its resource constraints to endure. The first is size. China's economy in 2012 is more than three times its size in 2000 in real terms (that is, controlling for the effects of inflation and exchange rates). But the impact of its economic footprint on the rest of the world is arguably larger than this suggests because the Chinese currency is stronger today than it was in 2000, magnifying the ability of Chinese demand to affect global prices.

The second relates to why China's economy has slowed: the government's deliberate strategy to "rebalance" growth away from investment and exports to serve domestic consumer demand. While the consensus seems to have coalesced around the fact that "rebalancing" to a more consumption-based economy will support more sustainable Chinese growth (that is, growth that is less likely to be interrupted by an economic crisis), it is unclear whether this will translate into a reduction of resource demand or whether it simply means that demand will have a different composition. Put another way, what would Chinese consumers want if their economy retooled to serve their needs more rather than government development priorities and consumers abroad? Spacious new houses, shiny new cars, wide new roads, as well as fancy phones and tablets to play with while they're stuck in traffic? Resource-intensive stuff.

Indeed, just as latecomers to industrialization can theoretically leapfrog to adopt the latest technological innovations, latecomers to the global middle class can just as easily ape the kind of resource-intensive lifestyles that exist in developed countries. The predicament that China now confronts is twofold and mutually reinforcing. Even as the hyperindustrialization that characterized the Panda Boom loses some steam, more moderate resource demand from extensive growth in industry will be supplemented by demand from an emergent consumption-driven economy. A slower and modestly rebalanced Chinese economy may not be enough to decouple China's economic development from the constraints of resource scarcity. It is these looming constraints to which we now turn: the intractable problems of managing land, energy, and water.

Land: So much yet so little

One of the CCP's first political campaigns when it secured power in 1949 was land redistribution. Rural landlords saw their assets seized and many were executed for crimes against the peasant class. Urban private property was also progressively nationalized, forcing most urbanites into state-owned housing complexes by the 1970s. Land redistribution was immensely popular among the poor rural majority, and remains one of the cornerstone symbolic steps that the CCP took toward an egalitarian society. In reality, however, even Chairman Mao Zedong could not socialize away the desire for ownership among the Chinese, a notion deeply embedded in historical and cultural roots. Indeed, in a meeting with U.S. President Nixon four years before his death, Mao presciently reflected on his legacy, remarking wistfully that "I haven't been able to change it [China]. I've only been able to change a few places in the vicinity of Beijing."[11]

The chairman's remarks aptly captured the land and property issues of the time. Soon after Mao died in 1976, the communes were dismantled, and with them the collective management of rural land and agriculture. The household responsibility system, which took its place, granted peasant households autonomy to manage agricultural production on a family-controlled plot. It also allowed them to keep any surplus production above the government-mandated target— call it tenant farming 2.0. Today, after years of inaction, the central government is once again experimenting with ways to return land to peasant owners with longer-term (that is, multidecade) leases, to encourage efficiencies in land usage and economies of scale that can dramatically improve agricultural yields. In cities, land remains state owned, but land-use rights of up to 70 years are privately leased and traded and essentially treated as the equivalent of real ownership. With de facto property ownership once again possible, it is vividly clear how little Mao was able to alter the average Chinese's enduring priorities. Deep-seated economic and cultural values dating from the pre-Mao era continue to make real property ownership tremendously important to average Chinese people.

Ownership society with Chinese characteristics

To untangle the social psychology of land ownership, a minor detour into Chinese economic history is warranted. As an avid student of history, Mao seemed to have understood better than his Soviet-trained contemporaries in the CCP that the class divide in premodern China was not between nobles and commoners as in Europe but between landlords and landless peasants. Land's importance was as much as, if not more so, an issue of power than of livelihood. Certainly the CCP's demagoguery of the predatory landlord is full of exaggerations: Not all landlords extracted exorbitant rents, charged usurious interest when a bad harvest or family illness delayed its payment, or manipulated their tenants into debts to indenture them to his descendants. But the unequal relationship between a landlord and his tenants left them much more vulnerable to misfortune, or to the unreliable quality of their landlord's character, than were farmers who owned their own plots. For small-scale farmers, owning a plot was a precondition of economic security, and by extension conferred the kind of autonomy that was far more elusive for tenant farmers.

Moreover, average Chinese have for centuries counted on land and property values to consistently appreciate because their supply is basically fixed, while the population that demands them keeps on growing. In the 500 years preceding the collapse of imperial rule, the Chinese population grew eight times. Generations of successive efforts in draining and irrigating swamps, clearing jungles, and terracing hillsides were only able to increase total land under cultivation by about half as much. And despite improvements in technological inputs and agricultural efficiencies, rising productivity was largely offset by the shrinking slice of land available to the average farmer. In per capita terms, the imperial Chinese economy had basically been in a protracted period of stagnation for half a millennium, even before the drastic decline in living standards caused by the war and dislocation of the collapse of the Qing dynasty. The only reason population didn't outpace cultivated land even more drastically over that half-millennia was the episodic declines in population during plagues, famines, and civil wars of dynastic transitions. Unlike in North America, where population pressures are an abstract concern, China has had intimate experience with overcrowding for half a millennium.[12]

The hyperinflation of the Republican era in the 1930s and 1940s reinforced land's superiority to paper money as a store of value. Money is an IOU from a government and becomes worthless when the government collapses, is overtaken by its enemies, or simply decides not to pay. Legal tender is also easily debased when a regime hits hard times. Land, however, is a real, tangible, productive asset; it retains its value regardless of who the emperor is.

Between 1949 and 1988, China's constitution prohibited land transactions, but the doubling population made land's scarcity obvious even without a rising market price. Over the subsequent 25 years, when transactions of land use rights became legal, China's population grew by 20% again. It is little wonder that the average Chinese today sees investing in real property as a one-way bet.

Legacy problems

With a population of 1.37 billion according to the 2010 census, China uniquely combines an incredibly dense crush of people with tremendous scale. Geographically it is the world's third- largest country after Russia and Canada, roughly the same size as the United States and about a tenth larger than Brazil. But China's population is more than four times America's and seven times Brazil's. To drive home the point, as many people live in China as combined live in the United States, Indonesia, Brazil, Nigeria, Japan, Pakistan, and Bangladesh. Compounding the squeeze, about half of China's land area is sparsely settled desert and treacherous mountain ranges.

What this means is mind-boggling population density, underscored by the statistic that 19 out of 20 Chinese people live in the half of the country near the Pacific Ocean. China has roughly one square acre of arable land per person, less than a third of the supply in the United States. In fact, the city of Shanghai is so dense now that it claims nearly 17,000 people per square kilometer in the downtown area, 2.5 more than in Tokyo.[13] Such density may be unfathomable to an average American, even a New Yorker, for whom space and land constraints are entirely moot in comparison. But it is a Chinese norm to which most have resigned (see Figures 1.2 and 1.3).

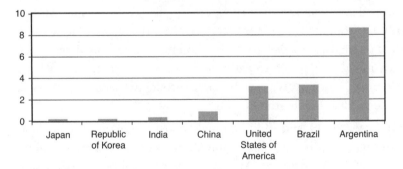

Figure 1.2 Agricultural land per capita (acres)

Source: FAOStat, authors' calculations

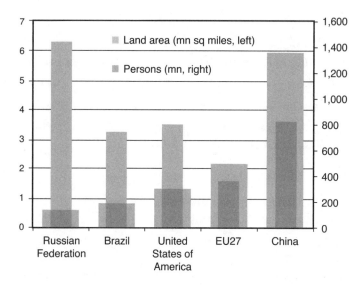

Figure 1.3 Population density across various countries

Source: FAOStat; data for 2009

Adding to historical anxieties over agricultural land adequacy is the pressure on land supplies from urbanization and industrialization. Lester Brown's 1995 study of China's food supply pointed out the daunting challenges the country faces as it modernizes. Japan, South Korea, and Taiwan, the East Asian tigers that preceded China on the road to modernization, all became major food importers as they industrialized and converted rural land to urban use.[14] Increases to agricultural productivity due to modern technology and crop varieties were more than offset by the loss of land to urbanization, industrial use, and road construction in those countries. The Chinese government, however, appears determined to prove Brown and other skeptics wrong, as they attempt to maintain domestic food production to guarantee food security as the Chinese government defines it—which generally means maintaining 95% self-sufficiency in the staple foods that form the basis of the Chinese diet, and within that, 100% self-sufficiency in grains.[15] This is in part driven by the political logic of the low-inflation bias that was so central to the Panda Boom. Relinquishing domestic food supplies to the whims of the global market could mean importing inflation, something that economic planners cannot yet stomach. Instead, the government is hoping to somehow engineer an escape from its resource fate.

Energy: From industry to transport and residential

In 2011, China's energy consumption grew 7%, its fastest pace in four years, and reached 3.5 billion tons of standard coal equivalent, about doubling what it had been a decade earlier. The previous year (2010), the International Energy Administration (IEA) stated that China had already surpassed the United States as the largest energy consumer in the world, leading to stern denials from Beijing and questioning of the IEA methodology. Whether China is already the largest energy consumer today is a moot point: The question is not if, but when.

Irrespective of breaching this psychological threshold, China's already formidable impact on global resource demand and pricing is undeniable. Over the next decade, what will it mean for global energy demand if the middle-class "Chinese dream" turns out to be a near-carbon copy of the American dream? Two cars per family, a house with a backyard, and a daily commute in from the suburbs? Among other things, it would mean a China that consumes ten times more energy than it does today. Even if there were enough physical space for Chinese consumers to live such American lifestyles, there are probably not enough traditional energy resources—oil, coal, natural gas—in the world to fully realize that dream.

The entry of hundreds of millions of Chinese into the global middle class in the first decade of the 21st century already offers hints of what an even modestly more Americanized Chinese consumer future will mean. For instance, although it accounted for less than a tenth of the oil consumed globally over the decade, China accounted for about half of all global growth in oil demand and an even larger share of demand growth for other types of energy (see Figure 1.4). Over that decade, the structural makeup of the economy—focused on manufacturing, heavy industry, and real estate—was primarily responsible for propelling unbridled energy-intensive growth, gobbling resources like a panda would bamboo. But the final demand behind this industrial restructuring—the ultimate customer for those manufacturers and real estate developers—was supplied by Chinese families buying cars and houses and the need for infrastructure to support their newly modern lifestyles.

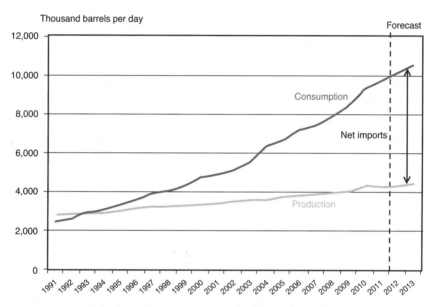

Figure 1.4 Chinese oil production and consumption, 1990–2013

Source: U.S. Energy Information Administration International Energy Statistics and Short-Term Energy Outlook (Aug 2012)

The oil market aptly illustrates China's effects on commodity pricing. With rising Chinese demand, oil prices shot up ten times faster than inflation in the first decade of the 21st century. Of course, blaming skyrocketing global oil prices on China is controversial, virtually taboo inside China, and oversimplifies global dynamics. In the high-growth emerging world, China does not exist in a vacuum: India, Indonesia, and Brazil also contributed to global resource demand growth during the Panda Boom. And policies pursued in the developed world were also pushing up oil prices. Central banks for most of the developed economies set interest rates below the inflation rate during much of the first decade of the 21st century, which inflated the price of oil along with other real assets. The growth of financial instruments making it easier for investors to indirectly purchase oil and other real commodities over the last 20 years has also pushed their prices up, by adding investment demand for commodities as a store of value to the real demand for commodities as inputs to economic activity.

Caveats aside, however, Chinese growth and industrialization is likely a bigger reason behind the oil price boom of the first decade of the 21st century than these other concurrent causes. That China was by far the biggest contributor to emerging market growth during that decade, and remains so today, most obviously implicates it.[16] But the more important link between the Panda Boom and skyrocketing oil prices was the role commodity prices play in linking China's economic conditions with the rest of the world. New wealth and spending power swelled rapidly, which in most economies would fuel inflation since the supply of goods grows more slowly than the demand for them. But the boom also kept manufactured goods rolling off of assembly lines even faster than Chinese consumers could buy them, holding down prices of manufactured goods instead of lifting them. By contrast, oil and the other imported natural resources essential to Chinese growth were not produced much more efficiently in 2010 than ten years earlier.[17] The Chinese government could control the value of the exchange rate and could prevent workers from organizing unions and forcing higher wages, but it could not control the U.S. dollar price of imported commodities.

It isn't simply or even primarily about oil. China remains a predominantly coal-based economy—about 70% of primary energy mix—and will continue to be over the next decade (see Figure 1.5). Even given the abundance of domestic coal supplies, China peculiarly became a reluctant net importer of coal over the past several years because transport bottlenecks drove up prices of domestic coal, making it uncompetitive with imports. If energy security has a similar emphasis on autarky as food security, then China has failed spectacularly at it. Same with natural gas, where domestic consumption has significantly outpaced domestic production, leading to a search for gas supplies from Australia to Russia. Indeed, if Chinese government projections are correct, China will need to import over 50% of its gas by 2020. Variations exist, but the Panda Boom's effects are visible across the menu of commodities: Between 2000 and 2010, prices of imported coal and oil tripled; imported iron ore prices rose almost four times.

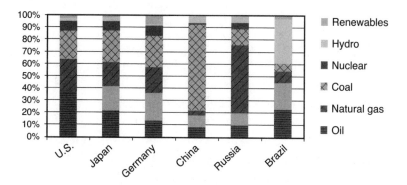

Figure 1.5 China's coal consumption overwhelms developed and developing countries

Source: BP Statistical Review of World Energy, 2012

A larger, slower-growing, more consumer-focused economy will not magically make the economy less energy intensive after the Panda Boom. True, energy demand is changing: What has been may not always be. It is possible that gradual de-industrialization of the economy combined with modest de-carbonization policies will lead to slower growth in the consumption of coal, gas, and oil. But slower-growing energy consumption by Chinese industry, directly tied to the Panda Boom, will likely be supplanted by the shift toward the consumerist future of energy consumption: demand from the transport and residential sectors.

The mode of urbanization that China has already chosen as the key driver of its economic growth over the next decade will crucially influence the type of energy resources around which its economy will develop. An oil-dependent U.S. economy was a consequence of the support of an auto industry and the attendant expansion of a national highway system. China, incidentally, already has a highway network that is second in length only to that of the United States and a growing middle class whose car envy is unparalleled, irrespective of government restrictions. Moreover, with another 100 million rural residents expected to move into cities over the next decade, the energy required to build, power, and move people around the traditional mega-metropolises and the new urban jungles will be substantial. Even if the lifestyles of individual Chinese only reach half of the resource intensity of Americans, China's enormity will still dramatically affect energy demand and commodity prices. The rise of a consumption-driven Chinese middle class is just a new chapter in the history of energy-intensive Chinese growth.

Scenario simulations are a common tool in the energy industry to manage the huge uncertainties and long time horizons required to plan for new energy development. The Lawrence Berkeley National Laboratory has compiled various scenario projections on China's energy consumption trajectory, including a set corresponding to the optimistic projections of Chinese National Development and Reform Commission's Energy Research Institute (see Figure 1.6). Within this large range of possibilities, none of the scenarios see energy consumption peaking before 2030, with the most optimistic projecting flat growth after that year. Such an optimistic scenario will require both considerable low-carbon policy incentives and rapid diffusion of disruptive energy technologies that could dramatically alter China's energy future. China's trajectory today suggests far more fossil fuel burning in the country's future than this projects.

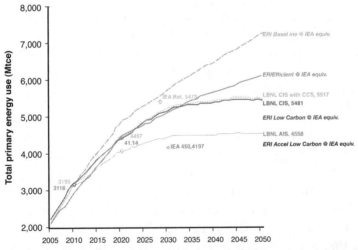

Note: AIS is Accelerated Improvement Scenario, CIS Continued Improvement Scenario, IEA Equiv. refers to converting EI's numbers EOIA equivalent given that EI follows the convention of using power generation equivalent, rather than IEA and LBNL's use of calorific equivalent, to convert primary electricity. This results in a 3.01 lower gross energy content for renewables and biomass.

Figure 1.6 Scenario projections of China's future energy consumption

Source: Lawrence Berkeley National Laboratory

To be sure, China has promoted extensive penetration of renewable energy, as well as nuclear power, as one method to diversify away from coal and reduce dependence on fossil fuels. By 2015, China hopes to have renewable energy account for 9.5% of total energy consumption, up from about 8% today. Nuclear will be only about 2%. But that leaves nearly 90% of energy demand to be satisfied by fossil fuels. The reality is that the current pace of renewable penetration is simply insufficient to meaningfully alter China's resource constraints over the next decade. To do so would require a transformative energy technology at a much lower cost than is yet on the horizon.

Import dependence as Achilles' heel

China's resource fate isn't simply a matter of supply and demand constraints. The Panda Boom's insatiable appetite for energy, a direct result of its economic growth model, has thrust China into an unwanted prominent role in 21st century energy diplomacy. China has swung from a tradition of economic isolationism to vulnerability to global volatility in a single generation, creating unanticipated complications for its foreign policy.

Chinese foreign policy was hardly imbued with such complexity before the Panda Boom. It was rhetorically aligned with the international movement of socialist developing countries, though in substance it amounted to not much at all beyond China's immediate neighborhood. Even before its modern era, China's foreign policy has for centuries supported a splendid economic isolationism. In the Ming Dynasty, the Chinese armada under Admiral Zheng He charted much of the Indian Ocean and Southeast Asia before Christopher Columbus was born, only to abandon looking outward when a new emperor found engagement with foreigners inadvisable. In the late 18th century, the Qianlong emperor snubbed a British trade mission bearing technologically advanced gifts, sniffing, "There is nothing we lack ... We have never set much store on strange or ingenious objects, nor do we need any more of your country's manufactures."[18] China's indifference to foreign imports so frustrated Western interlopers that the British eventually resorted to smuggling opium into China in the 18th and 19th centuries to balance their trade deficits; it was the only foreign product the Chinese could be made to buy.

In line with this tradition, until relatively recently Chinese leaders assiduously ensured an autarkical energy security policy, basically consisting of self-reliance. Only 25 years ago, China was a negligible player in global energy demand. In fact, it was a net exporter of petroleum products extracted from oil fields concentrated in its far west and northeast.

The massive accumulation of productive capital and real estate during the Panda Boom forced China to look outward to feed its industrial engine. The view they found is dismaying. The energy status quo beyond China's borders appears distinctly disadvantageous to the country, on both economic and security terms. The ease with which Western nations could disrupt Chinese access to Middle Eastern oil during a military conflict is deeply unsettling to a government used to energy self-sufficiency. More unsettling is that even the purported Western hegemonies, particularly the United States, are helpless to control the wildly gyrating prices of the global oil market. In its overseas sojourns, China has befriended oil-producing pariah states whose isolation makes them willing to enter into long-term exclusive supply contracts, at prices insulated from market fluctuations, in return for Chinese investment in local infrastructure and development.

This strategy has produced mixed successes; energy producers with broader choices of customers like Canada have occasionally balked at Chinese investment in domestic resources, and China (at least today) lacks the strategic influence necessary to compel its suppliers to play along. Energy diplomacy with Chinese characteristics, it turns out, is a huge pain to execute in reality. China has repeatedly found its overseas ambitions frustrated when backing the wrong horse in authoritarian petrocracies. Chinese oil companies experienced huge financial losses across the Arab world, from which it sources half of its petroleum imports, when the Arab Spring toppled the dictators who had agreed to Chinese investment.

Similarly, its courtship of the Sudanese government has been a huge headache. CNPC, the omnipotent state oil major, entered Sudan in 1996, taking ownership stakes and winning operator rights for several major oil fields. Their presence brought the Chinese government under intense international pressure for its support of the Sudanese government, which has been accused of genocide in southern Sudan. China turned a blind eye to Sudan's civil war, citing its policy of noninterference, but is now unable to ignore what it previously described as Sudan's internal affairs: South Sudan won its independence as a sovereign state in 2011. Subsequent to winning independence, South Sudan shut down the pipeline linking CNPC's oil fields to the Sudanese coast as the two governments argued over revenue sharing between the south and north; the South Sudan government is also pressuring China to finance a new oil pipeline that will reach the ocean through Kenya, circumventing China's friends in Khartoum in the north.

China's vast appetite for energy makes it increasingly impossible to live up to its stated policy of noninterference and neutrality overseas. Regardless of whether China accepts market prices or negotiates sweetheart deals, its demand is so vast that it cannot anonymously buy in the market; it is the market.[19] China's vast economic clout inevitably makes it a player in regional conflicts in which the participants are determined to force the Chinese to take sides. But China, still lacking diplomatic heft and military clout, is far from a new United States in the region. As the United States retreats from Middle Eastern oil dependence, China is confronted by its uncomfortable and growing vulnerability to the political vicissitudes of a volatile region.

Dependence on limited foreign resources is the Panda Boom's most serious weakness; it would be the panda's Achilles' heel if pandas had ankles. Former Premier Wen Jiabao famously criticized Chinese economic growth in 2007 for being "unstable, unbalanced, uncoordinated, and unsustainable," in part referring to its vast consumption of finite natural resources. Though Wen was referring to the domestic economy, his descriptive labels apply as accurately to a Chinese foreign policy held hostage by the pursuit of that elusive energy security.

Water

In a famous passage from his totemic *Wealth of Nations*, Adam Smith reflected on the paradox of water's cheapness: "Nothing is more useful than water: but it will purchase scarce anything; scarce anything can be had in exchange for it. A diamond, on the contrary, has scarce any use-value; but a very great quantity of other goods may frequently be had in exchange for it." Smith's observation that water is not priced according to its utility and intrinsic value is as obvious as it is profound. Like anywhere else in the world, water in China is essential for producing goods as disparate as the cement walls of a building, the coal that is burned to heat it, and the pork in the dumplings sold by vendors on its front steps.

As China sprinted toward an $8 trillion economy, its thirst for water has grown in parallel with demand for all resources. The cost of water, still viewed as a public good too important to be sold to the highest bidder, is not always readily reflected in its price. But water in China is considerably scarcer than in many other countries, triggering rising costs and pressures across the Chinese economy and society. Smith would have had a very different story to tell had he lived to see the water paradox play out as part of the Panda Boom.

Someone who did foresee how the water paradox would become a central challenge to Chinese growth was Brown, whose study in the mid-1990s focused particular attention on water. What he described was a perfect storm of swelling demand for a finite resource, predicated on a ballooning population, rising consumer demand for modern plumbing and water-intensive meat-rich diets, and burgeoning industrial demand as the Chinese manufacturing juggernaut strengthened.

Chinese officials and scholars hotly contested Brown's predictions when his book was published. The official position was that China would manage resource constraints as necessary to maintain symbolic food security, its ability to feed itself—that 95% self-sufficiency redline for staple foods. Rising agricultural productivity, scientific progress, and the organizational and leadership prowess of the CCP would allow China to overcome its resource constraints. The subsequent two decades of development have largely vindicated Brown's view.

Thirsty industry

That China is a water-scarce country is an open secret. In addition, the Chinese economic planners who decided to embark on industrialization seemed to have cast aside any concerns, compounding the scarcity manifold. When water supplies are overtaxed, they don't just dry up. Instead, they first run black, like the horrific environmental disaster in the Huai River in 2001 documented in Elizabeth

Economy's eponymous book.[20] Or sometimes they run other interesting colors. In 2012, the Quxi River in the eastern Chinese city of Wenzhou ran white after a latex factory spill. Zhengzhou's Qili River ran red the same year when heavy rains washed unidentified pollutants into the river.[21] Lax environmental regulations are rightfully blamed when water pollution disasters spring up in China. But ultimately, stricter enforcement will be confounded if demand on water supplies rises without limit. Each iteration of water recycled from a new plant or residential complex returns it to China's river basins a little dirtier and less usable.

China's water problems are measured in a variety of ways, and the results are universally alarming. The Chinese government tests water resources against standards set in an Environmental Quality Standard for Surface Water, which establishes five separate standards for water quality, ranging from I (most pure, for state natural protected zones) to V (suitable for agricultural use).[22] Levels II and III are considered suitable for human consumption. Level II allows, for example, a maximum lead concentration of two-thirds of the maximum concentration allowed in U.S. drinking water by the EPA, while Level III allows over three times the U.S. limit. According to the Ministry of Environmental Protection (MEP) 2011 report "Fresh Water Environment," more than half of China's largest lakes and reservoirs were contaminated at levels that make them unsuitable for human consumption (see Table 1.2).[23]

Table 1.2 Water quality of various water sources

Water quality	I	II	III	IV	V	Less than V	Main contaminants
China's great lakes: Tai, Dianchi, and Chao	0	0	0	1	1	1	
Large freshwater lakes	0	0	1	4	3	1	Phosphorus, organic compounds
Lakes in cities	0	0	2	3	0	0	
Large reservoirs	1	4	3	1	0	0	

Source: Ministry of Environmental Protection

Similarly, two-fifths of the 469 water testing stations on China's ten largest rivers showed water too contaminated to be safe for human consumption; for four major rivers in north and northeast China (the Songhua, Huai, Hai, and Liao), three-fifths of sites tested are unfit for human use.

The stark degradation of such a vital part of everyday life is apparent to any visitor to China as soon as the jetlag wears off. Anyone coming from a developed country will immediately be struck by the challenges and complications of just getting a drink of water when you don't trust what comes out of the tap: Do you buy bottled? Boil tap water? What about brushing your teeth? What about when you get home at midnight and didn't plan ahead? Longer into a visit, deeper complexities will present themselves: Do you trust all bottled water brands equally? What about the same product sold by a street vendor or your sketchy corner bodega instead of Walmart? It would all seem paranoid if you weren't meeting informed Chinese people worrying about the same things. Like most challenges of adapting to a new place, its novelty wears off as a stay lengthens.

But unexpected incongruities still jump out from time to time: for example, noticing the unsettling absence of birds along the beautifully forested banks of the Three Gorges Dam reservoir on the same day you taste the faint tinge of diluted sewage in a cup of coffee served on a river cruise. Or the foul smell of the Huangpu River coming from the showerhead of a dazzlingly modern five-star hotel room in Shanghai, or the port-a-potty stench that occasionally wafts out of the historic moat around the Beijing center city. The consequences of excessive demands on China's water supply are even tangible during your side trip to Hong Kong, which sits at the mouth of a river system inundated annually with billions of tons of raw sewage.

These anecdotal impressions are the immanent manifestation of residential water supplies stretched far beyond the critical point. China's 4,727 underground water-quality testing stations under 400 cities show three-fifths of all water supplies rated "relatively bad" or worse (see Figure 1.7).

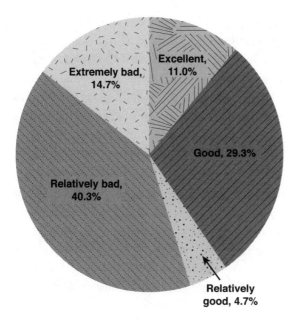

Figure 1.7 Groundwater quality, 2011

Source: Ministry of Environmental Protection

China's MEP also announced that roughly half of all rural residents lacked access to safe drinking water around the time it released the 2011 water-quality report. In some of the more arid regions of China—for instance, the Chinese capital—the repercussions of water overusage extend beyond pollution. The excessive tapping of underground water has led to serious land subsidence, a phenomenon that is basically equivalent to the earth sinking because groundwater is not replaced. Even Shanghai is afflicted with land subsidence, with the weight of its skyline compounding water overextraction to weigh down the land, an unpleasant thought as each additional skyscraper is erected to complete the futuristic skyline. Tianjin has severe subsidence problems in which offshore petroleum extraction compounds water extraction. For these and other coastal cities, subsidence brings large swathes of densely inhabited territory closer to sea level, or even below it, increasing their vulnerability to flooding and tidal surges.[24]

The Chinese government is turning to dubious feats of engineering to mitigate the constraints of scarce water on its development, most spectacularly with the South-to-North Water Diversion Project.

This massive public works project will divert water from the relatively water-rich south to the parched north. Like the Three Gorges Dam, the Diversion Project was first proposed in the 1950s, requires huge and technically complex feats of engineering to complete, and creates new vulnerabilities to Katrina-style intersections of natural disasters and failures of public engineering. But the dire straits of northern China water shortages—recall again that the most degraded river systems named by the MEP are all in the north—call for desperate measures.

China's government, like most governments, has avoided pricing the scarcity of water into user fees, partly because high water prices would regressively squeeze the incomes of millions of impoverished farmers still toiling in its countryside. But in the coming decade, it may have no other option.[25] Populations, incomes, and factories all continue to multiply across China, and they all demand water. Nothing is so useful yet so scarce.

H2O politics

Just as Chinese demand for oil is pushing the country into unfamiliar, messy foreign entanglements, its thirst for water resources stokes tensions with its Southeast Asian neighbors. The Mekong River Delta is the nexus of these tensions. The Mekong is the world's longest river, spanning most of Southeast Asia. It flows out of China's southwestern Yunnan Province into Burma, Laos, Thailand, Cambodia, and Vietnam. Mirroring their practices on river systems throughout the country, the Chinese have built a number of new dams along the Mekong in recent years. The difference is that China's renewable energy initiatives, particularly its focus on hydroelectric power, are slowing the river's flow when it reaches China's downstream neighbors, threatening the health of Southeast Asian fisheries and water security. Water levels in the Mekong Delta reached their lowest levels in 50 years in 2010, causing obvious discord between China and neighbors. The Chinese government attributes low water levels to drought, and Southeast Asian governments attribute them to unsustainable water use, with China as the obvious but unnamed culprit.

Longer term, China's neighbors will want their water back with interest. Poor countries across Southeast Asia are watching China enviously and taking notes on the fastest pathways to leapfrog from poverty to prosperity; their water demand will rise just as surely as China's when they crack the Panda Boom code. India is a prime example: 20 years behind China economically, with 1.2 billion people and faster population growth, and per capita water resources even more limited than China's own. After years of arguing that more developed countries (that is, the West) should wink at resource overexploitation in developing countries—after all, that's how today's wealthy countries developed in their day—China may find itself pushing back against its poorer neighbors in the coming decade because "there is not enough water in Asia for everyone to live a Chinese lifestyle."

Foreign analysis of the risks to China's economy usually focuses on growth: whether the Chinese government can maintain it, whether the statistics measuring it are real or fabricated, and whether the economy would collapse if it slows. But growth is not China's problem. The Panda Boom worked spectacularly by ramping up aggregate investment and concentrating it in infrastructure, capital equipment, and other real assets that increase the economy's capacity to produce in the long term. Rather than growth, the Chinese economy's greatest dilemma is scarcity—how to ensure sufficient supplies of energy, land, and water to support ever-expanding production and consumption. In other words, what is China to do when the panda eats through all the bamboo shoots?

2

Food: Malthus on the Yangtze

Ensuring the Chinese people have plenty of food arguably counts as one of the greatest achievements of the Chinese government. A book about scarcity also demands equal praise for the achievement of plenty. In countless conversations with disaffected or apathetic younger Chinese, nearly everyone notes his or her grandparents' deep loyalty to the state despite the litany of contemporary problems that the country confronts. Chinese people over the age of 70 today, who were alive during the tumultuous civil war preceding China's founding, often recount the mantra that "a full stomach is enough" (*neng chibao duzi jiu keyi le*). As simple as it may sound, it was an aspiration not to be taken for granted by Chinese of that generation.

That generation remains so intensely aware of the government's success at keeping the population fed partly because of the catastrophic failure to do so in the earlier years of the people's republic. The worst manmade famine in modern history remains deeply etched in the psyches of its survivors: the Great Leap Forward of the late 1950s, a colossal, self-afflicted atrocity that led to the deaths of close to 40 million Chinese.[1] In the long view of many older Chinese, guaranteeing a full stomach is of much greater significance than the many impositions and tribulations of a lifetime under authoritarian rule or the corruption and inequality of today. *Neng chibao duzi jiu keyi le.*

Younger Chinese, though, tend to have a much less visceral relationship with food security, and dramatically less gratitude for the government that has ensured it, than do their predecessors.[2] The Chinese government has virtually eliminated a fundamental form of scarcity so effectively that its achievement is fading from collective consciousness. Herein lies one of contemporary China's more interesting contradictions. Among these elderly loyalists savoring each day's full stomach live more overweight and obese Chinese than the entire population of the United States.[3] The health effects of changing diets on today's plump generation, living alongside a lean generation that survived extreme deprivation, is a striking reminder of the speed with which China is changing. It is a developing country that is now troubled by developed country problems.

From famine to relative abundance, food has always occupied an exalted place in the Chinese collective imagination. If there is a Chinese essence, then food defines a critical aspect of it. Few countries can compete with the Chinese obsession over their greatest cultural export. From Beijing's elaborate banquet diplomacy and banquet business deals to the ubiquitous greeting of "have you eaten yet?" (*chi fan le ma?*) food pervades Chinese political, economic, and cultural life. The preoccupation with food and historical memory of its severe shortage still heavily inform state policies toward food. Even absent these factors, the government faces the unavoidable daily reality of feeding nearly 1.4 billion mouths, a fact it does not take lightly. Few things are as politically sensitive and culturally imperative.

Unfortunately, food policy and food security are about to get harder. After spending most of the last century underweight, China is now burdened with an overfed middle class, a demographic that will exert new pressures on the country's food security and global markets. China's recent sense of abundance is likely to be fleeting precisely because the country's growing affluence begets behavioral changes that are difficult to correct once unleashed. At least a third of China's citizens, or about 450 million, have yet to attain a standard of living that includes being able to eat meat every day. As they do, swelling demand combined with a land crunch will strain China's capacity to produce its food supply domestically. Each subsequent wave of Chinese entering the middle class will feel entitled to a level of food consumption that could prove ecologically and economically unsustainable, or at least require enormous and risky changes to global agriculture. After sustaining inflated prices of hard commodities like energy and minerals in the past decade, Chinese demand will have considerable effect on prices of soft commodities, especially food, in the next decade.

What's more, though little is known about the precise effects climate change will have on agricultural production globally, signs have emerged that it won't be particularly pleasant. For instance, the extent and duration of the U.S. drought in 2012 caught many by surprise and drove up corn prices substantially. But what happens in Iowa doesn't stay in Des Moines; it is also felt in Henan. That's because corn is the primary feedstock for cattle and pigs, and the U.S.'s drought-induced corn price hike also fed into Chinese pork prices. Already prone to annual floods and droughts, and dependent on imported feedstock to raise the pork, beef, and other meats its population increasingly demands, China is one of the more vulnerable countries to the deleterious impacts of global warming. If climate change leads to more frequent bouts of natural disasters, knock-on effects on the Chinese food supply can be expected to be serious.

The laundry list of looming concerns has compelled the government to overwhelmingly favor supply-side food policies, and understandably so. Food inflation as a result of supply constraints—triggered by natural disasters or political corruption—has often served as a leading indicator of social instability, particularly in poorer developing countries where a disproportionate amount of income is spent on food. The population tends to get angry when a government cannot adequately deliver life's necessities. The global food crisis of 2007–2008, in which an unprecedented rise in the price of food stables led to rioting in a number of poorer countries, remains a fresh memory for most of the world.[4]

Still a developing country, China is well aware of such possibilities and has been particularly adamant about controlling food inflation. One of the first policies the State Council issues each year for the past decade has predictably focused on agriculture, as if to unequivocally stress the importance the government placed on maintaining food security and modernizing the sector that sustains it. But the focus on supply will face considerable limitations over the next decade as middle-class demand balloons. Chinese meat consumption has already risen several-fold, and China has long been an importer of soybeans to feed livestock. China's thin-stretched agricultural capacity could easily translate into a global food price shock should a prolonged natural disaster strike the Chinese heartland.

Allowing itself to be potentially dependent on imported food in a crisis is an unappetizing proposition for the Chinese government, whose attitude toward food security is one of the last realms in which Mao-era autarkic policies still hold sway. Can you blame them? Food *is* indispensable—a human right that the Chinese government staunchly defends, and dependence on food imports requires trust-worthy and stable suppliers. When China looks beyond its borders, such suppliers are far and few in between. But there may be little choice: Without imported food, the government's only other option during a crisis would be to impose rationing to ensure supply. Given the government's already stretched capacity to keep China's opinion-ated and ballooning middle class under control, rationing could be a combustible formula for getting people out on the streets.

Just as threatening to the government are the social tensions that spring from the country's supply-side food policies. Chinese agricul-ture, once famous for the green revolution that magically raised yields, is now becoming infamous for endemic food quality scandals instead. These scandals are in part a symptom of pressures on suppliers to meet rising demand. The government, anxious to maximize produc-tion and minimize costs, and lacking an effective regulatory apparatus to supervise the millions of small household producers in the food supply chain, has been either unwilling or unable to improve the safety of the food supply. As more and more Chinese citizens' expec-tations rise to match their world-class standards of living, third-world food safety is increasingly unacceptable and politically explosive.

That a Malthusian nightmare has not enveloped the world's most populous country can be attributed to the confluence of smart poli-cies and technology's contribution to raising the scale and efficiency of farming.[5] The Cassandras of a coming food crisis in China, such as Lester Brown, have not seen their worst fears materialize.[6] But were their dire warnings wrong or just premature? The scale of Chinese food consumption, questions over whether technological improve-ments can persist, critical water scarcity, and grave food safety issues conspire to make ensuring food security a precarious proposition. The coming decade will be a monumental test of whether Chinese food security will remain intact in the face of a food-obsessed middle class and their children. During the past decade, Chinese demand for fos-sil fuels was often blamed for rising oil prices. Will the next decade see developing countries casting blame on Chinese consumption for rising food prices? Either way, China's food problems will certainly be a global problem that could increasingly price the average Iowan's dinner table to Chinese demand.

Feeding one-fifth of humanity

With roughly 20% of the world's population but only about 8% of its total arable land, China's unmatched scale and density put it into a unique category when it comes to food security. The Chinese government, probably more than anyone else, understands where to prioritize agricultural policy: at the top. Leaders since Mao Zedong have deep scars from witnessing the horrors their botched food policies have wrought. An entire generation of Chinese survivors of the Great Famine, including one of the author's parents and the current Chinese president, will not allow for another monumental failure of public policy when it comes to food. Since the Deng Xiaoping era, China has been largely self-sufficient in providing many crucial foodstuffs to its exploding population, defying skeptics of the ability of the country to feed itself. It is a remarkable feat that validates the reform policies practiced under Deng.

Agriculture was the first and arguably the greatest beneficiary of the reform dividends generated by abolishing collective farming communes in the 1980s. The utopian commune system established in the 1960s and 1970s was meant to raise productivity by creating economies of scale, but instead hobbled the economy by removing farmers' incentives to boost efficiency. In the communes, village leaders assigned each farmer points based on labor hours worked, which then determined how much produce the worker received. Since each laborer basically worked the same amount of hours or days as any other worker in the collective, everyone received roughly the same amount of food provisions. Free-riding opportunities were numerous and agricultural production languished, leaving China barely able to feed a growing population.

Enterprising village leaders didn't always follow the rules, however. By the late 1970s, some farms were already experimenting with a land contract system that allowed farmers to lease land from the village and take control over its own grain production—tenant farming with Chinese characteristics. One of the poorest provinces, Anhui, is usually considered the pioneer of this contracting system. Despite opposition from other provincial leaders and conservatives within the government, these local experiments received top leaders' blessing in 1980 in the so-called Document No. 75. Over the next couple of years, the State Council reaffirmed support for the practice, rapidly making it national policy under the name of the *Household Responsibility System.*[7]

Farmers could suddenly contract plots of land and sell any agriculture production in surplus of their government quota for profit, creating powerful new economic incentives to transform the Chinese countryside. According to Jikun Huang and Scott Rozelle, by 1984, nearly all farmland was under contract to farmers, typically for 15-year periods.[8] Though far from privatizing land, the stability created by land-use rights was enough to provide assurance to farmers that they would be able to reap the benefits of at least some improvements they made to their plots of land. The government stopped short of conferring full land ownership rights, however. That was too bitter of a capitalist pill to swallow for a party founded by landless peasants.

The land contract system's impact on agricultural production was swift and profound. For the next couple decades, Chinese farmers maintained production growth rates for most commodities of about 4% per year, faster than population growth (grains and cotton being notable exceptions). Production grew rapidly after 1978 at the same time that the agricultural labor force shrunk by more than half, sustained by more efficient production (see Figure 2.1).

In addition to better policy, better technology also supported higher agricultural yields. From the mid-1980s on, the success of Chinese agricultural production depended much more on technological advancements, fueled both by adoption of foreign technology as well as indigenous research and development (R&D). Often, foreign agricultural technologies were difficult to adapt to Chinese cultivation. Substituting machines for people, for example, is an obvious low-hanging fruit of introducing technology into agricultural production. But in China, rice cultivation has always been labor intensive rather than capital intensive. The bucolic and Monet-esque rice fields terraced into hillsides, charmingly featured in the pages of *National Geographic,* resist easy application of off-the-shelf agricultural equipment developed in advanced economies. So, innovation in rice cultivation instead focused on devising hybrid rice and fertilizers, which China commercialized in the 1990s. These actions raised rice yields dramatically, though progress has slowed in recent years.[9] Meanwhile, Beijing stepped up R&D spending on agricultural biotechnology in the 1990s and continues to champion genetically modified foods. These efforts seemed to have paid off. The core efficiency of agricultural production, what economists call agricultural total factor productivity, increased by an average of 3% to 5% per year for major grains between 1979 and 1995 (see Figure 2.2).[10]

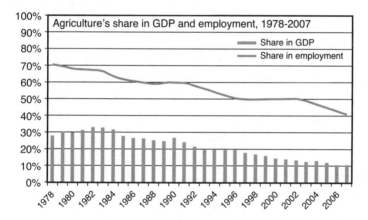

Figure 2.1 Agriculture declines as a share of total GDP and workforce

Source: National Bureau of Statistics and authors' calculations

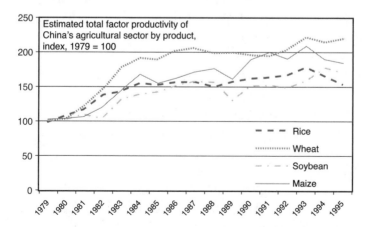

Figure 2.2 Production efficiency increased dramatically for numerous crops

Source: Huang Jikun et al.[11]

A diet for a land of plenty

Beijing's record of keeping its citizens' stomachs full is impressive. But rising incomes and standards of living are changing what goes into those stomachs, imposing a new kind of strain on agriculture. China will likely have to dramatically raise the productivity, scale, and efficiency of its farms. To this day, about one-third of China's labor force works in agriculture. In contrast, the United States is more than capable of feeding 300 million people, often a little too well, with only about 2% of its labor force. To mechanize Chinese agricultural production on a grand scale would require absorbing millions of farmers into other vocations over the next several decades—roughly another 280 million according to a Chinese Academy of Sciences study—jobs that may no longer be readily available as the manufacturing sector slows down.[12] If the sequencing of improving the agricultural mechanization process isn't properly managed, China could be left with both food production shortages *and* unemployed farmers with grim future prospects.

The meat of the problem

The Chinese food supply's central "known unknown" factor is the magnitude and pace of Chinese consumption growth, and in particular the eating habits of a burgeoning middle class that increasingly counts meat and dairy as essential parts of the diet. Consuming meat served as a status symbol of relative wealth in China when most people were too poor to eat it daily. Is meat's social role now encouraging Chinese people to consume more of it?

Despite stagnating population growth, tens of millions of new entrants to the urban middle class are adopting meat-rich diets each year. Accelerating urbanization, too, will mean rising consumption at the same time that the agricultural workforce is falling—requiring each farmer to do more with less. Barring dramatic cultural shifts, there will be hundreds of millions more regular meat consumers in the coming decade. Beijing residents, for example, consume an average of 60kg of meat annually, while the wealthiest top-fifth Chinese ate an average of 70kg. Taiwanese meat consumption is even higher, at about 87kg.[13]

Vegetarianism perplexes most Chinese, other than a small minority of die-hard Buddhists. The fact that an individual would deliberately *choose* to abstain from meat seems counterintuitive in a culture where meat was a rare note of variety in a diet of grains, rice, millet, and yams. Try asking for a vegetarian version of a meat dish on a typical restaurant menu and the Chinese wait staff will appear puzzled (and usually won't accommodate). Meat is now central to almost every middle-class meal, and fish also make frequent appearances, especially at lavish banquets.

It isn't simply meat consumption in the aggregate—the specific types of meat consumed can have more significant impacts on demand for land and feed, and ultimately on prices. Though China's diet has traditionally been pork and poultry dominated, beef consumption could accelerate with the introduction of Western foods such as steaks and hamburgers—common dining options for the post-1990s generation Chinese. There is also generally less incentive to raise cows because inputs are more expensive—abundant land and large volumes of feed—making beef more expensive than the other types of meat. Pork instead is to China's food industry what coal is to energy—the indisputable king, with half the world's swine consumed in China.[14] Chairman Mao himself was a pork aficionado and was responsible for the nationwide popularity of a fatty braised pork dish from his native Hunan Province. For Chinese urbanites, about 60% of their meat consumption is pork; for rural Chinese, pork constitutes 67%, though, of course, meat comprises a smaller share of the diet than in urban China. Pork is so important to Chinese diets that the government maintains a strategic pork reserve to stabilize prices during supply crunches and inflationary spells, most recently in 2008 and 2011.[15]

Rising affluence has fueled exponential growth of China's meat consumption in recent decades. Cultural factors—China's generational divide and approach to food—likely compound the problem of rising meat consumption as well. Younger Chinese have few qualms about consuming meat, loading up on burgers and pork chops, and their elders of the lean generation, after the crippling scarcity they personally faced, tend to encourage their children and grandchildren to "eat more meat, fewer vegetables" (*duo chi dian rou, shao chi dian cai*). Whatever the reasons, past projections of Chinese meat consumption, for example those of Huang, Lin, and Rozelle, have vastly underestimated the Chinese infatuation with meat and the pace of consumption growth:

> Per capita demand for red meat is forecast to rise sharply throughout the projection period [2000-2020]. China's consumers will increase 65% of their meat consumptions [sic] by 2020, from 17 to 28 kilograms per capita for pork, from 2 to 3 kilograms for beef, and 1 to 2 kilograms for mutton.[16]

Actual meat consumption growth outpaced the economists' wildest dreams. The U.S. Department of Agriculture (USDA) projected that in 2012, each Chinese on average consumed 4.1kg of beef and 38kg of pork.[17] Compare that to the low-end projections from those above: China has more than doubled meat consumption nearly a decade ahead of schedule. Over the past three decades, meat consumption has *quadrupled.* Total annual meat consumption in China is now 71 million tons, more than double that of the United States. China alone now consumes 60% more meat than the entire world produced in 1950 (see Figure 2.3).[18]

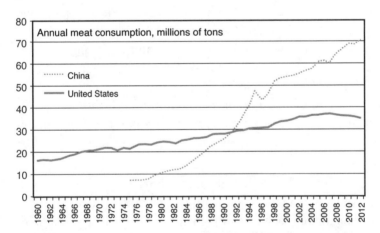

Figure 2.3 China has shot past the United States in total meat consumption

Source: Data compiled by Earth Policy Institute from U.S. Department of Agriculture Production, Supply and Distribution database

The stress to agricultural supplies grows when Chinese full stomachs are stuffed with meat. With rising meat consumption comes knock-on effects on China's corn and soybean demand, the key ingredients of animal feed. It isn't just pork, the Chinese are also drinking much more milk and eating more eggs, which require raising larger numbers of chickens and herds of cows. If it quacks, clucks, bleats, or moos, it was probably raised on corn or soybeans.

China used to be one of the world's largest soy producers up until around 1995–1996. Since then, Chinese production levels have languished while demand has outstripped supply five times. Over the course of about 15 years, China went from soybean self-sufficiency to one of the world's largest importers of the commodity, influencing agricultural markets and land prices from the United States to Brazil. Global supply has followed Chinese demand. Over the past half century, global soybean production reached 250 million tons, a 14-fold exponential expansion in production.[19] And over what period was growth fastest? From 1990 to 2010, the two decades during which China's middle class emerged. The "great powers" of Western hemisphere agriculture have capitalized on China's boom. Brazilian farmers have allocated more land to raise the crop—sometimes chipping away at dwindling acreage of the Amazonian rainforest. Soy, in the meantime, has become second only to corn production in the United States.

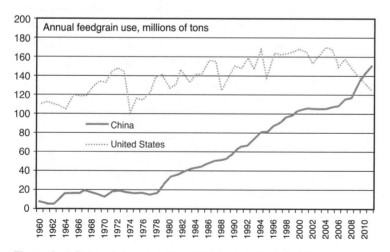

Figure 2.4 China also surpassed the United States in feed-grain usage

Source: Data compiled by Earth Policy Institute from U.S. Department of Agriculture Production, Supply and Distribution database

Millennia after discovering and domesticating the soybean plant, China now finds itself uncomfortably dependent on imports for about 75% of its consumption. Beijing still insists that China is a self-suffi-cient producer of its own food supply—*self-sufficiency* conveniently defined to omit the soy and corn that feed most of the meat on Chi-nese dinner tables (refer back to Figure 2.4). Is soy dependence a harbinger of a broader deterioration of China's ability to satisfy its appetite? Maybe so, if recent years are any indication. In 2012, for instance, the country surprised the world by importing an incredible 2.6 million tons of rice, nearly 400% more than in the previous year.[20] Just as Australia has benefited from Chinese demand for coal and iron ore, other Asian rice exporters such as Thailand and Vietnam may see demand for their rice production transformed by Chinese appetites. This is particularly so in light of the recent scare over high levels of cadmium, a poisonous metal, found in millions of tons of domestically produced rice.[21] Rice, unlike meat and fish, is indispensable to the diets of Chinese rich or poor alike—it is imperative for the govern-ment to ensure its supply.

Why would a country that produces about 140 million tons of rice, that is supposed to see rice demand growth slow relative to meat demand growth, and that has successfully raised rice yields for decades, suddenly import so much? The jury is still out. Chinese importers may have been exploiting arbitrage opportunities, with domestic rice prices (set high to subsidize farmer incomes and stimulate produc-tion) higher than global prices. Or perhaps the opaque Chinese rice reserve was running low and the government was simply restocking. Could it also have been a result of domestic demand exploding, imply-ing future price pressures on the global rice market similar to those affecting soy? Of course, the Chinese government wouldn't explicitly admit a supply shortfall at the risk of spooking countries that com-pete with China for rice imports or that fear another replay of the global food price shock of 2007–2008. A similar fate could befall corn, especially if a spike in China's demand growth coincided with another bout of unusually severe droughts.

Whether it be soybeans or corn, the meat of China's food problem is just that: meat. Peeking into the somewhat distant future, the USDA projects that global demand for coarse grains used as feedstock to raise livestock will increase by more than a third over the next decade, with China accounting for a third of the increase. The country's corn imports are expected to rise 15% annually, and more than triple in volume by the 2021–2022 season. Global trade in soybeans will also increase by about a third: The USDA projects that Chinese soybean imports will rise 60% by the 2021–2022 growing year and account for 80% of the global increase in demand.[22] By then, instead of just $2 extra for guacamole, your burrito bowl at Chipotle could come with a helping of made-in-China sticker shock.

Hot and bothered...and thirsty

China's food demand is set to take off just as new constraints loom on the supply side, principally among them water and land shortages. Alternating cycles of floods and droughts have long threatened Chinese farmers with famine, and Chinese emperors with the threat of revolution. For much of the 20th century, the government seemed to have conquered the vagaries of water availability with the damming of China's river systems. But over the next decade, pressures on water supplies from climate change and urbanization threaten to undermine the supply of this most vital agricultural input.

For those still unconvinced of climate change's impact on global ecosystems and agriculture, the past two years (2011 and 2012) likely provide a limited preview of how increasingly unpredictable climate patterns could affect the world's two largest food consumers and producers. The American heartland saw the worst drought in at least half a century in 2012, following on the heels of a severe dry spell across China in 2011. The protracted drought in China left at least 15 million people with water shortages and affected three to five million hectares of farmland. Just as the drought was easing, the coastal Yangtze River Delta zone was pummeled by biblical downpours, ruining vast amounts of crops.[23] Vegetable prices in much of China rose 40%, exacerbating supply-side inflationary pressures feeding into meat prices.

Droughts are familiar to Chinese farmers. Northeast China, including the capital Beijing, has lived in a perpetual parched state, a perma-drought, for hundreds of years. But the extreme swings of 2011 affected the agricultural core of China, an area where water was historically abundant.[24] Climate change is an equal-opportunity wreaker of havoc on ecosystems, and China is especially prone to its unpredictable downside effects because of its longstanding shortages of water and land. Chinese water expert Ma Jun commented on the drought of 2011:

> This drought tells us that water scarcity does not only exist in north China, but increasingly south China is also facing water challenges... It is a new warning signal because it shows the south is no longer a store with unlimited water supply.[25]

As climate change attenuates China's available water supply, an enormous new source of demand is competing with agriculture for a place at the watering hole: urbanization. Growth of Chinese urbanites, estimated to hit one billion by 2030, will increasingly wrestle with the agricultural sector for water.[26] Urban water consumption accelerates with every modern flush toilet installed and every washing machine brought into a middle-class Chinese home. Could urban China's dream bathroom undermine its kitchen? Diverting water for urban use takes water from the farmers raising the pigs and cows to feed urban elites. How will Chinese politicians balance these competing claims to a precious resource? Could water access become a new battleground of inequality in China?

Urbanization, too, will compete for another vital and scarce input for producing food: arable land.[27] China technically imposes a strict redline on land development, protecting a certain percentage of arable land—about 120 million hectares—but that is also what it claims on food security. Local Chinese officials grabbing land from farmers has been a common feature of Chinese economic development of the past decade and a key source of social frictions. Urbanization, if not pursued rationally, could leave shrinking farmland, riled farmers, and less-secure food supplies in its wake. Policy measures intended to protect rural land from urbanization are, as yet, insufficient. Even though the Chinese government extended rural land-use rights to 30 years and in 2006 codified land-use rights in a rural land contract law, following such rules is usually not in the interest of local officials.

Much can be justified in the name of development, even if it means undermining food security.

To the Chinese government's credit, its new leadership appears to fully grasp the potential trade-offs inherent in choosing urbanization and consumption as future engines of growth. But awareness of the situation alone won't address the negative externalities of accelerated urbanization. Whether the government can navigate a less-resource-intensive and rational urbanization process, or whether one even exists, remains an outstanding question.

Rise of the machines?

For foreign analysts such as your humble authors, it's useful to step back and acknowledge that the Chinese government has for at least 30 years been making fools of us and our dire predictions of their country's future. The Chinese government's ingenuity and pragmatism have gotten it out of many a public policy jam. Ingenuity is hard to quantify, but it seems likely that Beijing could find solutions to any of the individual resource constraints to agricultural production and protect food security. But what about all of them at once? The confluence of so many overlapping sources of scarcity poses the most formidable challenge to Chinese food policy since the agricultural reforms of the 1980s. Could China be approaching a food-supply tipping point?

For many Chinese policymakers, the answer to China's seemingly intractable food conundrums is better technology. After all, technology has come to China's, and indeed the world's, rescue before. Forecasters of food-shortage apocalypse, including Malthus himself, have consistently underestimated technology's ability to raise efficiency to once unimaginable heights. The United States strikingly illustrates how investments in agricultural sciences and mechanization have produced one of the most productive agricultural sectors in the world. In fact, U.S. agricultural production is so prodigious that the consumption of its products can afford to be hugely inefficient, wasting 40% of the food America produces, worth about $165 billion a year, and still overfeeding a population of 300 million and exporting plenty of soybeans to China.[28]

China certainly has ample room to close the productivity gap with more modern agricultural economies, and can continue to introduce mechanization and improve scale, tracing a path that others have gone before. For instance, the Chinese government can be expected to build on their successes with hybrid rice and other crops to improve yields without using up more land. China is also one of the few major countries outside of the United States to champion genetically modified foods, and has devoted substantial R&D to agricultural biotechnology.

When it comes to water, too, China's brightest minds—its intelligentsia, government policy wonks, and scientists—have novel, sometimes wildly ambitious proposals to keep the faucet running. China's gargantuan South-to-North Water Diversion Project, if successfully executed, could balance out the uneven distribution of water between China's two most populous regions. But it is a gamble with a long time horizon that is unlikely to matter over the next decade. And even if it is successful, it can do little to alleviate China's very low *average* availability of fresh water, only one-third of global levels (see Figure 2.5).

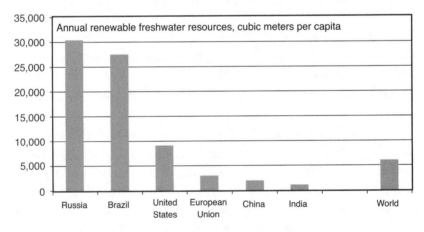

Figure 2.5 China will never be a water-abundant country

Source: World Bank World Development Indicators

New water recycling technologies or desalinization of seawater could potentially help preserve a scarce resource. China's latest industrial policies prioritize wastewater recycling technology for large cities, and a mega desalinization plant has been erected by the Bohai Bay near Tianjin in northern China.[29] More projects are planned, which could drive the market for desalinization technology and potentially create a bonanza for companies in countries like Israel and the United States that have advanced technologies. And obvious opportunities seem available to improve the efficiency of irrigation in China, which lags far behind other middle-income countries and even further behind the efficiency levels obtained in the United States:

> [While] agriculture is the main sector that withdraws water... only 45% is actually consumed by crops, owing to the low efficiency of the irrigation systems... [China's] relatively poor water productivity, US$3.6 per m^3, is lower than the average of US$4.8 per m^3 in middle-income countries, and much lower than the US$35.8 per m^3 in high-income countries.[30]

To adequately feed a population four times that of the United States who increasingly aspires to similar food consumption levels, while maintaining a stable balance of global food supply and demand, another green revolution beyond any of the incremental technological improvements currently being discussed for China would likely be required. The country and many of the other latecomers to economic development have already absorbed much of the gains from the mechanization and hybrid breeds of previous rounds of agricultural revolution. Without another leap or breakthrough to accommodate the ferociously rising consumption of first China, and then India and other developing countries, the world could well face increasingly frequent bouts of food price paroxysms.

Agricultural productivity growth seemed to have slowed globally, even in the United States. In *An Economist Gets Lunch*, economist Tyler Cowen argues that productivity in farming has been reduced by half in the United States during the 1990 to 2002 period when compared to the gains over the previous 40 years. Moreover, "estimates suggest that 35-70% of agricultural R&D is directed at 'breaking even'—protecting crops from various disasters—rather than moving forward and achieving new gains."

> Jonathan A. Foley, a food and environmental researcher at the University of Minnesota, put it well: "We've doubled the world's food production several times before in history, and now we have to do it one more time. The last doubling is the hardest. It is possible, but it's not going to be easy."[31]

The techno-optimists may be validated again, if Chinese scientists can develop and quickly commercialize safe genetically modified organisms, future food prices may even be lower than today's. Or perhaps a cloning technology breakthrough just around the corner will make it possible to consume test-tube swine and cattle. All of this *might* come to pass. But the evidence available today to support such optimism about the near future seems thin.

Of course, even if fanciful new technologies make manipulating seeds and pig embryos in a laboratory possible, it is far from clear that the world will feel safe eating them. Public skepticism toward government food safety claims runs even higher in China than in the rest of the world. That's because the Chinese government's credibility on food matters remains, deservedly, abysmal. From the government's perspective, *food security* means self-sufficiency and guaranteeing the population remains fed if a foreign conflict cuts China off from global agricultural markets. But for many in the Chinese middle class, food security means something more immediate: the fear that contaminated food will harm them and their children.

From Happy Meals to deadly dinners

Food (un)safety in China is a long and unhappy tale. Let's begin ours in 2004, when 13 infants died of malnutrition from eating adulterated baby formula with no nutrients.[32] They were rural children from one of the poorest provinces in China, a group that usually does not command sustained national attention. Although official media covered the incidents, the story quickly fell out of the public eye and was forgotten by all but those directly affected. But then in 2007, tainted Chinese food exports killed victims who were much harder for the Chinese government to ignore: American pets. Chinese pet food exports were discovered to be killing dogs in the United States, and Americans demanded an answer.[33] It lay in melamine, a chemical substance that up until then remained a mystery to everyone except chemists. It turns out that melamine is synthetically manufactured and when added to certain food products will increase their protein content as measured by conventional tests.

Literally hundreds of thousands of small producers sell into China's food supply chain, making it difficult for the government to regulate food supplies even if it tried. The struggle against cutthroat pricing to earn a living and the near-certainty that adulteration in the food supply would be hard to trace back to those responsible were irresistible temptations for intrepid suppliers. A little melamine artificially juiced their products' protein content, reducing the amount of (expensive) real meat or milk needed in it at the same time:

> "Many companies buy melamine scrap to make animal feed, such as fish feed," said Ji Denghui, general manager of the Fujian Sanming Dinghui Chemical Company, which sells melamine. "I don't know if there's a regulation on it. Probably not. No law or regulation says 'don't do it,' so everyone's doing it. The laws in China are like that, aren't they? If there's no accident, there won't be any regulation."[34]

Mr. Ji's brazen candor reflected the government's tacit tolerance of the existence of such a cottage industry of melamine suppliers. And as long as they only hurt dogs and cats in America, the pressure on the Chinese government seemed like it could be managed by playing defense and deflecting criticism, without rooting out the problem. That perception proved misguided and naïve, when just a year later, melamine started hurting Chinese babies again. This time, it didn't affect just a dozen poor infants: More than 6,000 across the country fell ill, many of whom contracted kidney stones.[35] Adding insult to injury, it was revealed that the government had knowledge of tampered baby formula and related illnesses but chose to scuttle reports because the 2008 Beijing Olympics were about to begin. China had to put its best face forward for the world, and nothing could derail its carefully crafted, pristine image. But the effort to smother the issue before it could go public backfired; parents were rightly outraged by an attempted cover up that put their children's lives at stake. The government realized that it had walked into a political firestorm. It had botched handling of what every average Chinese felt entitled to: sufficient and safe food.

Beijing sprung into action and ordered a massive recall of dairy products that could've been tainted. Eventually, the culprit of the doctored baby milk was found to be a company called Sanlu Group in Hebei Province just outside of Beijing (a company that had sold a substantial ownership stake to New Zealand dairy firm Fonterra). Given the gravity of the situation, the government took extraordinary measures. For selling these substandard and dangerous products, two men were executed, and the former chairwoman of the company was sentenced to life in prison.[36] The harsh punishment meted was meant to show the government's resolve, finally taking the issue seriously. That might have been enough if Sanlu were an outlier or a one-off, but it was merely a manifestation of a much deeper systemic failing of China's food supply chain. Sanlu was unlucky and got caught red handed. But who knew how many more Sanlus were flying under the radar or how widespread their practices had become?

The milk scandal of 2008 became a watershed, unleashing a barrage of media and public scrutiny of this life-and-death issue. Since then, so many food safety violations have been uncovered that they inspired an enterprising and technology-savvy college student to begin a website dedicated solely to tracking Chinese food safety incidents on a map.[37] The cringe-inducing headlines exposing each new case shocked many Chinese. The parallels between China today and the meatpacking jungle that Upton Sinclair so pungently described in his classic on the U.S. food industry at the turn of the last century are palpable.[38] As one report had it:

> Accounts of dubious or unsafe food in China are as mesmerizing as they are disturbing—"artificial green peas," grilled kebabs made from cat meat, contaminated chives, chlorine showing up in soft drinks. There have been stories of imitation soy sauce made from hair clippings, ink and paraffin being used to dress up cheap noodles, and pork buns so loaded with bacteria that they glow in the dark.[39]

One category of food violations that has lately captured the public eye is the phenomenon known as *gutter oil,* a product so offensive that it is difficult to describe accurately without resorting to obscenity. Gutter oil is the used cooking oil dumped by restaurants into gutters or drains and then scrounged up by underground entrepreneurs to be reprocessed (sometimes with animal parts) and resold to unsuspecting or uncaring restaurant managers to be used as cooking oil. Photos of the oil's production process surfaced and went viral on the Internet in late 2009, creating yet another ugly embarrassment for a government that was supposed to be eradicating these harmful practices.[40] To cap off China's terrible eight years of food hazards, the country's favorite meat, pork, also became embroiled in safety issues. In 2011, some pork purchased in Shanghai was discovered to freakishly glow in the dark, which some experts believe was caused by the growth of unidentified bacteria.[41]

Public concern about the failure of the Chinese food system continues to mount. Meanwhile, the government continues its "whack a mole" approach with symbolic punishment of violators who make the evening news but is unable to satisfactorily resolve the fundamental deficiencies of a food supply chain in tatters.[42]

Astronauts get Tang, taikonauts get grass-fed beef

With few easy solutions to ensure strict compliance of food safety standards, the government and well-connected elites decided to protect themselves in the meantime. Food, and its access, became another proxy indicator of inequality between the elite few and the average *laobaixing*.[43]

In June 2012, China joined a very exclusive club of nations that have successfully completed a docking mission in space, a mission that also launched China's first female *taikonaut* into space. This marker of national prestige has been captured by only two other countries before—the United States and Russia—capping a triumphant, Kennedy-esque moment for then-President Hu Jintao.[44] Yet the euphoria of China's technological achievements was punctured by the revelation that an exclusive organic farm had been supplying the astronauts' food. An intrepid reporter from the *Beijing News* visited the farm in Inner Mongolia, not far from the launch site, and described its pastoral scene of free-range chickens, roaming cattle, and a pristine manmade lake that prohibited motorboats.[45] Unauthorized personnel and vehicles were not allowed to enter the area. The report set off a public uproar on the Chinese Internet, with the contrast between the privileges reserved for taikonauts and what was being fed to the proles, dramatizing what Chinese officialdom thought of the general food supply. One typically wry and cynical comment on the Web read:

"Come on, all the high-ups eat food from special suppliers, okay? We shitizens [sic] can only eat things from the periodic table."[46]

Of course, this wasn't the only exclusive farm serving elite customers and authorities. Other documented farms were found just outside of Beijing, with fences erected to deter intruders or unauthorized visitors. As Barbara Demick of the *Los Angeles Times* reported:

> "It is for officials only. They produce organic vegetables, peppers, onions, beans, cauliflowers, but they don't sell to the public," said Li Xiuqin, 68, a lifelong Shunyi village resident who lives directly across the street from the farm but has never been inside. "Ordinary people can't go in there."[47]

Many of life's necessities and niceties are available to officials through "special provision" channels (*zhuan gong*), a legacy of the communist planned economy. It's one thing for senior officials to get special Cuban cigars in plain wrapping unavailable to the public. But unlike other types of inequality, food inequality is literally an issue of life and death, a question of human necessity affecting all Chinese. It is for this reason that the discovery of these food farms for the entitled was so shocking and unpalatable for a public already feeling short-changed by officialdom in countless other ways. It also exposes the hypocrisy of government officials responsible for assuaging the Chinese public that food is safe: If that were the case, why are those officials eating from a farm behind enclosed walls? In a political system that promises the population a secure livelihood in return for acceptance of the status quo, allowing the proverbial well to be poisoned calls the government's competence, credibility, and maybe even its fundamental legitimacy into question.

The scarcity of safe food is but a reflection of the larger challenges China faces in managing its food supplies.[48] Food scares are not unique to China. But the country's scale and chronic inability to ensure a sound food supply chain add another layer of immense burden to an already overstretched food production system. Overlap and lack of coordination in bureaucratic oversight is one problem. But with many food companies owned by (or under the protection of) local governments, the absence of rule of law is another equally powerful factor. As long as the incentives for making quick profits by flouting the law remain fundamentally unchanged, improvements seem doomed to be temporary and conditional. Momentary improvements will be inevitably followed by new and equally stomach-churning revelations.

Indeed, at the end of 2012, another food violation case surfaced. This time it was blamed on perhaps one of the best known American brands in China: KFC.[49] The Shanghai government claimed that one of the company's subsidiaries had used too much antibiotics in their chickens. While the brand was American, these chickens weren't imported. They were raised in the same broken food system that produced glow-in-the-dark pork, gutter oil, and poisoned baby formula and dog food. The latest food incident to befall China's flagship metropolis Shanghai is the appearance of more than 10,000 dead pigs floating in the city's key waterway, the Huangpu River.[50] The government has denied that disease was the cause of the swine deaths, but few are convinced. If China's most cosmopolitan and developed city can get flooded by dead pigs, what are the laobaixing being fed in Hunan?

Rising Chinese demand that leads to national and global food scarcity and price spikes is anything but a consensus view. The economist's proverbial "on the other hand" is captured by the quintessentially anti-Malthusian outlook argued by Rockefeller University economists: the world has reached *peak farmland,* a tipping point after which global agricultural land use will gradually decline:

> Expecting that more and richer people will demand more
> from the land, cultivating wider fields, logging more forests,
> and pressing Nature, comes naturally. The past half-century
> of disciplined and dematerializing demand and more intense
> and efficient land use encourage a rational hope that human-
> ity's pressure will not overwhelm Nature.[51]

The core hypothesis is that land use, over the next 50 years, will decouple from food demand as efficiency gains become so enormous that output on a fixed acreage of available land can triple. The Rockefeller economists expect technological advancements to keep pace with the doubling of global food consumption needed to accommodate the world's population peak at nine billion in 2050.[52] It is, of course, impossible to rule out scientists stumbling upon unprecedented supply-side technological breakthroughs sufficient to bend nature to humanity's whims. Yet even the Rockefeller economists' optimism is punctuated by many caveats, chief among them the unpredictable nature of consumption patterns. "Most wildcards probably will continue to come from consumers. Will people choose to eat much more meat? If so, will it be beef, which requires more land than poultry and fish, which require less? Will people become vegetarian or even vegan?"

For China, we suspect the first question will be answered in the affirmative, especially over the next decade, fueling continued growth of per capita food demand. Having started at a low base, beef consumption will almost certainly rise as the first generation raised on Happy Meals start buying groceries for their own households. Just as the last three decades of catch-up growth in China created a wealthy middle class, the hundreds of millions of Chinese who will join its ranks in the coming decade are likely to practice catch-up food consumption, particularly of meat. Meat will be an integral part of most meals in a country with a long and resonant cultural fixation on it; vegetarianism seems unlikely to attract mass appeal. Perhaps the expanding middle class's attitudes toward eating meat will shift for ethical or health purposes. Yet developed East Asian economies with sizable middle classes, from Taiwan to Japan, have not moved to vegetarian diets. Incidentally, Chinese food was the original influence for these East Asian food cultures.

It likewise is difficult to see how China breaks from the path toward a constricted agricultural land supply. The process of creating more consumers and rebalancing the growth model in China will likely come at the expense of agricultural land. That's because policymakers, particularly Premier Li Keqiang, believe that the key driver of consumption, and by extension of economic growth over the next decade, will be urbanization.[53] One hundred million more Chinese are expected to become urbanites over the next ten years, the equivalent of creating a New York-sized city every single year. The government has stated its determination to preserve arable land in the face of such urbanization, just as it proclaims its commitment to food security. While victory will likely be declared on both fronts ten years from now, what that *victory* will entail remains an outstanding question. It seems inevitable that farmland will be encroached upon during the process of urbanization, implying that China will have to generate even greater production efficiency on each remaining acre of land (or land classified as unfarmable today will, at least on paper, become part of agricultural production tomorrow). Competing claims to limited water resources as part of urbanization will also require technological wizardry to overcome.

Such competitive priorities deeply concern Chinese policymakers confronting the challenge of maintaining food security in the daunting decade ahead. Within the State Council, rural China expert Chen Xiwen has warned against projecting past success into future outcomes, believing that accelerating urbanization will severely test Chinese food supplies. For instance, even though against many odds, China produced nearly 160 million tons more grains in 2012 than it did a decade earlier, it also imported 45% of grains needed to meet total demand that same year.[54] The collision of rising Chinese food demand with potentially slowing domestic food production will have considerable ramifications beyond China's borders as well. China's voracious appetite, if unrestrained, will especially affect the developing world if higher food prices mean citizens of poorer countries have to spend a higher percentage of limited disposable income on necessities such as food.

Within China, domestic scarcity will seem all the more daunting under a food system that is unaccountable and potentially dangerous to individual livelihoods. Beijing not only needs to fix a highly fragmented supply chain but to also untangle the institutional knots at the top that govern food safety. Bureaucratic coordination and enforcement remain messy, uneven, and weak. Local producers can easily exploit loopholes or escape notice, particularly in the absence of rule of law. Reflecting the public distrust of their own food system, Chinese mothers have flooded Hong Kong to buy trusted brands of infant formula. The new Chinese government, to be fair, has not stood idly by. In March 2013, the government unveiled a new high-level agency similar to the U.S. Food and Drug Administration tasked with tackling food safety. While the agency's success is far from assured, its very existence shows that the government certainly understands what a combustible issue food safety has become.

Received economic wisdom tends to view a consumption-based China as the right path for economic development. But is China's food system, and indeed the world's, ready for another one billion American-style food consumers? We must hope it is. But we must also be prepared for the possibility that Chinese food scarcity will exert massive pressures on the country and the world at large.

3

Labor: Where did all the migrants go?

It became fashionable after the Soviet Union's collapse to say that breakneck economic growth was the only thing postponing the Chinese Communist Party's (CCP) day of reckoning. Communist ideology was discredited, went the saying, but as long as the economic pie kept growing, the citizens would set aside broader concerns and take their piece. But what if growth were interrupted by, say, a global financial crisis, collapse of world trade, and mass layoffs on the Chinese factory floor? The music would stop, the masquerade party would come to an end, and Jennifer Connelly would smash her way through David Bowie's bubble prison, so to speak.[1]

Except that it didn't. The Chinese economy faced exactly this cataclysmic scenario in the final months of 2008: Venerable Wall Street titan Lehman Brothers collapsed in September, sending global capital markets into a tailspin and terrifying business managers around the world. Collapsing confidence and financial dysfunction forced businesses around the world to cancel orders en masse. It was a huge blow to the Chinese manufacturing industry, compounding the weaknesses of a domestic economy already fragile after months of government tightening policies intended to cool a real estate bubble and overheating inflation. Tens of millions of Chinese migrant workers were laid off in the lead up to the Lunar New Year holiday in late January 2009.[2] They returned to the countryside, passed the holiday with relatives, and then waited for the crisis to abate.

Meanwhile, Zhongnanhai's poobahs sweated.[3] The global economy was plunging into the worst recession since the 1930s. China responded hastily with an outsized stimulus package that, although it boosted confidence, was in and of itself insufficient to create jobs for both the laid off workers as well as the millions of college graduates and young migrant workers who had flocked to urban job markets every year for decades. Early in 2009, Chinese officials were openly worrying about maintaining social stability in the Chinese countryside.[4]

The economy in 2009 was indeed shaky by Chinese standards, although much better than in the rest of the world. China's real GDP growth slowed to single digits and was the slowest in nearly a decade. The China bears rose from hibernation and emerged from their caves to swarm op-ed pages and talk show panels, predicting a jobs crisis, an economic crisis, and a political crisis. Even the more temperamentally optimistic economists found it hard to see how China would avoid an extended period of high unemployment and heightened social unrest in rural areas.

Instead, the labor market overheated. China's economic policymakers flooded the economy with bank credit for the next two years, funding countless new housing projects, amazing feats of infrastructure modernization, and of course, some fantastical white elephants mixed in with the infrastructure bonanza. Migrant workers gravitated toward the millions of jobs created on construction sites, or back to the factories whose order books were filled by investment-led demand. The slack in the Chinese labor market was absorbed by early 2010, and job postings began to outnumber jobseekers for the first time since the Panda Boom began at the turn of this century. Suddenly, it was a lack of workers rather than a lack of orders keeping factories from running at full tilt.[5]

Concerns about crippling social instability evaporated as breathtakingly quickly as did the slack in the migrant labor market. But it was unclear in the heat of the moment exactly what had saved the country from disaster. Was it simply the sign of a massive stimulus program pulling the economy from the brink of recession? Or did the crisis fundamentally transform the labor market in some unanticipated way? With the benefit of several years' hindsight, it seems clear that the labor market had been transforming all along—it was just that short-term cyclical swings of the economy, buffeted by a global recession and a steroidal stimulus, were obscuring the structural sea change.

No sooner had China dodged a cyclical economic disaster did it find itself running short on a crucial input essential to keeping its growth machine humming: abundant labor. China's slow-burning demographic crisis, which experts Chinese and foreign alike had long warned would someday transform its economy and society, has turned out to be not as slow burning as previously thought. The structure of the Chinese labor force is changing much faster than the government anticipated, shifting the economy from one that enjoyed an enormous labor surplus to one of labor scarcity—call it China's *demographic hangover*.

The change is most dramatically demonstrated in the migrant workforce, with a younger generation bringing higher demands and aspirations as an older generation exits. Rising labor costs are pushing manufacturers to replace workers with more machines or to reconsider earlier decisions to relocate production from advanced economies. Within China, this oncoming structural scarcity is forcing a major reevaluation of the country's growth model—the only long-term antidote to what otherwise would likely be chronic economic ills. Over the next decade, the progression of China's labor market from demographic dividend to demographic hangover will impose pressure on business models, economic policy, and China's role in the world.

Socialist employers' paradise...

During the Panda Boom, all the major factors affecting Chinese labor relations had swung in employers' favor, foremost being supply and demand. Tens of millions of state-owned enterprise (SOE) employees laid off in the late 1990s helped keep "true" unemployment in urban China (as opposed to what the meaningless official unemployment statistic said) elevated for most of the 2000s. Add on top of this millions of migrant workers trekking to find work in the dense factory jungles along the coastal provinces, as well as millions of teenagers aging into the workforce each year, and the buyer's market for blue-collar labor was assured. The persistent overhang of excess labor kept manufacturing labor costs, or wages from the worker's perspective, low in China (see Figure 3.1).

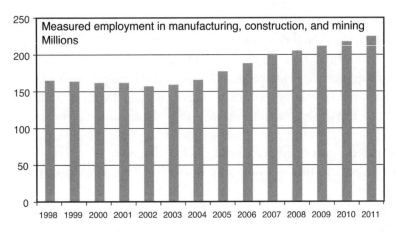

Figure 3.1 SOE layoffs in the late 1990s shrank the manufacturing labor force
Source: China Statistical Yearbook 2012

The above figure most likely overstates the stagnation of industrial employment in the late 1990s. Chinese employment statistics historically measured SOE employment much more accurately than private employment, so a shift of workers from SOEs to the private sector could cause a drop in official measured employment when the full truth had to account for the growth outside of the measured economy. But even if employment was not falling in absolute terms, the massive SOE layoffs observable through the weak employment in the late 1990s hurt workers' bargaining power and kept wage growth modest.

With China so large relative to the rest of the global economy, the ripple effects from China's transformation held wages down globally, as multinational companies flocked in to set up operations in the "employers' paradise" of China. It was a symbiotic arrangement. The shiny new factories sprouted on the back of foreign capital could quickly absorb Chinese workers and the "China price" of products that incorporated a steep labor discount helped foreign companies improve profit margins. There was little to complain about for all parties involved.[6]

Longer-term factors similarly supported a glut of workforce entrants just as China embarked on its market reforms. The country experienced a baby boom amid the relative peace and social stability of the decade following China's 1949 reunification, which, later in the century, echoed in a mini-baby boom that boosted the number of annual workforce entrants around the end of the 20th century. So too did the liberalization of agricultural production play a significant role in fortifying China's workforce. The earliest market-oriented reforms of the 1980s began on the farm and dramatically increased productivity per worker, freeing up underutilized laborers who gravitated toward factory work on the coasts.

During China's demographic explosion, maintaining job growth was the government's paramount priority. Occupational safety, collective bargaining rights, and other costly labor protections were vastly less important, and summarily ignored. The party-controlled umbrella union organized in all Chinese firms, the All China Federation of Trade Unions (ACFTU), existed more to co-opt and control employee complaints than to represent them in negotiations with management. Employment conditions were much more favorable for employees of the central government owned SOEs that survived the late 1990s. They enjoyed considerably better job security and occupational safety than the average Chinese worker (and often much higher salaries). But these exceptions applied only to the fortunate few, accounting for a tiny minority of Chinese workers. The overwhelming majority of Chinese workers were employed in private firms or local government-owned firms, where labor protections are an afterthought and unions a farce.

Policy first began to favor employers less universally with the Chinese Labor Contract Law of 2008, the centerpiece of a stronger labor regulatory package that increased worker protections against layoffs, obliged employers to negotiate with the party-controlled ACFTU over pay rates and benefits, and provided workers with new avenues to enforce their rights against employers in courts.[7] Fully enforced, the regulation's provisions were estimated to increase the cost of employing Chinese workers by some 10% to 20%.[8] But at the time it was enacted, the law appeared only a minor adjustment for the highly elastic labor market. After all, there were still nearly 200 million migrants and millions more waiting to move off farms. As long as the supply remained abundant, the employer's paradise would endure. At least that's what most thought.

...Becomes socialist employers' paradise, lost

By 2010, cracks were starting to show in the paradise's foundation. This became most visible in a string of highly publicized wildcat strikes at foreign-owned factories. Multinational and Chinese manufacturers had cut wages during the downturn of 2008–2009 and had been slow to raise them as production began normalizing over the following year—even as inflation had taken off in a hurry without waiting for wages to catch up.

It was a double shock for foreign employers. First, they were flummoxed that workers were emboldened to shut down production so soon after many manufacturers had been driven to the brink of bankruptcy. Managers were still twitching at the memories of 2008, when the economy was so bad that many owners in Shenzhen had snuck over the factory wall in the cover of night, leaving their unpaid workers behind. Multinational managers were caught off guard by such demands in particular because many of them were still negotiating with headquarters over whether their global salary and headcount freezes would be subject to exceptions in the event Chinese demand recovered as quickly as it fell off a cliff. Second, that the strikes happened at all turned preconceived notions on their head: China was not supposed to have strikes or collective bargaining actions whatsoever! The head of the Chinese labor union is a CCP official with a seat at the proverbial banquet table that manages the company's employee affairs. So long as a company maintains good relations with the official union, Chinese workers weren't supposed to be allowed to organize against management, just as they were not able to exercise free speech, the right to vote, or other basic employee rights. And yet the protests happened.

Double-digit wage increases eventually ended the strikes, but they didn't bring back the old labor market. Factory employers who were slow to keep wage increases in line with market rates quickly saw their workers walking down the street to another plant to earn the market wage. Annual workforce turnover at factories of half or more were not uncommon.[9] After lagging behind GDP growth for the previous decade, average Chinese wages grew faster than GDP in 2011 and 2012, right alongside a marathon slowdown of the economy as a whole. Those who counted on another decade of cheap labor were perplexed at the speed with which dynamics shifted. What gives?

Migrants came, saw, and some are saying see ya later

China's migrant drought has to a large extent revealed that the usual explanation of how the Chinese labor market works rested on a longstanding fallacy, one that significantly overestimated the amount of excess labor. Many Chinese economists like to use the theories of Nobel Prize winning economist Arthur Lewis to explain their country's rapid growth.[10] Lewis thought of economic development as the interplay between a traditional subsistence sector and a modern capitalist sector. When industrialization begins, labor flows from the subsistence sector to the productive sector; becomes vastly more productive with the benefits of economies of scale, mass production, and technology; and contributes to rapid GDP growth. Wages remain very close to the subsistence levels because a glut of underutilized workers stand ready to take the jobs of any worker in the industrial sector who demands higher wages. The gains from higher productivity then accrue to the owners of capital, fueling further investment. It is only after the *Lewis turning point*, when the flow of excess labor from the subsistence sector slows to a trickle, that employers are forced to compete for access to the finite supply of unskilled labor, prompting sustained rise in wages.

It is easy to understand the appeal of this theory in China. The Lewisian subsistence sector feels intuitively familiar for the Chinese, who have long understood their countryside to hold a glut of underutilized workers, many of whom were itching to test their fortunes in the big city. The underlying motivation for the household registration (*hukou*) system was, in fact, to tie peasants down to their land and prevent urbanization from outpacing the government's ability to build the hard infrastructure and institutions that distinguish Chinese cities from the often unsafe, unsanitary, and politically unstable slums encircling the megalopolises of other developing countries.[11] Similarly, the

Lewisian industrial sector, where rapidly growing profits allow industrialists to reinvest in a more abundant and technologically sophisticated capital stock, fueling a virtuous cycle of higher productivity
and more profits, sounds like many of the hyper-growth era industrial
parks that encircle China's mega cities.

From a high level of abstraction, the Lewisian growth model
goes a long way to explain the persistence of low Chinese wages amid
rapidly rising labor productivity. But like many simple economic
models, it's best for explaining what will happen—so long as you don't
need to know when. Before the migrant drought, the data most commonly cited to determine when the Lewis turning point would be
breached was the urban-rural divide of the Chinese labor force (see
Figure 3.2).[12]

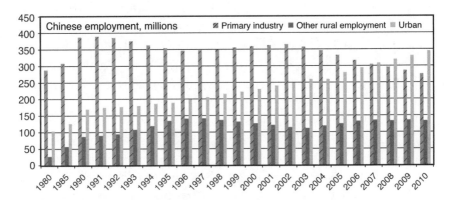

Figure 3.2 High-level data implied large pool of untapped rural labor

Source: China Statistical Yearbook 2011, authors' calculations

Looking simply at the urban-rural divide, China's labor force
seems reassuringly far from a turning point. Workers employed in
agriculture and related industries fell by over a fifth between 2000
and 2010, but still accounted for about two out of every five working Chinese. The reserve of low-productivity, low-wage agricultural
workers available to flock to cities and coastal factories should remain
full for another decade at least.

But this simple quantitative analysis ignores an ugly truth of how
the Chinese workforce functions, or at least how it functioned historically. By Western standards, China would be considered a racist,

sexist, ageist place to try to find a job, since nondiscrimination is a legal concept foreign to Chinese employers. Matter-of-fact discrimination in hiring along these dimensions is perhaps one of the most familiar and jarring experiences of expatriates on their first rotation in China. The header of a standard Chinese resumé or professional biography is laid out with six bits of information: name, gender, race, date of birth, party membership status, and place of birth. It was, and probably still is, standard practice to affix a headshot to the application, implying that physical appearance is another determinant in the hiring decision. During the previous decade of unrelenting growth, many factories would only hire female Han Chinese workers under the age of 25, because they were believed to be more easily managed than men and more energetic than older workers. Even today, Chinese female flight attendants are subject to explicit height and weight criteria. For migrant workers over the age of 40, finding work was exponentially more difficult than it was for younger migrants (and sometimes impossible). The distinct role of age discrimination in the Chinese labor market means that a smaller sliver of the job market, workforce entrants, paints a truer picture of the dynamics affecting the supply of factory workers. The conditions among the youngest cohorts in the labor market show that it is being upended much more clearly than does the aggregate view of all workers.

The transformation of demographics among the younger cohorts of Chinese workers is a legacy of China's overall demographic transition, one that has long been known and predicted but which had been expected to affect the economy only gradually over a period of several decades. For economic forecasters, demographics is a bit of a redheaded stepchild: The predictions it produces materialize much more slowly than do calls about next month's industrial production figures. And gradualism rarely moves a market preoccupied with today and tomorrow. No one, as far as we can tell, ever made a buck in China by sneaking an advanced copy of the annual household population sample survey and placing speculative futures trades ahead of its release. As such, demographics are remarkably underexamined outside specialist circles that consider their crucial role in growth and development.

Yet without China's demographic dividend, the Panda Boom could never have been. Indeed, it overlapped with a rapid rise of young people aging into the Chinese workforce, something of a baby boom echo generation. While the labor supply appeared endless in the 1980s, 1990s, and 2000s, economic policy increasingly favored the interests of enterprises at the expense of their workers, whether the interests were wages, fringe benefits, job security, or occupational safety. But, with a few egregious exceptions, workers were not forced to accept their jobs. Migrants took whatever work was available in the cities, where many of the opportunities turned out to be in construction. The work was a more attractive option than staying home in the countryside, where crowded plots of land would become even more so as a glut of young people aged into working years—subsistence living and a dearth of opportunities.

Westward they go

Just as the lightning-hot economy of 2005–2008 was absorbing the millions of workers laid off during the late 1990s, the schoolhouse gate opened wider to unleash larger and larger classes of high school graduates to take to the factories and construction sites. The cyclical shock from the global financial crisis and recession in 2008 and 2009 and subsequent stimulus program masked the dramatic trend of declining labor market entrants that characterized this period. By the time the crisis had passed in 2010, China's annual cohort of 18 year olds (as good a proxy as any for how many young people are "really" aging into the workforce) had fallen by a fifth from 2008 (see Figure 3.3).

For China's factories, the squeeze on the workforce was actually even more profound, a side effect of the explosion of higher education in China over the first decade of the 21st century. From 2000 to 2010, the number of young people enrolling in higher-education programs rather than entering the workforce after high school *tripled* from 2.2 million to 6.6 million. With so many young people hitting the books, the usual squeeze through the factory gates became more spacious; the number of 18-year-olds not enrolled in school fell by more than a third (see Figure 3.4).

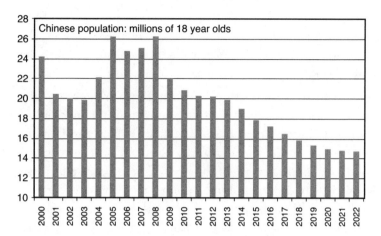

Figure 3.3 Labor force entrants fell rapidly after 2008

Source: U.S. Census Bureau International Database

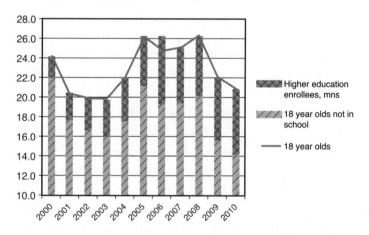

Figure 3.4 With more young people in school, fewer are working the factory floor

Source: China Statistical Yearbook 2011, U.S. Census International Database, authors' calculations

Chinese factory managers have more or less adapted, willingly or otherwise, to the new reality. Employers are, of course, raising wages as necessary to keep their workers from walking off the line. Some foreign manufacturers are contemplating relocation to Southeast Asia, where wages remain much lower than in coastal China. But the lack of Chinese-quality ports, roads, and electricity supplies in less-developed Southeast Asian countries limits the appeal of this choice to the most labor-intensive operations. Manufacturers are also shifting factories further inland, away from the largest Chinese cities where costs of doing business (and wages) are highest.

Moving inland appeals for three reasons. First, urban wage rates in southwestern Chinese cities such as Chengdu or Chongqing are markedly lower than in Shanghai, Shenzhen, or Beijing, despite rapid increases. The immediate discount is an appealing short-term payoff of relocation. Second is a more "strategic" reason. Locating factories in a large inland city can appeal to local migrants who would rather work 6 hours from their home village instead of 26 hours away in Guangdong. These quality-of-life concerns are compelling to older migrant workers, who feel more pressure to visit home. Their sense of familial obligations is generally more acute than the migrants in their late teens or early twenties, who are often unmarried and usually childless. Third is that local governments in poorer hinterland regions are more welcoming to factory employers than governments in the vicinity of Shanghai and Beijing, which reserve preferential tax and other policies for employers creating high paying, high-skilled jobs (that is, not manual labor).

One prominent case of relocation is the now-infamous and controversial Taiwanese firm Foxconn. It is the machine behind Apple's brain, the blaster to the late Steve Jobs's master—a link visible but unseen in the Cupertino tech giant's supply chain. The performance of Foxconn—whether it could meet the exacting standards of Jobs's perfectionism as well as produce enough units for a new product launch—mattered greatly for Apple's reputation and company value. It is also the reason that Apple could slash the prices of its products repeatedly: Foxconn could control production costs, including labor. But as worker discontent and demands crescendoed in 2011, Foxconn made the highly public decision to relocate most of its production facilities from Guangdong Province to inland China to keep labor costs down. Given the city-sized scale of Foxconn operations, with about 400,000 in its Shenzhen campus, the firm's actions served as something of a bellwether for the thousands of other manufacturers that dot the Guangdong landscape.

Workers with attitude

If a job close to home appeals in particular to older migrant workers as a practical way to balance work and family obligations, it also appeals to migrants of the post-1980s and 1990s generation, but for different reasons. The younger migrants tend to weigh lifestyle considerations heavily and approach the workforce with radically different expectations and attitudes than previous generation of workers. Early on in the post-1978 reform and opening period, migrant workers often left their parents and siblings (the one-child policy was less strictly enforced in the countryside than in cities) for life in the factory town or the city. The labor they found in Chinese factories was tough and mind-numbing work to be sure, but still compared favorably to the exhausting rigors of farm life in a remote, low-tech, labor-intensive agrarian village economy.

The new generation of migrant workers, by contrast, hardly worked the farm, if ever at all, and often never saw their parents working it either. Many of them are already second-generation migrants, either born in the cities or following their parents to more developed parts of China on a long-established path after growing old enough in their "home" village to work. Many of China's 30-year-old migrant workers today actually migrated a decade ago, and have now lived more of their adult lives in urban China than in their rural villages.

The generational divide has ushered in important behavioral and psychological changes in the younger migrant labor pool. Of the roughly 262 million migrant workers, more than 35% are between the ages of 16 to 30.[13] Their mentality and attitude toward manual labor differs significantly from that of their parents. Recent studies from Chinese think tanks have shown that these new migrants are less motivated by simple financial opportunities, but are in pursuit of career advancement and individual interests. Moreover, they tend to put a premium on social justice and fair treatment, implying that their tolerance for longstanding tensions in the Chinese employer-employee relationship is on a shorter fuse.[14] Even the Chinese government can no longer ignore this emerging cohort. In the State Council's annual number-one document in 2010, which for the past decade or so has predictably focused on rural sector development, for the first time mentioned the issue of the new generation of workers.[15]

Laid-off migrant workers were strikingly resistant to returning to the farm during the short-lived downturn of 2009, either because the livelihood the government assumed was waiting for them there did not actually exist or because they were too accustomed to the comparatively posh modern lifestyle of urban China.[16] Many of them have more in common with their hukou-wielding urbanite contemporaries than with earlier generations raised in their villages. A 2011 study by the former National Population and Family Planning Commission found that more than 1 in 20 of China's post-1990s generation of migrant workers holds a college degree.[17]

The penetration of technology is also transforming this relatively new Chinese factory labor force. Today's factory workers are overwhelmingly participants in the hyper-connected world of mobile communications, benefiting as much as any other Chinese from the ability to instantly connect with their colleagues and friends across the country and share information on wages, work conditions, all within the bounds of the government censors. On their mobile phones or in Internet cafes, migrant workers have an unprecedented ability to communicate with each other and to access information relative to previous generations of "proletarian" Chinese. These new tools have given the younger migrants more leverage, or at least awareness of changes in the labor market, and they are behaving accordingly.

Warmer, cuddlier policy for migrants

Government attitudes toward migrants in the cities have changed dramatically from a decade ago, when it was still technically illegal for migrant workers to live in urban China without authorization. Members of the *floating population,* as they were called, were subject to intense scrutiny and frequent harassment by the police. Migrants who were caught without proper identification cards used to be detained in prison-like houses, and many simply disappeared, never to be heard from again.

These unsavory practices were exposed in the seminal Sun Zhigang case in 2003. A recent art school graduate from central China, Sun arrived in the southern city of Guangzhou as a migrant. On an evening stroll in the city, he had left his identification card home. A local official, most likely a *chengguan,* one of the authorities most despised by the Chinese public because they are often involved in forcible removal of people from their homes for property development, spotted Sun and sized him up as a migrant. Unable to produce his identification, Sun was swiftly taken to a shadowy detention center. Within days, his family was informed that he had fallen ill and died under detainment. Yet his autopsy revealed severe wounds and internal bleeding, strongly suggesting a violent death. The relatively liberal press in Guangdong championed the Sun case in an effort to advocate reforms of the detention system and humane treatment for migrant workers. Although in its infancy at the time, the emergent Chinese blogosphere played an important role in making a legal issue out of the Sun tragedy.[18] The top leaders in Beijing paid attention and eventually rescinded the detention policy.

In recognition of the ugly reality of migrant lives, government policy subsequently began to shift in the mid-2000s, in part because of the economic need to leverage urbanization as China's next driver of economic growth. The State Council promulgated a notice in 2011 (only made public a year later) that encourages municipal governments of smaller cities to create a pathway for migrants to obtain urban household registration after they have fulfilled minimum periods of contribution to social security and tax programs and have proof of local residence.[19] The tolerance of strikes against foreign-owned employers in 2010, when local governments intervened minimally to force the workers back to the production lines and did not severely stifle press coverage, also illustrates the modestly rising status of workers in the Chinese political pecking order.

For obvious reasons, the government has not publicly announced an official change in policy to better accommodate the needs of workers rather than employers, because doing so would be tantamount to an admission of the government's earlier inadequacy in protecting workers' well-being. And few things irk the Chinese government more than having to publicly admit a policy mistake. But if one were to connect the dots of less-draconian reactions to strikes, modestly less-anti-migrant urbanization policies, and less-oppressive police treatment of migrant workers, it paints a new de facto policy regime elevating workers' rights. This new world both reacts to a changing reality and helps to shape it. The government's newfound tolerance for workers' demands and actions, in part exemplified by the longer leash permitted for labor activism, will undoubtedly shape factory worker attitudes and tactics in future labor negotiations.

School of hard knocks

The flip side of the dearth of blue-collar labor has been the glut of recent college graduates that scarcely qualify for work in China's competitive job market. China is new to the notion of the democratization of higher education, as it is to many aspects of what most in the West would consider modern institutions. During the beginning of the market economy era in the 1980s, less than 3% of Chinese young people received a four-year university education. This exclusive cabal of credentialed elites was placed into high-flying careers and lived lifestyles befitting their social status. Even in the 1980s, an advanced education commanded a high income and access to the best housing, healthcare, and education for one's own children when they arrived. What's more, in the city where the lucky few completed their studies, they had relatively easy access to urban household registration; a local state-owned work unit could easily secure an urban hukou booklet for an employee with an advanced degree.

That was then. Recall those 4.4 million additional higher-education enrollees since 2000? They now face a life that would be totally unrecognizable to graduates a generation earlier, who had the fortune of first-mover advantage. Tripling the size of the higher-education system in only a decade has meant a rapid proliferation of new institutions, most of which provide educations—and professional prospects—that can't compare with those of the graduates of the top-tier institutions. A massive riot staged in 2006 illustrated how important the qualitative difference between lifestyles of graduates of elite universities and those of graduates of newer, less-prestigious institutions are to new graduates. Some graduates of the satellite campus of a university in central China apparently went berserk when they discovered that their diplomas designated them graduates of the satellite, not of the prestigious parent university as they were originally promised.[20] Everyone understands the professional benefits of belonging to the second category.

In a situation that would sound familiar to Americans, graduates of lower-ranked, newly founded universities have struggled to find good entry-level jobs. Beijing University researcher Lian Si coined the poignant phrase by which these struggling young people are known in China: *the ant tribe*—industrious, intelligent, yet anonymous and deprived of humanizing membership in a coherent society.[21] They live in small, crowded, shared apartments at the edge of major cities, scraping by to make rent. The plum university graduate jobs at SOEs, in government, or working for glitzy multinationals are no more attainable for these young people than for migrant workers of the same age. And without a good employer to secure their place in urban China, these young people are no better integrated into the economic and social fabric of their new urban societies than are migrant workers. In fact, average starting wages for college graduates were actually lower than average migrant worker salaries in 2011.[22] So much for the premium placed on intellectual pedigree. The mismatch between labor supply and demand in this particular segment generates a sense of scarcity of its own.

What happens when your key economic input shrinks?

China's demographic hangover poses an existential and tangible threat to the current growth model. This challenge was vividly apparent in China's key economic indicators in 2012: while growth was only marginally slower than in 2011, the simultaneously tight labor market and sluggish aggregate demand benefitted working Chinese over their employers. In nominal terms, GDP rose 9.8% from 2011, but in a change for China, more of the gains from growth accrued to workers than they did to the owners of capital.

Median urban disposable incomes rose by 15%. Corporate profits of industrial firms, by contrast, rose by only 5%. The balance of supply and demand in China's urban employment centers, a useful quarterly indicator of the tightness of the job market, reached an all-time high in 2012 (see Figure 3.5).

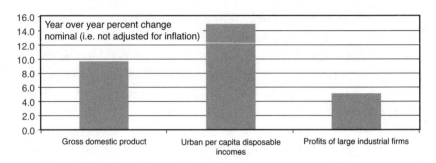

Figure 3.5 Rebalancing good for workers, challenging for employers

Source: National Bureau of Statistics[23]

The impact on manufacturers was even more painful in the export-oriented private sector than for domestically oriented manufacturers, often in heavy industry and selling to meet demand from Chinese infrastructure and real estate investment. Much of this is evident when comparing the HSBC China purchasing managers indexes (PMI) compiled by Markit, which are more representative of trends in smaller, private, and export oriented firms, to the PMI compiled by the state-controlled China Federation of Logistics and Purchasing Managers, which disproportionately tracks conditions in large, capital-intensive, and state-owned manufacturing firms. An appreciating currency and several years of inflation persistently outpacing that of China's major export markets have already put upward pressure on the cost of doing business in China. Rapidly rising wages reinforced that dynamic by further accelerating the country's shift from an export-oriented to domestically focused economy. Economic underperformance in the United States, Europe, and Japan also did China no favors. The country was getting hit from both sides—internal structural changes and external volatility—unambiguously validating the need to adjust China's economic model.

To a great extent, China's demographic hangover is actually good news for rebalancing its economy—from the dependence on investment and exports as the source of final demand that characterized the capital-intensive model toward household consumption. Tight labor markets are spurring very rapid wage growth, an essential component of this transition. After all, a consumption-fueled economy cannot materialize without income growth; otherwise, consumers don't have the money they need to consume the products they need and want. But the process of transition does not benefit all, to say the least. Rebalancing means households living on their salaries get more of the economic pie. Entrepreneurs, "red capitalists," multinationals, and the tax collector, however, will be left with less.

Cashing out on the demographic dividend: an "uh oh" moment?

All governments would prefer to avoid governing a country at the end of the demographic dividend. In the United States, the end of the demographic dividend is coinciding with a contentious fight over the funding and distribution of public goods. In Europe, the rapid growth of unfunded pension obligations is making the Eurozone's currency crisis all the more difficult to contain. In Japan, the depths of the demographic deficit have turned the government balance sheet into Swiss cheese, decimating its ability to fund anything besides the welfare of retirees. Simple demographic arithmetic underlies the complex politics of austerity: fewer workers paying into social welfare programs, more retirees consuming their services.

Governing and encouraging economic development are much easier with an enormous demographic windfall blowing at a government's back, propelling its economy forward even if policies are less than optimal. At the end of the windfall, individual policies and economic decisions start to matter much more. Any government in this situation will need to be a whole lot smarter and more creative in designing policy incentives once its working age population is shrinking and social spending obligations growing.

The challenges the Chinese government faces at the end of its demographic dividend are in many ways quite similar to those of other countries. Economic growth has already slowed after the end of the Panda Boom era and will slow further in the decade ahead. A deceleration in the growth of the working-age population would translate into slower GDP growth even if efficiency per worker rose in line with historic trends. But in a demographic hangover, productivity growth (that is, growth in output per worker) is likely to slow markedly. This is partly because of a less-productivity-friendly mix of economic activity. Expanding demand for services for retirees means that more share of Chinese GDP will be generated by retirement homes, community activity centers, dialysis clinics, and geriatric care institutes. It's much harder to double GDP per person employed in these parts of the economy than it is in the manufacturing sector, the part of the global economy where productivity growth has been consistently fastest since the industrial revolution.

What's more, the demographic hangover will have an indirect but hardly negligible impact on the financial system. Working people are net savers as they prepare for retirement, and then they become net dis-savers—that is, spend down their savings—when they retire. During China's demographic dividend, a bulge of net savers contributed to a flood of financial system liquidity that was channeled through the banks into a proliferation of investment in productivity enhancing infrastructure: factories, roads, ports, you name it. As those workers retire, the supply of savings will shrink, as will the capacity of the Chinese economy to invest. It is nearly impossible to overcome this huge secular trend, even if the Chinese economy were to magically become more efficient at allocating investment. More constrained financial liquidity will increase inflationary pressures because the amount of credit growth that would have been normal in years past now exceeds the funding capacity of China's savers.

Public policy: A dash of creativity and wisdom needed

Some of the government's conundrums are particular to China, however. Slower economic growth, which will be a direct legacy of the demographic hangover, will blunt some of the government's most effective tools at managing its hybrid market economy. Beijing has been incredibly successful at growing out of economic problems. The bad loans crippling the banking sector at the dawn of the hyper growth era weren't fully repaid, for example—they just shrank relative to the rest of the financial industry as the economy raced ahead and gradually became small enough that they no longer posed a systemic risk to the economy.[24]

Similarly, even after the wrenching changes of the late 1990s, the state sector continued to shrink as a share of GDP because the private sector grew much faster.[25] All indications are that the government plans to deal with the fallout from the credit boom of 2009–2010, which will inevitably generate hefty bad loans, in the same way as, for example, how the banking sector was restructured in the late 1990s and early 2000s: Spin off nonperforming loans into "bad banks" that the Chinese call asset management companies, have the government guarantee the bad banks' liabilities to the economy's more sound financial institutions, and wait for the economy to grow, making the debt problem shrink relative to the size of the economy.

This becomes a much less-effective strategy for crisis resolution if the Chinese pie grows half or a quarter as fast as it did during the Panda Boom. Geriatric societies from Japan to Greece to the United States have struggled with the impossibility of "growing out of the problem" when fiscal or financial crisis looms. There is no magical switch to flip and return growth to boom-era rates. China is already vastly more cautious about allocating debt financing in 2013 than it was in 1993, but it will have to become more cautious still to prevent the dismal math of slowing growth from overwhelming its national balance sheet.

Another uniquely Chinese policymaking conundrum will be what kind of institutions need to be concocted to provide the vast amounts of social services needed by an elderly population. Before the end of the 20th century, care for the aging population in China was understood to be a responsibility of the family unit, not of the government. Multigenerational households, large families, and a relatively small share of the population living beyond their 70s or 80s made this a manageable proposition. But this arrangement will no longer work. China's elderly population is already exploding, more than doubling from 86 million in 2000 to 172 million in 2020.[26] Older Chinese people will increasingly have only one or two children who could take care of them, not the large extended families of earlier generations. And most crucially, the children of China's aged are increasingly likely to live far from home.

The newly installed government of President Xi Jinping and Premier Li Keqiang continues to look to rapid urbanization to fuel economic growth, a point of continuity from the previous administration. But urbanization means migration from country to city, a journey often lasting more than a day from a village in the Chinese interior to the traditional manufacturing hubs of southern or eastern China. Wealthier Chinese migrants have the possibility of moving their parents to the city to take care of them. For the vast majority of Chinese rural families whose young people go to the cities for work, however, that is not economically feasible. The greatest need for retirement homes, and for services for the elderly, is concentrated in the country's poorest backwaters, where neither rural families nor the resource-poor local governments (state resources are proportional to the level of development of the local economy) can afford them.

Challenges to companies, both foreign and domestic, likewise constitute a mix of the familiar and the unique. Companies are already moving factories inland and raising wages to adapt to the new balance of power between migrant workers and employers. Inevitably, many companies will also start incorporating business practices for managing a mature workforce, analogous to those adopted in the United States or Europe. In addition to locating their factories closer to migrant worker hometowns to help members of the sandwich generation of middle-aged migrants, with both children and parents back in their home village dependent on them, companies will likely eventually pursue more flexible work schedules that appeal to older workers no longer able or interested in working a traditional factory shift.

More broadly, corporate strategy is adapting to the end of cheap Chinese labor at the same time that demographic changes are contributing to slower economic growth. Such a shift matters most for multinationals, which are allocating investment, R&D, and managerial resources between China and other markets. A lower-growth but more-expensive China won't drive the multinationals away, however. The value proposition of being in China will still be largely driven by proximity to the world's largest high-growth market, the one that adds the most to global aggregate demand each year. Even as China descends from stratospheric growth rates, it will almost certainly retain this role in the global pecking order for another decade.

However, China's role as an outsourcing paradise has begun to turn into a merely normal vacation spot. In the United States, this is encouraging companies to contemplate shifting production back onshore or relocating the lower-value-added and more labor-intensive processes to other emerging markets such as Mexico or Vietnam. China's demographic hangover will also mean increased mechanization of the production remaining in China. As labor becomes more expensive, machines become relatively cheaper and a more attractive option for maximizing efficiency.

Finally, China's demographic hangover could coincide with a right-sizing of expectations about what China can mean for a multinational's business. This seems most likely to affect multinational managers' willingness to accommodate Chinese characteristics—the combination of regulatory uncertainty, intellectual property violations, and the risk of becoming embroiled in corruption scandals that seem much harder to avoid there than in a developed market. A deeper and protracted bout of foreign disillusionment with the China dream of 1.4 billion customers could paradoxically serve as a catalyst for the government to renew economic and institutional reforms.[27]

When 150 million workers unite

China's demographic hangover is here, as unexpected and unpleasant as the morning after a thirtieth birthday. A drought of labor force entrants is ushering in profound and sweeping changes to China's society and economy: empowering migrant workers, rebalancing the economy, and challenging the government and Chinese families alike to manage unfamiliar terrain in the family structure.

Some of these changes will be welcome in naturally facilitating long-term economic sustainability. A glut of urban-born college graduates and a dearth of rural-born blue-collar workforce entrants may unintentionally narrow the inequalities between urban and rural and highly educated and less-educated workers that have ballooned after a generation of divergence. It must be a relief for the government that a secular force such as the demographic transition has arrived to accomplish what its own policies have not. However, the strains of a rapidly changing population also bring new and unfamiliar complexities. Given the facility with which the government has managed difficult economic transitions in the past 20 years—forcing the military out of the market economy in the 1990s and initiating the Panda Boom later that decade—the purely economic dimensions seem daunting, but no more so than similar problems that have been managed adequately during China's reform and opening process.

Instead, it's the social and political dimensions of the demographic hangover that seem most perplexing. If given to informed speculation, the rise of an independent labor movement could potentially trigger the most revolutionary of these sociopolitical manifestations. Its organization would probably be less through traditional command and control institutions that the CCP has effectively managed and co-opted over the years and more through social media and "flash mob"-style informal arrangements. Regardless, the reality today is that China's newly empowered migrant workers are new participants in urban civic life. Although their interests have long been poorly represented in Chinese politics, migrant workers are awake, albeit still groggy and unclear about precisely what they want. Will they shake the world or, at the very least, push China into a new stage of people-oriented development?

Part II

Social Scarcity

4

Welfare: Socialism with Chinese... actually no, not socialism at all

An otherwise uneventful spring afternoon in Harbin #1 Hospital was shattered when a 17-year-old brandishing a fruit knife barged into an administrative office. Li Mengnan attacked the closest bystander, a 28-year-old medical intern named Wang Hao. Absorbed in his studies and caught off guard, Wang had no time to react as Li's knife punctured his carotid artery, a wound that proved fatal later in the day. Three other office staff also sustained injuries while fending off Li's attack. When the police found Li, he was in the hospital emergency room, patching a neck wound he had inflicted upon himself in an apparent suicide attempt.

Li, a teenager from rural Heilongjiang Province, which borders Siberia, had accompanied his 62-year-old grandfather on a ten-hour train ride to the provincial capital Harbin for specialist treatment. The grandson was afflicted with ankylosing spondylitis, a debilitating chronic condition that in China can be effectively diagnosed and treated only in major urban hospitals, a financially crippling prospect for a poor rural family. Regardless, Li's grandfather was determined to use his savings from a life of labor as a coal miner to cure his grandson. Li's attack, made during their third such trip in March 2012, followed his doctor's refusal to admit him for an extended stay, instead telling him to return in another month. Li later recalled that he was particularly angry at the doctor's dismissal and lack of concern for the toll that repeated travel to the hospital was having on his sickly grandfather, who took the grueling train ride despite battling gastric cancer himself. Li snapped. His revenge was as existentially indifferent to his victims' identity as the hospital had been to his: his murder victim, Wang, wasn't even the doctor who shunted him. He was just a randomly chosen hospital employee, in the wrong place at the wrong time.

This tragedy in Heilongjiang was the cover story of an April 2012 issue of *Caixin,* a trailblazing investigative and feature magazine.[1] The issue led with the story not because it was a horrific and isolated incident, but rather the opposite. Hospital violence now occurs so often in China that individual incidents are almost ceasing to shock. The routineness of Li's violent outburst epitomizes why Chinese hospital violence has become an acute public concern.

Indeed, a similarly bloody scene rocked a hospital half a year earlier in another corner of the country. A former patient of an ENT (ear, nose, throat) specialist in Beijing, who seemed to blame the recurrence of his medical conditions on the specialist's ineffective surgery, slashed his doctor 18 times with a cleaver in an attempted revenge killing. The attacker, Wang Baoming, was subsequently handed a 15-year prison sentence, a verdict that the prosecutor argued was too lenient. According to the prosecuting attorney, defendant Wang demonstrated no remorse in the courtroom, insisting instead that the hospital be held accountable for what happened.[2]

Doctors everywhere face a high-risk environment when taking patients' lives in their hands. In the United States, the risk of medical malpractice lawsuits can indirectly incentivize doctors to recommend unnecessary tests and procedures for patients as a kind of "insurance" in the event an upset patient takes a case to court. Chinese doctors don't worry as much about being sued. Instead, they work under the regular occupational hazard of retributive violence at their patients' hands. China's spate of hospital stabbings reveals an uncomfortable truth about the state of Chinese healthcare: The same institutional reforms that have created a vibrant and massive manufacturing and investment-led economy have been much less successful when applied to the healthcare system.[3] Instead of blossoming under the Panda Boom's laissez-faire liberalization, Chinese healthcare is strained nearly to the breaking point and unable to accommodate rising demand.

The perverse incentives of hospitals operating as profit centers rather than public-interest-minded service providers have pitted hospital and patient interests against each other. Doctors are sandwiched between revenue targets that they can meet only by prescribing unnecessary drugs and procedures from above and resentful and distrustful patients from below. Little wonder that a 2008 survey showed two-thirds of Chinese doctors have symptoms of depression.[4] The exorbitant cost of medical care without a functioning social safety net also deepens the stratification between China's haves and the have-nots (like Li and his family). Although Li's and Wang's extreme actions, with intent to kill, are outliers, the pressures that drove them to deadly violence are painfully familiar to countless participants in the Chinese healthcare system.

The current reality was hardly preordained. In fact, until the late 1980s, China boasted a remarkably good healthcare system for a poor country, which dramatically raised life expectancy from just 41 years in the 1950s to 73 years in 2009, and considerably reduced death rates at birth.[5] Impressive achievements of yesteryear, however, are now overshadowed by public outrage and a crisis of confidence in the government's ability to meet citizens' expectations. What happened?

The disintegration of the public health system directly resulted from policies that prioritized spending to feed unrelenting market-driven growth over public-interest social welfare institutions. China's seeming abundance of "hard capital" has come at the expense of starving the welfare state. The flourishing economy of the past 15 years was funded by funneling resources away from public welfare and toward productive investment and industrialization: call it *beating stethoscopes into plowshares.* Underfunding and lack of public trust are problems that are not merely confined to the healthcare system. Indeed, the end of the extraordinary growth era will spread the health system's ailments throughout other components of the social safety net. Even if policy shifts resources away from hard investment and back into social spending, the "Floridization" of Chinese demographics will intensify the shortage of healthcare provision over the next decade, worsening the frayed social contract between patients, providers, and the government.

Dismantling the welfare system...

While maintaining a nominally socialist regime, the Chinese Communist Party (CCP) has long abandoned the trappings of a socialist economy, a reality particularly evident in the provision of social welfare such as healthcare and pensions. Under Chairman Mao Zedong, when communism dogma still flourished and inspired idealism, the delivery of social welfare in urban China ran through the state-controlled *danwei*, or work unit. It was an all-encompassing system that essentially dictated an individual's social and professional life, public and private. The danwei dispensed housing, education, and entertainment. Though usually not of high quality, danwei public services were at least guaranteed, secure, and nearly free, with the trade-off being that the reasonable range of human activities—from work to play—fell under the watchful eye of the CCP.

Healthcare in urban China was also provided via the danwei. While access to medical benefits was employer based, the state fully subsidized and determined how benefits were disbursed. Public hospitals designated to serve work units provided the necessary care. Service was far from global standards or sophistication, but it was easily accessible and affordable; drug prescriptions, for example, were largely reimbursable. In short, it was a socialized healthcare system that, at a minimum, gave adequate and effective basic care to the urban population.

In rural China, social services were delivered through a system of agricultural communes. The CCP organized the hundreds of millions of farmers in the agricultural sector, the largest part of the economy under Mao, into collectives to improve delivery of services, organize production, and facilitate political control. Collectives were assigned production goals and required to submit their surpluses to Beijing according to state-determined prices and quota targets. Because people were cheaper than machines—and rural China had plenty of people—there was little incentive to mechanize or produce at scale. Rural life was technologically primitive, and public health services were no exception. Part of the communes' revenues were set aside to finance commensurately meager local health clinics and the so-called barefoot doctors, rural health providers trained to manage simple conditions and make home visits to treat the sick. If a health issue was more serious or complex, patients would be triaged up a hierarchical system to a county hospital, which maintained better quality staff and more advanced facilities than those available in rural clinics. In these ways, most rural residents had access to some form of healthcare, albeit generally inferior to what was available in cities.

When Chinese patriarch Deng Xiaoping initiated major market reforms in the 1980s, the commune system was dismantled and replaced by a household responsibility system, devolving production targets to the household level and allowing producers to keep their surplus above government targets. The retreat of the state left a healthcare service vacuum in rural China. As the communes disappeared, a fairly functional and effective financing system for rural healthcare vanished with them. Farmers and the rural population at large soon found themselves forced to fend for themselves in securing healthcare. Even the barefoot doctors were forced to seek private opportunities.[6] A decade later in the 1990s, the danwei system crumbled too, as state-owned enterprises (SOEs) were absolved of the responsibility to shoulder social obligations, such as providing employees' healthcare or reimbursing medical bills, to encourage them to focus on lifting industrial profitability.

Change happened so rapidly and constantly that city-dwellers and rural Chinese alike had little time to digest what the dismantling of the old system meant for their lives. Few realized that it marked the end of the social contract that the government forged with Chinese citizens.

The end of the planned economy health delivery system was one facet of a larger government strategy to allow many of the social welfare institutions of the pre-1978 era to atrophy as it transformed agriculture, industry and commerce into market-oriented systems. Destroying the work unit-based welfare state was instrumental to the country's transition from planned to market-oriented economy. It was state-guided creative destruction, or what might be called

"Schumpter with Chinese characteristics."[7] The financial burden of providing free housing, education, healthcare, and pensions—some employees didn't even have to buy their own groceries—was a huge drain on SOEs' cash flow, constraining their abilities to invest in their businesses. But more fundamentally, SOEs' expansive responsibilities for their employees' lives outside the factory were a distraction from the factory floor itself, one that the ailing state sector could not afford. During the period of political and economic turmoil in the late 1980s and early 1990s, the central government was struggling desperately to avoid the kind of stagflation that would wrest its control over a rapidly changing society.

From containing a potentially disastrous economic contraction amid the Asian Financial Crisis of 1997–1998 to acceding to the World Trade Organization in 2001, the Chinese government's major priorities did not emphasize social welfare policies. The state believed it must choose between ordering work units to serve as a foundation of the welfare state or remaining viable commercial concerns. Fearing a Soviet-style economic collapse, it decisively chose the latter. The Panda Boom policy mix channeled state sector money (fiscal budgets, state-owned bank loans, and SOE operating surpluses) away from social spending and into industrial projects, property, and infrastructure, the tangible building blocks of economic growth. It was an incredibly effective growth-at-all-costs strategy, and its costs were substantial. The old health system withered in the 1990s, and the government neglected to implement a new one in its stead. As the social safety net was pulled out from underneath Chinese households, out-of-pocket costs of healthcare ballooned from only 20% of all health spending in 1978 to 60% in 2001 (see Table 4.1).[8]

4.1 China's healthcare spending

	Total spending (100 million yuan)	Government spending	Social spending	Individual spending	% government	% individual
1995	2,155.1	387.3	767.8	1,000.0	18	46.4
1996	2,709.4	461.6	875.7	1,372.2	17	51
1997	3,196.7	523.6	984.1	1,689.1	16.4	53
1998	3,678.7	590.1	1,071	2,017.6	16	55
1999	4,047.5	641	1,146	2,260.6	16	56
2000	4,586.6	709.5	1,171.9	2,705.2	15.5	59
2001	5,025.9	800.6	1,211.4	3,013.9	16	60
2002	5,790	908.5	1,539.4	3,342.1	16	58
2003	6,584.1	1,116.9	1,788.5	3,678.7	17	56
2004	7,590.3	1,293.6	2,225.4	4,071.4	17	54
2005	8,659.9	1,552.5	2,586.4	4,521.0	18	52.2
2006	9,843.3	1,778.9	3,210.9	4,853.6	18	49
2007	11,289.5	2,297.1	3,893.7	5,098.7	20.4	45.2

Source: Ministry of Health Statistics Yearbook, 2009[9]

Although the individual share of healthcare costs has dipped modestly from its turn-of-the-century highs to around 45%, China's total spending on healthcare remains meager—only about 5% of GDP as recently as 2010, according to official figures. This stands in stark contrast to the 8-9% of GDP that the United States currently spends on healthcare.[10] Chinese spending is only barely above the 3% average for middle-income countries at similar levels of economic development and that have far smaller elderly populations consuming disproportionate shares of healthcare, according to the World Bank. It's even worse in terms of per capita government healthcare spending, about $240, though consultancies such as McKinsey & Company anticipate that spending will increase.[11] The burden on households for healthcare spending inevitably rose. For most urban residents now, it is still common to pay 50% of healthcare costs out of pocket. Although its total spending on healthcare is below average, China's out-of-pocket expenses are much higher than average, even when compared to OECD countries.[12]

Rising personal costs weren't the only change. The manner in which public hospitals functioned also experienced a makeover, largely as an adaptation to increasing marketization of the economy. Politically, the public hospitals were supposed to continue serving "social functions" and were officially discouraged from being profit-driven enterprises. Yet economically, the disappearance of heavy state subsidies forced them to generate their own revenues. The dissonance between the political and economic logics created perverse incentives that warped the behavior of hospital systems and doctors.

As hospitals increasingly became semi-private entities, the de facto profit motive has overwhelmed their *de jure* purpose of providing a public good.[13] The absence of a robust health insurance system forces hospitals to directly squeeze the patients. Complicated surgical procedures generally require a down payment, sometimes in the form of a red envelope stuffed with cash, before the surgeon lifts a finger. And when doctors lose money on services provided under cost at government-regulated rates, they often push unnecessary and expensive drugs onto patients and skim off the top to hit their revenue targets.[14] Rather than discouraging the practice, hospitals often push doctors into it because the hospital-run pharmacy is a profit magnet. Little by little, public hospitals have degenerated into pay-as-you-go rackets rather than patients-first servants of the public good.

Even if the drugs that hospitals sell are necessary, their costs are often astronomically out of proportion with the average Chinese income. In Li's case, his grandfather supported a family of four on a minimum social security income—called the *dibao*—that meted out a mere 1,000 yuan ($158) per month. And the cost of filling the prescription to treat Li's spondylitis? More than ten times the grandfather's salary.

Rampant over-prescription of drugs and treatment not only imposes higher costs on patients but may also lead to physical harm. A recent study that surveyed hundreds of health clinics and city hospitals and pored over 230,000 prescriptions found that hospitals were regularly overprescribing items like antibiotics at about double the rate recommended by the World Health Organization.[15] Even when compared to other developing countries, China apparently has a high rate of prescribing injections, particularly of steroids, whose overuse can trigger serious adverse effects. Unlike in the United States, where the always-present threat of medical malpractice lawsuits tends to mitigate blatant and egregious abuses of medical authority, the possibility of fatal patient retribution may become the only factor that dissuades a Chinese doctor from peddling expensive, unnecessary, or dangerous treatments.

It is little wonder that the public has hardened its perception of healthcare professionals as profit-mongers with few moral scruples. Yet the blame cannot be placed entirely on the doctors, who command meager pay and even less prestige. They are operating in an environment in which supply is constrained and demand appears endless, yet the doctors are underpaid and severely overworked. Their salaries have lagged behind those earned by similarly educated professionals in urban China, only reinforcing the tacit understanding that they can supplement their income by pocketing extra fees from patients. Meanwhile, a staggering six billion total outpatient visits occurred in 2011, equal to an average of five visits per Chinese citizen.[16] One doctor in Beijing recalled seeing 60 patients in a single day, while a colleague served 40.[17] Under these circumstances, patients are shuffled in and out to maximize the number of patients served rather than attentive care—a fast food model at premium prices.

Demand is so overwhelming that hospitals must impose strict registration processes for patients, a Kafkaesque "take a number" system. Anyone who has stepped foot inside the Chinese embassy's visa office in Washington, D.C. will immediately understand the hospital's numbers system. The embassy's cramped room is usually filled with visa applicants, anxiously clasping their tickets and eyeing the digital counters, while casting intimidating glances at each other as if to warn against line cutting. Nevertheless, every applicant assumes the pounce-ready position before his or her number is called, because all assume that a nanosecond of hesitance means that *someone* will swoop in their place.

Now, imagine that the waiting room is rationing life-and-death health services, rather than visa stamps. Unsurprisingly, the numbers approach has spawned a cottage industry that profits off of reselling "good" numbers to visitors to the hospital so that they can actually have access to a doctor. Like scalpers who roam outside Fenway Park or Yankees Stadium, these Chinese scalpers are in the business of monopolizing a scarce resource, which they provide with great convenience—and at a significant markup. To see a specialist, for example, a typical registration for an appointment officially costing around 10 yuan ($1.60) could have a street price of hundreds of yuan.

To be sure, such illegal scalping is not new, and in fact has created headaches for both the hospitals and local law enforcement for years. An intrepid Chinese reporter went undercover in 2005 to profile scalper activities.[18] When he arrived outside a Beijing hospital around 9 p.m., the scene looked like a stadium the night before premium tickets go on sale, with concertgoers parked in lawn chairs lining up to wait to buy. At the Beijing hospital, the lawn chairs were available to rent for 5 yuan ($0.80) per hour and a deposit of 200 yuan ($31.50). Within minutes, the reporter was approached by a young man who asked if he needed a number to see a specialist. The reporter declined initially, confident in the fact that his early arrival would mean that he would be able to see a doctor today. Yet the young scalper only chuckled at what seemed to be the reporter's naiveté, replying that it mattered little how early he arrived; the scalper has seen patients wait for days and even weeks before getting access.

The scalper boasted about the fact that his group occupied the front of the line and that he guaranteed success or the fee will be returned. So what is the fee? First, hand over a personal identification card (the hospitals require real-name registration) and 14 yuan (~$2.00) for the normal registration fee. Second, when picking up the registration number and personal identification, a 300 yuan ($47) fee for the scalper's "labor" is demanded. When the reporter tried to haggle over the price, he was spurned. According to the scalper, his business's operating costs included paying his people 50 yuan (~$8) to stand in line, another 60 yuan ($9.50) to rent a lawn chair, and with only ten specialists available, 300 yuan ($47) is the absolute minimum. Much like a drug dealer, the scalper had the buyer in his hands, fully aware of the leverage he commanded as a result of supply constraints and the necessity of health services for the sick.

Over the years, these microscalping rackets and patient/doctor tensions have worsened, compounding the strain on a healthcare industry confronting acute supply shortages. The Ministry of Health recently reported that *hospital incidents*—a vague term that encompasses everything from violence to public disturbances, similar to the societal mass incidents tabulated by the Ministry of Public Security—rose to 17,243 in 2010, up a whopping 150% since 2005.[19] This figure alone reflects a deterioration of a system that creates vast insecurities at both ends: Patients fear that they will receive improper care or bankrupt themselves by seeing a doctor; doctors fear that their personal well-being is being threatened.

The latter dynamic is underscored by the fact that retention at hospitals has become challenging, as numerous doctors have abandoned their trade in favor of becoming pharmaceutical drug representatives or selling medical devices. A 2011 China Medical Doctor Association survey found that nearly 80% of parents do not want their children to pursue medicine, in contrast to "just" 54% in 2002.[20] These trends imply that the situation will likely deteriorate, further pitting the overextended doctors against lines of angry patients.

The Chinese medical profession, instead of bearing a stamp of pride, has been stained by blood and overwhelmed by institutional dysfunction. Indeed, a patient-doctor relationship that is supposed to be predicated on mutual trust has evaporated. Prioritizing growth over welfare has come at a terrible, socially destabilizing cost. A discontented Chinese middle class, large enough in numbers now, increasingly feels its social and economic freedoms are curtailed by a highly inadequate and expensive healthcare system. As one highly educated member of the Chinese middle class told the authors, her every visit to a hospital brings about such anxiety that she tries to avoid hospitals as much as possible.[21] That anxiety and discontent is poised to exacerbate over the next decade, as demand grows unabated.

...And stitching it back together

The Chinese government now faces a combustible social issue—encapsulated in the Chinese expression *kan bing gui, kan bing nan* ("seeing a doctor is costly, seeing a doctor is difficult")—that has society on edge. In reaction to the latest violent episodes, the health and public security ministries issued an Emergency Notice in May 2012 calling for heightened security and ensuring safety at hospitals.[22] But improving security presence and enhancing surveillance are cosmetic and reactive measures that are unlikely to solve the problem.[23] The daunting predicament for the government is how to devise, in the words of healthcare professionals, a set of preventive policies so that these hospital horrors won't occur in the first place. In other words, devising a solution that addresses the systemic and institutional roots of hospital violence.

Doctors slain in hospitals have a way of getting attention at the highest levels. Not only has the central government taken notice, it is sufficiently concerned to prioritize reforming the social welfare system, particularly healthcare. But the fixes won't come easy. For Beijing's mandarins, one of the initial decisions is whether to tackle demand- or supply-side policies. Judging by the reform plan that was unveiled in 2009, the government has decided to tackle the supply side first.

That isn't particularly surprising, as addressing supply issues is the low-hanging fruit of reform. It primarily requires spending money, $125 billion to be specific, the price tag of the reform package introduced several years ago. Since 2009, the first phase of healthcare reform has expanded basic healthcare coverage to 95% of the population, or near-universal coverage. (Unlike the vigorous debate in the United States over public options and mandates, no such debate took place in China; the government simply enrolled urban and rural citizens into the program by fiat.) Still, even after enrollment into the scheme, the government is only able to subsidize $19 per person, far from sufficient in covering personal spending on healthcare.

Beijing deserves credit for expediently expanding coverage across the country. But its efforts to improve public welfare also serve to reinforce inequality between urban and rural households. Although basic rural healthcare coverage has expanded over the past decade, it nonetheless stood at just $16/year for an individual in 2009, less than half the average amount received by urban adults.[24] Unlike during the old danwei days, the distribution of health benefits today is based on the urban or rural residence permit, or *hukou,* a system that stands in the way of equal access more often than not, particularly for China's migrant population. Similar to the debate over illegal immigrants in the United States, China has to deal with hundreds of millions of "domestic aliens" with ambiguous legal status, their existence only made possible by the Panda Boom. But mere universal coverage is far from sufficient in tackling the central issue: cost (see Figure 4.1).[25]

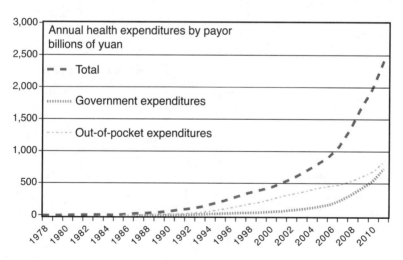

Figure 4.1 Healthcare spending breakdown since reform and opening up

Source: China Statistical Yearbook 2012

Indeed, opening the fiscal revenue taps is little trouble for a Chinese government that has become capital rich. Total fiscal revenue rose 25% to an all-time high of $1.64 trillion in 2011, or about the size of the Canadian economy. The rosy budgetary picture has even allowed the government to spend a little more than originally planned to $173 billion, according to former Health Minister Chen Zhu, a world-renowned hematologist.[26] As a result, the government subsidies cap was modestly raised to $32 per person in 2011. According to Chen, 432 million urbanites and 835 million rural residents were covered under basic healthcare as of the end of that year. He also touted improvements in rural access to healthcare, where supposedly 80% of the rural population can reach a hospital within 15 minutes. What's more, rural residents' out-of-pocket costs have apparently been reduced from 73% to 50%.[27]

An early 2012 assessment of the healthcare reform effort in *Lancet* seems to largely corroborate Chen's comments. But while noting that the reforms are progressing along the right path, particularly highlighting the speed with which China increased health coverage of its population, the study also struck a cautionary note:

> Evidence so far suggests that as long as inappropriate health care and health-care expenditure escalation are not controlled, no insurance scheme will be sustainable and patients will continue to bear heavy costs of medical care. A predominantly fee-for-service payment system coupled with a distorted fee schedule and drug mark-ups are the core culprits of rapid inflation of health expenditure caused by overuse of tests and drugs of unclear clinical indication.[28]

In some sense, the policies enacted are simply reconstructing a system that had been dismantled over the preceding several decades.[29] A key emphasis is on recalibrating the vast inequality in access to clinics and doctors between rural and urban China. It is moving forward into the past, with the state assuming a larger role. And as far as achieving minimal universal coverage is concerned, consider it mission accomplished. At least this is what the Beijing bureaucrats claim, to project an image of success and accomplishment. Yet just months after Minister Chen gave his optimistic assessment of the state of healthcare reform in January 2012, Li's fatal stabbing happened. It turns out that from rural Heilongjiang it takes 10 hours on a train, not 15 minutes, to see a specialist.

Decades of sharpening the growth-conducive policy tools make it easy for Chinese policymakers to fund the construction of new clinics and other "hard" health infrastructure. Staffing those new rural clinics and, more to the point, preventing urban public hospitals from operating as hubs of social Darwinism, is much harder. Mollifying the public's deep dissatisfaction with the public health system, and with social welfare programs in general, requires much more than just letting the fiscal spigot flow. It demands a new design for incentives that retain and attract human capital to feed hospitals and to alter the behavior of health professionals to reestablish trust between experts and patients, including creating norms of expectations. Technocratic wizardry won't do anymore. A suite of public policies will have to accompany the new clinics and upgrades in advanced medical equipment. Like so many other areas of contemporary China, the health system requires a shift in emphasis from hardware to software.

Of course, the level of public scrutiny that the overhaul of a national healthcare system invites is not for faint-of-heart politicians, in any country. Public perception, directly informed by individual experience of improvement, deterioration, or stasis, tends to lag behind measured improvements in effectiveness of a new policy. Just ask President Barack Obama. The American president championed and achieved a major healthcare reform package but earned little political capital from it. A similar fate could fall on Chinese policymakers, some of whom have staked their political capital on meaningfully reforming the healthcare system. Politically, a perceived lack of progress on this important agenda could expose politicians to critiques in the inner sanctum of the party for being incapable. The success or failure of this reform may even affect progress on other social welfare agendas, including pensions. The challenge for the new Chinese leadership, in fact, is much greater than that which faced Obama.

That's because China requires two very different approaches in all matters of public policy: one for developed China and another for developing China. Rural China still remains vastly underdeveloped across nearly every dimension when compared to urban China. From glitzy Shanghai, where the per capita income approaches that of South

Korea, to peasants who still get by on $2 to $3 a day, China contains a multitude of stages of development. Traditional infrastructure such as roads is woefully inadequate in underdeveloped regions, not to mention healthcare infrastructure like clinics and hospitals. For the have-nots, the disappearance of the rural health cooperatives means dire straits even with a new basic health insurance program in place. In addition to scarce access to healthcare facilities, even modest health-care costs could prove financially catastrophic for a typical rural family. This is why equalizing healthcare access and coverage between rural and urban China was the top priority in the latest reform package. In essence, the central government began rebuilding, piece by piece, a rural system that existed before its self-destruction and neglect amid the gale force of market reforms.

Yet even as Beijing pursued these actions, with all the right intentions, criticisms over the inadequacy of progress are common. A more pluralistic Chinese society no longer shies away from critiquing government policies, particularly on socioeconomic issues. The public has held the government's feet to the fire to force it to address glaring social welfare deficiencies, and with good reason. Despite paying lip service to prioritize healthcare reform for years, changes have not been forthcoming. The government's attention was captured by the bounties of economic growth even as the Chinese public grew less equal and less secure about their future.

Meanwhile, incidences of hospital disturbance and violence splashed across front pages, in both official and unofficial Chinese media. In fact, another bout of stabbings took place in September 2012 in a Shenzhen hospital, with four injured victims including one employee who was slashed across his head.[30] Clearly, somewhere between rhetoric and reality, China's brave new healthcare system didn't stack up. If anything, the perception was that the situation was static at best. It mattered little that people were minimally covered under a government plan, the core problems of the rural-urban divide and doctor-patient mistrust persisted. The situation is poised to worsen, in part because the size of China and its unbalanced development will lead to ballooning demand for healthcare services. As a result, it is unrealistic for the central government to sustain the kind of public spending necessary on healthcare without breaking fiscal coffers. Nor would the SOEs reprise their roles as the ultimate guarantors of social welfare provision; they have liberalized to the extent that returning to the good old days of socialism is impossible.

Yet lurking in the not-so-distant future is a powerful structural force that can make current scarcities even more pronounced. It is a looming dynamic that no amount of economic planning and foresight will likely escape: the country's demographic fate. Beating stethoscopes into plowshares was a wildly successful development strategy when China remained an authoritarian society with a young, productive population. It is a less-certain proposition in an environment in which public opinion, combined with the Floridization of Chinese demographics, becomes an ever more important driver of public policy.

From youth bulge to geriatric bulge

In front of the Workers' Stadium in central Beijing, old men and women dance to cha-cha music blasting from a boom box. A circle of younger onlookers materializes, some joining in the revelry. For anyone who has spent time in a major Chinese city, such a scene is immediately familiar. Old people in China have an affinity for dancing; they dance in parking lots, in parks, in just about any public space. A form of organized exercise and entertainment, dancing provides a community for the millions of older Chinese who can no longer count on their children for unconditional financial and psychological support, to say nothing of companionship. Beyond the cha-cha, retirees are often found in Beijing's numerous parks exercising, playing Chinese Hacky Sack, or pleasing observers with rousing rounds of Chinese chess. Wander a park or plaza and China may seem like it is proliferating with the elderly. In another 30 years, that perception will align with reality, when as much as one-third of all Chinese people are expected to be over the age of 60.[31]

Over the next decade, the Chinese government has to grapple with the peculiar paradox of being an older but still developing country. China's transition to a prematurely aging society will have far-ranging consequences across all dimensions of its political economy. The most obvious effect will be on the labor market—China's crucial and leveraged comparative advantage. But an equally profound consequence of a rapidly aging population is the weight it will load onto a social welfare system already stretched thin. Such a monumental shift is poised to dramatically affect the government's spending and policy priorities in the near future.

In contrast to Western developed countries, China managed to basically complete its demographic transition—from population boom and high fertility to low fertility and mortality rates—in about two generations, a historically unprecedented pace. What took most countries a century China accomplished in half that time. Japan, another aging Asian country, is facing a similar demographic challenge, but as a developed country with a per capita income of $46,000. China, in contrast, is expected to become the world's first old but relatively poor country. According to Wang Feng of the Brookings Institution:

> In 2005, China's rate of population growth was around 0.5%, down from over 2.5% in 1970. For China, the historical importance of completing its demographic transition in such a compressed fashion has many dimensions. One of these is that in less than 15 years from now, for the first time in history, China will no longer be the most populous country in the world.[32]

The extraordinary speed with which China made the transition has to be credited to state intervention on a staggering scale. Although the omnipotence of the Chinese state was always exaggerated, demography is arguably one area in which the formidable powers of the state matched their reputation. The large-scale public health programs, supported by mass mobilization campaigns, had remarkable effects on raising the overall life expectancy of the nation (see Figure 4.2).[33] However, state intervention has not only generated success, it has also been the target of much controversy.

More than three decades after its introduction, the illiberal one-child policy officially remains in place. A policy that may have made some sense in curbing explosive population growth in the 1980s now appears anachronistic and unfit for China's present conditions.[34] More than outliving its utility, the policy has been responsible for externalities such as harsh family planning practices. Following a population explosion in the 1960s and 1970s—when China added 200 million people in just a decade—CCP social engineers sought to fix an immediate problem. While the government may pat itself on the back for having avoided a Malthusian catastrophe, it also failed to account for the natural correction in birth rates as a country grows wealthier. The latest indicators show that China's birth rate has already fallen below the replacement rate—generally assumed to be 2.1—as the millions of rising urban elites, like their contemporaries in other countries, have delayed families in pursuit of professions and individual interests.

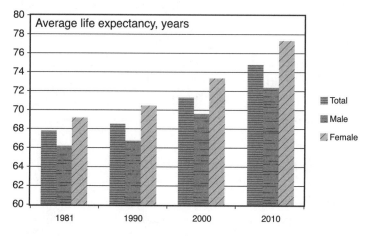

Figure 4.2 China's life expectancy since reform and opening

Sources: China Population and Labor Statistical Yearbook 2010 and Statistical Yearbook 2012

The latest 2010 population census bore this out. The data were not encouraging: China may be aging even faster than previously assumed. Although China added roughly another Germany worth of people between 2000 and 2010, the population's annual growth rate halved from the previous decade. But the share of population that are 60-years-old and above rose from 10% to 13%, or 174 million, a figure that will mushroom to 250 million in less than two decades. In other words, China will be able to fill up two Japans with old people by 2030. In the same decade leading up to 2010, the portion of population that are 14-years-old and younger declined from 23% to 17%, or 222 million. Much slower population growth and a shrinking 0–14 year cohort underscore the disconcerting fact that the Chinese birth rate is already well below the replacement rate, with some estimates putting it as low as 1.4.[35] There's also little indication that these trajectories will reverse any time soon, implying that Chinese sexagenarians could well outnumber teenagers by the time the next census is conducted in 2020. In economist-speak, China's era of demographic dividends is drawing to a close: A youth bulge is rapidly giving way to a geriatric bulge.

These dynamics present a predicament for the sons and daughters of the Chinese baby boomers. Frequently referred to as the *4-2-1 problem,* today's Chinese young professionals are in the unenviable position of having to support four parents and usually an only child. Cultural norms such as filial piety form enduring social expectations that elders will be cared for by their progeny. In fact, a law from 1996 even mandates that children care for their elders. Even the official mouthpiece *People's Daily* has not shied away from identifying the issue as a matter of serious social concern:

> Mr. Wang, 30, now works in Huizhou of Guangdong Province after moving there with his wife from Hubei Province several years ago. He soon got used to the life in Huizhou and has made significant advancement in his career. However, as the only child in his family, he is very concerned about his parents in his hometown.
>
> He said that as his wife is also the only child in her family, they have always sought to bring their parents to Huizhou to live with them after they got married, but their plan had to be postponed for various reasons. Now, their child will soon be 2 years old and the living pressure facing them is growing heavy.
>
> They feel extremely tired because they are under the mental pressure of supporting their aging parents and have to face the realistic difficulties in raising their child. Like Mr. Wang, many of those who are the only child in their family have to face the issue of supporting their parents. They are worried that they can neither afford to raise their child nor support their parents.[36]

With the family unit deeply embedded in China's cultural roots, social pressures that demand supporting parents are increasingly at odds with economic and professional realities. Career pursuits, as well as preoccupation with a child's development (only one shot, can't afford to screw up), mean less time and patience devoted to the elders. And despite the gravitational pull of filial piety, modernity and growing individualism are quietly upending long held traditions. For instance, the *Guardian* reported in March 2012:

> In a more individualistic society relationships face new challenges. Children and their spouses can find their parents' demands excessive or intrusive.

> He Daxing's daughters complained he had favoured his sons. And even when personal relations are good, practicalities may intervene. Children may work far from their parents, like one of He's sons, or simply lack time to help.

> "I have one daughter and there's no way she will be able to take care of me. I will be in a care home when I get older," predicted Liu Zhongli.[37]

Compounding the issue is that the 160 million or so only children, commonly referred to as the post-1980ers (*balinghou*), have only known rising prosperity and material progress. They have been the recipients of China's accumulated wealth of the last three decades, giving this generational cohort a quality of life far surpassing that of their parents. Better-off urban 20-something Chinese now regularly travel abroad, spend time studying in the West, and expect to inherit the property and assets of the family. Their cosmopolitanism stands in stark contrast to the relative parochialism of their parents, whose childhoods and teenage years were defined by a very different kind of scarcity: food, clothing, and the general niceties of life.

Indeed, their very lifestyles are going to exert more pressure on the health system: They are getting fatter. As Paul French documented in *Fat China,* diet patterns have changed and so have the kinds of diseases.[38] Once battling developing country diseases such as tuberculosis, China now faces diabetes rates approaching those of the United States, according to recent studies.[39] But unlike in America, where obesity is an epidemic associated with poverty, in China it is a physical symptom of wealth.[40] Such prosperity-induced ailments could further weigh down an already creaky system. "Becoming fat before it becomes rich" appears to be another paradox that will bedevil the Chinese healthcare system.

Given the accelerated demographic transition, and the associated change in cultural attitudes, the extent to which the children of today are prepared to assume the role of providers to their parents tomorrow could have larger social implications.[41] Social norms are in fact changing at a time that will only make existing institutional deficiencies more pronounced. To the extent that the post-1980ers are unable or unwilling to keep their parents under the same roof, alternatives like nursing homes and hospices will be appealing options. Yet existing high quality elderly accommodations are woefully inadequate to handle the likely spike in demand for such services. For instance, the World Bank estimates that China only has enough homes for 1.6% of the sexagenarian population. And according to *Xinhua,* China's total nursing home beds can accommodate merely one-quarter of the 12 million who are considering such an option.[42] Shortage of supply also means that the cost for nursing homes—some run as high as $800/ month—is generally out of reach for many Chinese families. Will competition for nursing home spots spawn the same sort of psychological duress and pay-for-access schemes that hospital admittances have?

While the Chinese government is well aware that the country is amid a huge demographic transition, Beijing's response seems disproportionate to the scale of the potential crisis. Or at least it isn't readily apparent that the government is driven toward meaningful action, yet. It is entirely plausible that Beijing believes that it can still buy time before being forced into drastic moves. And so, incrementalism will do for now. To be sure, the Chinese government has by no means remained on the sidelines, and has made noteworthy progress in expanding the pension system—making it at least on paper comprehensive for most workers for the first time. In pensions as in healthcare, the government has begun to reconstruct institutions of the socialist system that were dismantled during the last decade when growth took flight. Between 2009 and 2012, the government launched a basic social pension insurance program for urban workers and a new rural social pension insurance program for rural workers, which, combined with existing enterprise-sponsored pension programs, now cover about 80% of the workforce and provide some form of retirement benefit to almost 200 million people.[43]

Yet the system in place now is underfunded, fragmented, and inflexible. Although elements of the pension system are nominally prefunded, it is effectively paying current-year benefits with current-year contributions, meaning it will likely contribute to the government's rising fiscal burdens as China's geriatric bulge expands.[44] Wary of its ability to manage complex investments of pension funds, the government has prohibited their investment in stock markets and other financial instruments, instead investing funds in very low risk (and low return) assets. It is easy to understand why: Politicians occasionally pilfer from the fund to finance urban housing and infrastructure development. A particularly dramatic case of this type of corruption brought down the powerful Shanghai party secretary and Politburo member Chen Liangyu in 2006.[45] The disgraced party chief of Shanghai was accused of tapping the municipality's pension fund and disbursing it to property developers in his patronage network. Ultimately, Chen was found guilty of siphoning millions of dollars from the pension fund for his cronies and sentenced to 18 years in prison.[46]

The system's fragmentation multiplies opportunities for corruption, a symptom of China's decentralized public welfare system that allows provinces to exert considerable power over local funds and resources. Management of pension funds is convoluted and uniformity of standards difficult to impose, with each level of the local government down the hierarchy asserting some control (because funds are pooled at the county and district levels) and providing some opportunity for an enterprising official to skim off the top without drawing attention from central authorities. In addition, the lack of a nationally centralized pension system disadvantages migrant workers, or even registered urban households who relocate within China, because their contributions to the system in one locality are unlikely to count toward their eventual retirement benefit in another.

In an effort to centralize pension management at the national level, the government created the National Social Security Fund (NSSF) specifically as a cushion to deal with future social welfare liabilities. It is a centralized pool of money intended to offset funding shortages in other pension plans like the old age insurance scheme. China isn't unique in creating a centralized pension fund; developed countries such as Canada and Norway (in the latter's case, the pension fund manages the country's oil revenues) have formed similar entities. But in contrast to funds in developed markets, the NSSF has assets that amount to just 2% of GDP, compared to 7.6% in Canada, for example. This low figure is even more striking when contrasted with estimated unfunded liabilities of as much as 140% of GDP. Moreover, NSSF investments are primarily limited to bank deposits and equities in China's largest commercial banks, garnering low returns.[47]

It is far from clear that the NSSF can be an adequate demographic buffer and absorb the shock to the system when the demographic tsunami hits. Where there are three workers for every pensioner in China now, that ratio will dwindle to only two workers for every pensioner by 2030.[48] Already, funding shortfalls are popping up across provinces. According to a study by an influential Chinese state think tank, 14 provinces saw a combined total pension contribution deficit of $11 billion in 2010. Consequently, many provinces still rely on fiscal transfers from the central government to make up their unfunded mandates, a dependency that cannot be sustained indefinitely. Indeed, with China's tremendous population and diversity, a pension and retirement system that relies largely on endless state largess is unfathomable. And the government knows that to be the case—the sheer size of the country will require a flexible and smarter approach. Recent estimates that show the funding shortfall is already getting worse underscore the enormity of the challenge. While the NSSF has available funds of about 773 billion yuan ($122 billion), the pension system's unfunded personal accounts may have already exceeded 2 trillion yuan ($315 billion) at the end of 2011, up $79 million from 2010.[49] And this is a benefit that, for public pension insurance program participants, is currently as little as a hundred dollars a month.

China will likely be forced to create a larger role for the market and foreign investors in providing for its elderly. Chinese financial regulators lately have championed putting NSSF assets into stock markets and enhancing its management to transform it into a high-performing institutional investor.[50] With only $135 billion in assets, better returns on NSSF investments will be necessary to realize the fund's intended purpose of demographic buffer. Foreign investment could well play an important role too. The anticipated rising demand for care homes, hospices, and quality elderly services could afford numerous opportunities for investors.

For all of China's success in raising life expectancy, it now must manage the consequences of that success, which, ironically, is turning into a constraint. The Chinese government will need to step in to untangle the contorted system, which will demand a solution beyond simply throwing billions of yuan toward it. Making sure that China's grandmothers and grandfathers feel secure under a robust pension system is already a tall order; Beijing also has to contain costs in securing the future of nearly one-quarter of humanity.

Mo' bling, mo' honeys

As if an overabundance of the elderly wasn't enough of a conundrum, China also has to reckon with the fact that it will have fewer mothers to replenish the young. Chinese women are in short supply. And if the trend isn't reversed, future generations of Chinese men will inherit a bachelor nation. For every 119 men, only 100 women are available, a gender imbalance that is an outlier by the standards of most other countries. (Generally, a ratio of 105/106:100 is considered normal.) The persistent imbalance could leave 24 million unwed men over the next decade, according to the Chinese Academy of Social Sciences. That is a prodigious amount of potential Chinese bachelors.

Statistics like these are having profound effects on the traditional institution of marriage, which now often serves simultaneously as a marketplace for a commercial transaction. In an extreme case, the bride was awarded with a $12 million wedding and took home a "dowry" of six brand new Ferraris.[51] The scarce supply of women has, in economic terms, dramatically raised the marginal value of an individual bride. Chinese women appear well aware of their appreciating gender stock, which in turn drive up the expectations of a future groom's financial assets. As early as 2004, a joke swirling among 20-something Chinese men was that BMW actually stood for "be my wife," gallows humor that carried with it a sense of helplessness.[52]

Entering into a marriage, it seemed, required a luxury sedan as down payment. The situation has further deteriorated over the past several years—home ownership is now a baseline criterion for a potential groom. Even the Chinese government corroborates this noticeable shift:

> In a survey released by the Civil Affairs Ministry of China on January 4, more than 80% of single women interviewed believed that a man "does not deserve" to be in a romantic relationship if he makes less than RMB4,000 (around US$650) a month. Almost 50% believed that a man needs to shoulder the full cost of an apartment (or at least the down payment) before he is eligible to marry. That's bad news for millions of "bare branches," a Chinese term for bachelors, since the national average income of urban residents in China was only about RMB1,750 (around US$300) in 2010.[53]

Two economists in a recent paper underscored the increasingly monetized nature of Chinese marriage and hypothesized that this was another explanatory variable behind China's infamous high savings rate. Applying evolutionary biology theories, the authors contend that it is now the size of the male wallet, not physical size, that proves a better mating strategy in China:

> A rising sex ratio imbalance, by increasing competition among men for potential wives, can stimulate households with a son to postpone consumption in favor of wealth accumulation... The point estimates suggest that approximately 68% of the increase in rural savings rates, and 18% of the increase in urban savings rates in the recent years can be attributed in the rise in sex ratios.[54]

Not only are millions of Chinese men ineligible based on escalating pocketbook criteria, even those who have the financial wherewithal may be hard pressed to find willing brides. Elite urban Chinese women, who tend to be the highest educated, seem to be following a pattern similar to female counterparts in developed countries: They are delaying marriage or simply choosing to not marry at all. Although Mao Zedong was once fond of proclaiming that "women hold up half the sky," China remained a deeply sexist traditional society under his rule. Today, a belated wave of feminist ethos may finally be sweeping China as women are more comfortable with independence than ever. As *Foreign Policy* recently reported, "In 2005 fully 7% of 45-year-old Shanghai women with college degrees had never married, according to Wang's research. 'That's a harbinger of what's going to happen in other places [in China] for more educated women... there's a common joke that there are three genders in China: men, women, and women with Ph.Ds. Men marry women, and women with Ph.Ds don't marry."[55]

It is no surprise that marriages are tilting toward the transactional rather than the emotional, generating an ad hoc market in which parents assume the role of middlemen. Matchmakers have had a long history in China and were once the common conduit by which men and women entered into matrimony. They have now returned.

In a Shanghai park, droves of gray-haired men and women can be seen mingling, conversing, and exchanging pieces of papers, a scene that is easily mistaken for aging bachelors rekindling romance. It is, in fact, a blind date of sorts. Except the parents—armed with profiles and criteria—are standing in for their white-collar and career-driven children, in the hopes of striking the right target for a future son- or daughter-in-law. But one soon discovers that market conditions are tough. In one interview, the National Public Radio spoke to a participant of the matchmaking in the park events. "Ms. Yu's already given up hope for today. Chinese men won't consider marrying a woman who earns more than they do or is too highly educated, she confides. And there aren't enough men here, anyway."[56]

Ms. Yu's concern is shared by millions of parents and reflects a microcosm of the sweeping demographic challenge facing China. So far, practical solutions do not seem forthcoming, while the sensationalist has mused over wild ideas such as imposing a "babe tax" to prevent the outflow of Chinese women to other countries.[57] That is, young Chinese women should be treated as national strategic resources and therefore protected rather than exported into the arms of foreigners. As xenophobic and strange as the proposal is, it manages to hint strongly at worries over China's future vitality.

Serving the people

The return of matchmaking is but one of many unintended consequences of the state's simultaneous pursuit of partial market reforms and its dogged intrusion into the most private of human affairs: procreation. That the Chinese state has been very successful on both fronts is paradoxically engendering socioeconomic cleavages that could seriously erode the gains China has made to date. Deng may have said "to get rich is glorious" nearly 35 years ago, but that pithy slogan may have run its course. A more apt epithet of the times may be that "to get equal is *more* glorious."

For all the praise heaped on China's economic miracle, its social development has been much less miraculous. Surprisingly, a government that is usually preoccupied with how to secure enough of everything has only exacerbated the supply scarcity that affects the core of its society. From reproductive constraints and managing an aging society to altering the marriage landscape, the Chinese government's fortitude in economic engineering and purported prescience have become sizable liabilities on matters of life, death, and love. Yet these are precisely the looming issues for which the public is looking for answers and solutions. Not only do these constraints have obvious implications for the country's economic prospects, they can also easily upset social stability.

When becoming a physician can be considered a life-threatening choice, or when an excess of 20-something males become frustrated with their failure in an unforgiving marriage market, the already tenuous social fabric becomes increasingly threadbare. What's more, the typical social adhesive of a common values or belief system is either nonexistent or undergoing reflective reevaluation. The broad and vague notion of Confucian ideals have little resonance, while many "average Zhous" seem to be re-imagining the halcyon days of communist equality. At least all were equally poor, so goes the socialist nostalgia. That such disastrous history and suffering could be re-imagined with rose-colored glasses implies either selective amnesia or deep deficiencies in the current state of certain institutions. Perhaps like Americans before them, the Chinese public is hankering for a New Deal moment. Such a sentiment is particularly salient in the Chinese context because of its unfinished evolution from a socialist state and the Rawlsian sense of fairness that is also emphasized in traditional Chinese morality. Consequently, the government must respond or risk damaging its own competence and sapping its credibility.

And respond it has, though perhaps with more modesty and less urgency than expected. Even as Beijing has initiated some reforms in healthcare and pensions, doctors are still being stabbed and provinces are in the red for funding local pension schemes. But if left to the whims of the market, would things be even worse? This longstanding anxiety over unforeseen consequences continues to grip a government that prefers a steady and even hand to manage change over potentially uncontrollable market forces.

At least for now, the state seems to prefer a more cautious sequencing and step-by-step approach to reform. The public, meanwhile, has become more relentlessly critical of government credibility and more impatient with the government's inability to deliver on its word. This mismatch between public expectations and government capacity could grow more contentious, precisely because the single party controlling the government has ownership of the responsibility to deliver and there is no alternative to scapegoat.

For the coming decade, therefore, it will likely matter less for the Chinese government to finely calibrate GDP growth. Instead, it will be more imperative to find a better balance between men and women, the old and the young, and welfare and growth. Because China has deliberately leveraged its massive endowment of people to build an unprecedented growth engine, the government will now have to begin paying back its people for their tireless nation-building, especially the aging generation who largely built the country. It is these matters that will demand Beijing's energies and resources.

5

Education: Give me equality... but not until after my son gets into Tsinghua

A thought experiment: Turkmenbashi for a day

Imagine for a moment that you woke up this morning to discover that you are now the autocratic ruler of a large developing country. Congratulations! Like us, you will probably spend your time in the shower daydreaming about what kind of stone to use in the massive statues and busts of yourself that are to be installed in city centers, town squares, and other points of public interest. Marble? Classic but a little cliché. Alabaster? Beautiful but impractical; you're an autocrat, but not an insane one (or at least not yet). Decisions!

By breakfast, though, weightier matters will start to occupy your mind, foremost among them being how to maintain social order. You can probably count on the support of your political party and military, or at least its senior leadership. You share an ideology and hatred of the regime you've replaced, and more to the point, they would be first up against the wall with you if you lose control. What about the peasantry in the countryside? You consider them, but decide that no, they aren't your biggest problem either. While peasant revolutions have toppled many governments, the formula to control the countryside seems well established. Guarantee a basic livelihood; keep a tight control over the flow of people, goods, and information; and relentlessly emphasize through your state-controlled media how much better you are than the rapacious dictator you replaced. If all those actions are executed, you can probably prevent the rural millions from getting too restless.

By the time you get into your office, you decide your chief concern is actually the urban masses. They live closer together than the rural majority and have an easier time communicating and organizing, potentially against you, or at least the current order. They tend to be better educated and more receptive to outside ideas that you may consider inimical. The policies you use to limit mobility and communication in the countryside would not only be more difficult to implement in the city, they would be much costlier to an urban economy more dependent on the free flow of information and people than the rural subsistence economy. And to varying degrees, many of the remnants of the old regime live on among the urbanites, nursing grudges and waiting for a chance to reclaim their lost glories. It would be nice to have the urban masses love you, believe in you, and support you, but what you need is for them to cooperate with your rule—and fear whatever might replace you.

You spend the morning in meetings with your advisors, and by lunchtime you have a plan: You will buy them off, not necessarily using money exclusively but also relying on providing social benefits to urbanites. You will reserve premium slots in the education system for children of urban households and use your levers of control over the economy to improve their livelihoods, both at the expense of their rural counterparts. After this, your country's urbanites may think you're a rotten crook, but they will have too much to lose to be willing to support a populist political insurgency that would jeopardize their privilege. Back to more pleasant concerns: Where will you build your next palace?

No, seriously, there is a real thing called urban bias

If this is how you decide to spend your first morning in charge of your developing country, you will be in good company. Governments in poor countries with rural, agricultural majorities routinely enact policies that disproportionately benefit the urban minority at the expense of the rural majority. It is a phenomenon called *urban bias* in social science parlance and is one of the most appealing and powerful political processes in poorer countries.[1] Given limited resources, it is vastly cheaper, after all, to shower favors on a minority of your population than on a majority. With urbanites living closer to the seat of political power than the rural peasantry, governments often judge urban support to be valuable enough to the continuity of the existing sociopolitical order to justify distributing an outsized share of the spoils of the political process to secure it. While details vary from country to country, this practice is especially pronounced under governments that don't require votes to secure their power.

Today's China is of course a far cry from that imaginary country you briefly ruled with an iron fist; urban bias there was never so crude or explicit. But it is nevertheless a real phenomenon that has colored a whole range of social policies, education chief among them, since the founding of the People's Republic of China in 1949. Mao Zedong may have ridden to power on the back of the proletariat and rural folk, but the Chinese Communist Party (CCP) was relentlessly preoccupied with maintaining the support of urban elites and the intelligentsia under his rule, though the bouts of anti-intellectualism under Mao's capricious revolutions showed there is more than one way to skin a felinologist.

Carrots were often supplemented by sticks, and examples of suppressing the opposition to maintain control are easy to find. During the "Let a Hundred Flowers Bloom" campaign in the mid-1950s, the CCP invited intellectuals to freely express their opinions and criticize the party and government, and then promptly imprisoned many of those gullible enough to reveal their opposition to the status quo. But the generous and persistent privileges that urban Chinese have enjoyed at the expense of rural Chinese constitute a powerful reason why China's present form of government enjoys more substantial support from the urban middle class than popular accounts of, say, online protests or rage over official corruption would suggest.

An educated and urban middle class usually anchors most democratic societies. But in China, cutthroat competition for scarce public resources creates pervasive insecurity, making the middle class generally ambivalent about the types of popularly elected governments that predominate in the Western world. This is because the middle class is fully cognizant of its privileged access to public health, better infrastructure, and, of course, the education system, a direct result of China's undemocratic politics—one person, one vote would surely treat the rural majority more fairly.

Despite its increasingly uneasy relationship with how the government functions, the urban middle class, acutely sensitive to concerns of scarcity and inequality, has become the government's unlikely champion. Consequently, the urban middle class that benefits the most from this system retains a huge stake in the continuity of the status quo. This is particularly true of the education system, where urban bias offers a sharp lens through which to examine the distribution of China's scarce education resources.

In spite of being invested in perpetuating the urban bias, the middle class is paradoxically discontented with the current predicament of educating its children. China's economy and society have transformed so dramatically over the past generation that although winning the middle class is necessary, it is increasingly insufficient to guarantee the current sociopolitical order. Urban Chinese society has become vastly more complex and stratified. At the bottom of the heap, many of the newest Chinese urbanites are locked out of mainstream institutions; at the top, it is becoming common for the wealthiest Chinese to opt out of mainstream institutions in pursuit of lifestyles more readily available overseas. Nowhere are these tensions more apparent than in the educational system, which plays a definitive role in placing young people onto a track that will determine the course of the rest of their lives.

China's education system was designed to maintain urban bias in a country with an overwhelmingly rural population and agricultural economy. It was, and remains, a far cry from the meritocratic ideal that China's dynastic education system purportedly realized, but that is neither here nor there. With a predominantly industrial and service-oriented economy and a majority of its population in urban areas, today's China looks less and less like the country for which its educational system was designed. This tension makes education a key arena in which China's social and economic transformation will expose the government's increasingly scarce social and political

resources to command, coerce, or cajole cooperation from the growing urban majority over the next decade.

The social equalizer that isn't

The urban biases of China's educational system are such powerful tools of political persuasion in part because of the disproportionately determinative role education plays in the life trajectory of each
Chinese person. The material benefits of a good university degree in
China are familiar enough to people from other societies: a comfortable income, better job security, a safer and more pleasant work environment, and more dependable access to the same secure lifestyle
for his or her own children. But Chinese peculiarities imbue higher
education with a value that extends beyond the expected financial
returns from such an investment. The value of educational achievement resonates in China for powerful cultural and historical reasons
that both complement and transcend its tremendous influence on
material welfare.

To illustrate, let's take the supposed controversy over Amy Chua's
idea of "Chinese" parenting.[2] When discussing the brouhaha Chua
created in the United States, your humble authors' highly educated
Chinese colleagues were confounded. Why was America suddenly
aghast at what they considered fairly typical parental attitudes? But
they also added that Chinese-style parenting was becoming less popular for its own virtues in China. The elite of the elites who can afford
different options for their children are increasingly choosing them.
But for the vast majority of middle class Chinese, there seems little
choice other than to push their children hard—viable alternatives are
either limited or beyond reach.

Educational attainment, much like food, has long held a unique
status in Chinese society. The imperial examination system, which was
essentially a standardized humanities test that focused on Chinese culture and letters, was the gateway to a life of power and affluence as an
official of the dynastic court.[3] Peasant families made huge economic
sacrifices so that their most promising sons could forgo farm work and
focus on their studies to try their luck at winning one of life's precious
lotteries. The examination acted as a social leveler, since the cream of

the political elite was drawn from anyone able to prepare their child for the exam, rather than a narrow hereditary aristocracy. It served as a force for social cohesion because it trained imperial China's political and cultural elites in a coherent intellectual and ideological canon. The classical texts taught by the exam reinforced the prestige of continued learning. Like the exam takers who followed them, the sages of the Confucian tradition were philosophers, scholars, and officials. And probably most importantly, the examination system legitimized the rule of China's bureaucrats. In a culture that did not traditionally value all persons equally, the most talented and the most qualified had a special claim to the right to rule. The logic was rather simple: Those who have earned their status and privileges through a rigorous process of scholarly and intellectual competition surely are also entitled to govern the country. It was in fact a legitimizing and meritocratic force that was notably absent in other political systems during the same era, an age when the aristocratic privileges of the *ancien regime* were still alive and well in Europe.

Now, the path to an advanced education in China follows a terrain that should be as familiar to foreigners as are its tangible payoffs, at least on the face of it. Indeed, a cursory glance makes it seem so deceptively simple. Like passing the ancient imperial examination, admission to elite institutions is devilishly difficult to win, requiring a superhuman score on a single national standardized test, referred to as the *gaokao*. Where college entrance exams like the SAT or ACT in the United States usually take several hours, the gaokao lasts several *days*. Applicants are tested on all of the major subjects of the high school curriculum in one comprehensive, monstrous exam. For the vast majority of Chinese young people, their gaokao score will be the only criterion by which universities judge their academic merit relative to the millions of other college applicants in their cohort.

Anxious over the influence university admissions will have over their children's prospects, many families stretch themselves financially to send their children to rigorous after-school cram sessions or hire private tutors. The children themselves bear the incredible psychological pressure of averting failure, studying long into the night to improve their chances at a better score and paying in stress, exhaustion, and lost health for their single shot at the future. The intensity is often compounded by the fact that individual failure means implicating an entire family's loss of honor. Each June, newspapers profile the sacrifices families make to try to give their children an edge in the exam—like the family of a boy from a small town in Anhui Province who didn't tell him until after he had finished sitting for the entrance exam that his mother had died in a car crash 12 days earlier.[4]

The moment when a Chinese high school student receives his score on the university entrance exams is one of the most pivotal of his life. Anxiety, pain, sacrifice, drama: It's a shared trauma for nearly all aspiring university students in China, endlessly dissected and discussed in the popular media, although the spin varies depending on the type of media. Chinese accounts, in particular those from government-run media, emphasize that while standardized testing is traumatic, perhaps a bit excessively so (what a pity!), it is an unavoidable and integral component of ensuring equality in an environment of acutely scarce opportunities. The justification usually goes something like this: Personal essays can be bought online or copied, and enriching academic experiences abroad open doors only to students whose parents are able and willing to pay for them. A standardized test, however, with clear right and wrong answers, can provide a level playing field to divide up the educational spoils. The *test* keeps the meritocratic doors to China's elite educational institutions open to talented young people of all stripes—city or country, intellectual's daughter or factory worker's son, peasant or migrant alike.

Will it surprise you that the official narrative misleadingly omits some key details?

Yes, the moment when Chinese young people find out whether they earned a score high enough to gain admission to their dream school is crucial. But even more important in determining the young Chinese's future, and less remarked upon, is a much quieter event that occurs many years earlier. Within a month of his birth, his parents took his birth certificate to their neighborhood police station and had his name added to the family's household registration (*hukou*) booklet.[5] From birth onward, this quintessentially Chinese instrument of political and social control plays a sweeping role in determining which of life's opportunities are open to a Chinese citizen and which are shut, especially where educational opportunities are concerned. The hukou determines where a Chinese is "legitimately" entitled to an education and all other public services. Unsurprisingly, the quality of the primary education on offer in rural Henan Province is considerably inferior to that available to denizens of the provincial capital Zhengzhou, to say nothing of its gap with China's cosmopolitan urban centers along the coast. Chinese people holding the best hukou—primarily the urban middle class—enjoy a vastly disproportionate concentration of public spending on education that would be diluted in a more egalitarian political system.

Inequality begins at birth under this restrictive policy, one meant to manage population flows, not distribute social and public goods. It deepens when young people age into their middle school years. China's compulsory primary and secondary education is designed to guarantee the equivalent of a ninth grade education. The additional three years of secondary education necessary to prepare for college entrance exams are not compulsory, and admittance to high school programs is, like university admissions, largely test based. Although the admissions tests seem standardized, the outcomes for two students with the same score show enormous variance depending on whether they hold urban or rural residence permits and their specific locale of residence (see Figure 5.1).

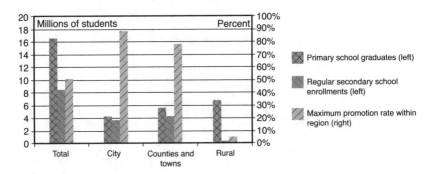

Figure 5.1   Rural four-year secondary schools offer slots for only 5% of primary school graduates; four-year secondary schools in cities can accommodate 90% of graduates

Source: China Statistical Yearbook 2012 and authors' calculations

For every two students who graduate from primary school nationwide, about one student is admitted to an academic secondary high school (a.k.a. regular secondary middle school offering college preparatory instruction, as opposed to a vocational school). But these high schools are overwhelmingly concentrated in cities and towns, where 16 to 18 entrance slots exist for every 20 children who graduate from primary school. In the countryside, conditions differ dramatically: There are only enough college preparatory high school admissions to accommodate 1 in 20 primary school graduates, or about 5%. This is not to say that rural students are entirely shut out of urban classrooms if they fail to win one of the few-and-far-between entrance slots to a high school near their rural home. Many Chinese "public" high schools offer boarding school programs that can accommodate rural students, albeit at a much greater cost to their family than a public day school in the same city.[6] But opportunities are clearly and overwhelmingly concentrated in urban areas, where urban households get first dibs on them.

And then comes college. An overlapping set of inequalities come into play when each high-strung high school student receives his score on the university entrance exam. Cutoff scores for university admission vary dramatically from province to province: A high school student in Hunan seeking admission to a humanities program at a national first-tier university such as Sichuan University would have needed a score of 583 out of 750 in 2011 to qualify (see Figure 5.2). For the most prestigious of Chinese universities among the first tier, admission is nearly impossible. But that same student could have won admission with a score of just 524 if he had the good fortune to be born in Beijing.[7]

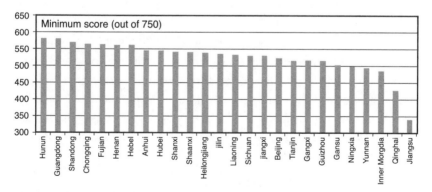

Figure 5.2 Select cutoff scores for admission to first-tier humanities university programs, 2011

Source: *People's Daily*[8]

Minimum qualifying scores are highest in the most populous provinces, and lower in Beijing and Shanghai, where applicants are fewer and where a relative abundance of highly rated universities reserve a disproportionate number of admission slots for local students. One of the authors' wives, a Beijing-born graduate of Beijing University, China's most prestigious university, vividly recalls the cynical attitude of students from the provinces toward the Beijing "townies" who won admission to the university with such comparative ease. Economically underdeveloped regions with large minority populations such as Tibet or Xinjiang have lower qualifying scores, a modest attempt at Chinese-style affirmative action to offset the disadvantages of birth in a poorer rural region with weaker and scarcer educational opportunities.

Other exceptions, complications, and backdoors distort the system even further. Many Chinese universities will, for example, have an affiliated middle school—somewhat akin to "feeder" schools in the United States—that enjoys unusually lavish educational resources, including admission slots reserved for its own students at the university when graduation approaches. In addition, several graduates of each city's most elite middle schools will each year receive guaranteed admission (*baosong*) for some of their students to the most prestigious schools without requiring passage of the national admissions test. These tony middle schools, in turn, grant a quota of their own admission slots to their affiliated elementary schools and other highly sought-after institutions. For children fortunate enough to land in one of these networks, which again depends significantly on the hukou and parents' political connections, securing placement in an elite higher education institution becomes much easier.

It is hard to quantify the exact *impact* of this complex and overlapping system of privileges, preferences, and priorities. But an academic study of the family backgrounds of students at Beijing University, known to locals as Beida, presents an appealing Rorschach blob for decoding this mess.[9] Well over half of Beida students are from households headed by government officials, professionals, or highly educated technical experts. These types of households collectively account for less than one-tenth of China's total and live overwhelmingly in urban areas (see Figure 5.3).

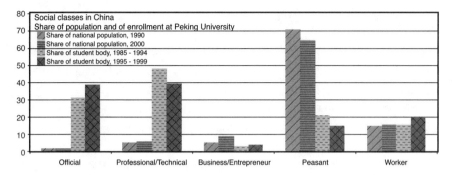

Figure 5.3   Perpetuating privilege at elite Chinese universities

Source: Liang and Li et al.[10]

The Chinese education system inspires intense competition, pressure, and anxiety in young people and their families. For those living in it, the scramble for scarce spots in each round of applications is its defining characteristic. In this respect, China's educational system seems not so different from that of the United States, Japan, or other countries where the lifetime economic return to education is large.

But as far as education's role in stabilizing society as a whole is concerned, the system's defining characteristic isn't competition, an aggregate lack of educational resources, or the pressure they produce. Its defining characteristic is its institutionalized inequalities—its artificial scarcities. At the highest level, China's educational system puts urbanites ahead of rural families. Within the cities, institutional inequality benefits the offspring of public officials, who enjoy preferential access to elite educational institutions. It just as clearly benefits the urban intelligentsia, who possess the educational savvy and economic resources to help their children prepare for China's grueling standardized tests. The experience of navigating the educational system is disorienting for a typical urban Chinese family because it resides in a duality between frustration with its extreme unfairness and reluctant submission to its bitter calculus. For the average Chinese in the middle class, awareness of the easy access to educational resources enjoyed by those higher on the socioeconomic ladder burns. But simply knowing that there are countless masses crowded onto even lower rungs, enviously eyeing the spot you hold, is a strong enough motivation to grit your teeth, close your eyes, and hold on tight right where you are.

From urban bias to urban household bias

China's educational system is well calibrated to foster support for the political system from an urban minority that fears losing its hard-won privileges to an agricultural rural majority. Like all urban bias policies, the education system serves to redirect resources from a majority to a minority. It was attractive to the Chinese government at the time it came into being because it could take a little from a lot of people, who will only mind a little bit, and give a lot to a few people, who appreciate it much more. Urban bias made the urban middle class into a willing and loyal political constituency.

The incredible successes of China's economic development have turned it into a country that looks less and less like the one this finely calibrated education system was designed to help manage. And as Chinese society has changed, so has the system of bias, from one that stabilized the country into one that can potentially destabilize it.

China today has more workers employed in urban areas than on the farm, becoming a majority urban country for the first time in 2011, according to government statistics.[11] And because most Chinese agricultural workers are less productive (that is, produce less GDP per hour of work) than workers in industry or services, agriculture's share of GDP has shrunk to a meager one-tenth in 2012. To make redistribution from rural to urban areas happen today would mean shifting resources from a poor minority, who would resent the acute squeeze, to a wealthier majority, whose loyalties would be at best little affected by government transfers that seem miniscule next to the wealth of the roaring urban economy. The math of traditional urban bias has become politically impossible. The flip side of a shrinking rural population, with less potential to have its resources further divided and redistributed to the cities, is a growing urban economy and city population, many of whom earn higher incomes and expect higher standards of living—in particular, better public services than were on offer in the past.

Here the mechanism that Chinese policymakers relied on to operationalize urban bias becomes crucial: again, the hukou system. Public goods are distributed according to a household registration status that, for most people, is passed down "original sin"-style from their parents. The hukou is used to tether the rural population to its place of birth. Relocating from the countryside to the city without proper authorization was a serious crime and often resulted in jail time or repatriation a la illegal immigrants. Now China's public security apparatus no longer discourages rural Chinese from assuming the status of the floating population of migrants who now flood Chinese cities.[12] Instead, the pervasive denial of the economic rights conferred upon holders of the urban hukou slows the flow from country to city. By delineating who has a right to public goods and where, the hukou system as enforced today has transformed urban bias into urban household bias. This is a fundamentally different political system than urban bias-based geographic distribution of public goods, and it has profound implications for social stability.

It's worth reemphasizing that the whole point of traditional urban bias embedded in policymaking was to create a class of haves among the most difficult to control part of the population, which had the greatest potential to threaten social stability and the status quo. The hundreds of millions of Chinese living on farms, producing food for the urban minority, were relatively less menacing because they were isolated and their movements geographically constrained relative to the urban minority. In contemporary China, however, where a majority of households with urban hukou own a home,[13] the typical urbanite is much less mobile than the migrant class of rural hukou-holders and their families who live in factory towns or shanty slums encircling cities, sometimes moving every couple of months or years in pursuit of better economic opportunity.

To give a sense of the scale of the migrant presence in major urban centers, one only needs to ask the average Beijinger or Shanghainese to play the "guess the population of your city" game. Many will answer in the range of 13 to 15 million, only to quickly follow with "but really, it's maybe anywhere between 18 and 21 million." That reply not only reflects the difficulty with which it is to ascertain the certainty of Chinese data, it also underscores the reality of the extent to which the migrant class has filed into the cities. This new class of semi-permanent residents now pose a potential threat to urban social stability for the same reasons that the Chinese government favored urban bias policies in the first place: They live close together, can communicate and organize easily, and are geographically mobile. Yet there is no migrant-class bias policy to forestall the withering of their support for the status quo. They live on the economic and social fringe of urban China, without the preferred access to public services granted to urban hukou-holders: housing, healthcare, and of course, education. The hole in the social safety net through which they slip seems to gape wider each year.

Turn on, tune in, and study abroad: Life at the top

Just as the fraying fabric of the educational system has increasingly pushed the migrant class to slip through the seams of educational opportunity and of political control, some Chinese families at the top of the socioeconomic pyramid are deliberately opting out of the education system. Many of them are seeking greener and more abundant pastures by sending their children overseas. With the flood of wealth that accompanied the Panda Boom, overseas education, unimaginable and unobtainable in decades past, is now within the financial reach of a growing number of Chinese households. Between 2000 and 2010, the number of Chinese students studying overseas leapt 700% (see Figure 5.4).

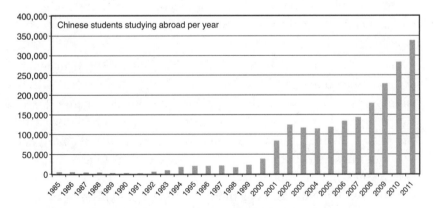

Figure 5.4   Newfound Chinese wealth showers on foreign university campuses

Source: China Statistical Yearbook 2012

Some of the interest in studying abroad reflects the desire of China's nouveau riche to claim a foothold in a foreign country, providing a possible plan B insurance policy of escape if they run afoul of the law in China or the political climate becomes less hospitable to the wealthy. (Diverting their wealth to a country with strong legal protections, in contrast to China, is usually another underlying consideration.) For other more intellectually minded Chinese families, providing an overseas education for their children is prompted by the perceived advantages of educational systems in more developed countries. Indeed, the Chinese educational system has long been believed to be weak in critical reasoning and innovation, instead overwhelmingly emphasizing rote memorization and imitation. These characteristics are epitomized in the modern era by the gaokao and before it by the ideal Confucian scholar whose correspondence was composed entirely of quotations from and references to the ancient classics. Foreign education promises immersion in a valuable foreign language environment (usually English), cutting-edge technology and curricula, higher-quality instruction, and a stronger, more rigorous emphasis on critical thinking and creativity.

For young Chinese people at the very top of the social ladder, an increasingly well-worn trail leads from the halls of China's elite middle schools to those of the West's most prestigious undergraduate universities and back to high-powered careers in Beijing, Shanghai, Hong Kong, or Singapore. Roughly 70 graduates of the toniest institution in the Chinese capital, the Beijing #4 High School, reportedly enrolled in undergraduate programs in foreign universities in 2012, which translates into roughly 20% of the graduating class.[14] The majority of Chinese students studying abroad, however, matriculate into more "ordinary" schools overseas.

The benefits of urban bias change little the fact that Chinese university admissions remain extremely competitive even for those who start the game on second or third base. Language barriers notwithstanding, it is much easier for many Chinese students to be admitted to a respected foreign university with an established academic track record in the United States or Britain than in their home provinces. The number of young Chinese people studying abroad each year now equals 1 in 20 of the students enrolling in domestic undergraduate programs, a telling sign of how much demand for education outstrips its supply in China. Unfortunately, such scarcity is made all the worse by a system that, willfully or not, incentivizes discrimination in already limited education opportunities.

The internationalization of the Chinese elite will mean many things for China's future, among them a more cosmopolitan ruling class in another generation. Those in that class can be expected to be abundantly armed with the types of skills that Western education and Western businesses prize: critical thinking, creativity, teamwork, and leadership. Even with overseas Chinese students concentrated in science, engineering, and business programs, many upon returning to China remark on the influence that liberal arts ideals and values had on them.

The future abundance of these ingredients is shaping an innovative society and economy, a reason for guarded optimism about China's ability to assume a larger role in the global economy and its governance. The immersion of a critical mass of Chinese elites in Western societies during their formative years may even change Chinese values, but any expectations in this area should be couched in some skepticism: the Western educations of many of the managers of China's leading state-owned enterprises have not prompted them to contest their employers' privileged access to their industry for the greater good of the economy or general public welfare. The experience of other countries as well, such as the crop of autocratic regimes run by returnees schooled in Western pedagogy, suggests that the relationship between elite cosmopolitanism and social transformation is at best a complex and indirect one.

Whatever the economic and social consequences of the growing ranks of Western-educated Chinese elites may be, they are likely bad news for the educational system's capacity to preserve social stability indefinitely. Privileged access to the education system is a double-edged sword for elite Chinese, just as it is for the middle class. Generally speaking, the more privilege someone has in Chinese society, the more they stand to lose if they step out of line, and the stronger their impetus to support (or at least tacitly accept) the existing order and the system's demands. For 21st century Chinese elites, though, the unprecedented possibility of opting out of the shared educational institutions is now possible, inside track notwithstanding. As the options available to elite Chinese expand, the government's influence over them wanes—just as does the government's ability to control the rural Chinese who each day become more and more indistinguishable from the 700 million or so other residents of China's immense urban jungle.

Running out of levers to pull

Analyzing the Chinese education system's shortcomings isn't intended to render normative judgments about its deep inequalities. The grossly uneven distribution of opportunities in China feels viscerally wrong to many Chinese who count themselves as part of the emergent middle class and who are concerned that upward mobility has become too treacherous a path for those with average means. But for an aspiring young person born in a developing country, the inequality of opportunity available to him relative to a peer in Bethesda, Maryland, or Westchester County, New York, could easily feel just as stark.

Moreover, it would be remiss and inaccurate to imply that the Chinese educational system is designed purely as a Machiavellian device for social control. In fact, educational attainment in China has advanced steadily and dramatically since the founding of the republic, and has been both an achievement in and of itself and a foundation on which China's supercharged economic performance has been built. Relative to many other developing countries, China has managed crowning achievements in ensuring an educated workforce and enrolling nearly all of its children in compulsory primary education. The country also remains a world leader in scholastic tests. And human progress in China's education system continues, most tangibly embodied in the government's ambitious plans to achieve near-universal upper secondary education and to have 40% of young people receive some sort of post-secondary education by 2020.[15]

But equally clear is the immanent reality that the education system is part of a set of Chinese political and social institutions that exist, at least in part, to perpetuate themselves. And this is as it should be: pragmatic tools that can turn ideas into reality are the difference between a political party that can change the world and a mob of people debating how to run a leaderless movement in Zuccotti Park. The design of China's educational system serves many goals, and one of them is maintaining social stability.

Judged purely on its capacity to achieve this goal, education in China is in trouble.

The system contributes well to the goal of keeping the middle class from getting overly restless and disgruntled. It grants urban Chinese, and in particular, the better educated urban middle class, privileges far in excess of those they would likely enjoy in a popularly controlled political system—for example, one that gives equal representation to Chinese holding rural household registration. They pay less than rural Chinese to get their children into school, the bar is set lower to pass the tests for admittance, and the instruction available is higher quality once their children are admitted. The larger and more developed the city, the greater the middle-class privilege that accrues to its inhabitants: Residents of Beijing and Shanghai worry about what kind of university their children will attend, not whether their children will attend at all. Were it put to a question, it seems doubtful that many middle-class Chinese would choose an electoral democracy that erased their claims on preferential access to education, or the many other public goods that are distributed in similar fashion.

But basing China's future social and, ultimately, political stability on the acquiescence of the middle class alone seems a risky proposition. This is true in particular as the migrant class achieves so many of the distinctions that made the middle class such a wobbly brick in the political wall in the first place. Young migrant-class Chinese, like Chinese of all socioeconomic stripes, are increasingly educated, mobile, and able to communicate freely with like-minded people around the country through the ubiquity of the Internet. These rural hukou-holding Chinese are not entirely locked out of the education system. Proliferating new institutions of higher education have made post-secondary education more available to Chinese people of all backgrounds, including those without access to the urban education system.

But policy bias is a relative, not absolute phenomenon. The biases against Chinese peasants, which were once effective and pragmatic anchors of social stability, have become sparks showered on a powder keg now that they disadvantage a migrant class that is far more capable of catalyzing social disruptions. Could the increasing educational opportunities available to young migrant-class Chinese ease the social tensions caused by this system? While education may provide them with a better livelihood than their parents achieved, it seems unlikely to become a path toward enduring social mobility. Similarly, the education system's influence over the behavior of the Chinese elite is waning as they increasingly pursue global lifestyles beyond the reach of traditional domestic institutions.

The tensions caused by hukou, and its role in education, are obvious in China, and the government is taking a number of incremental steps to defuse them. Notably, three of the most developed regions, the municipalities of Shanghai and Beijing, and the province of Guangdong, published plans at the end of 2012 to allow migrant children to enroll in local high schools and sit for the college entrance exam locally.[16] The contrast with recent Beijing government-initiated closures of schools for migrant workers is striking, and gives a sense of the conflicting demands being placed on local governments.[17] Even as the government tentatively tweaks the hukou system around its edges to better accommodate the legion of younger migrants who now dot China's urban landscape, it is politically difficult to manage if the system wants to keep peace with the urban middle class.

Fundamentally, it remains to be seen whether reforms of the education system merely facilitate geographic mobility of the Chinese upper and middle class or actually narrow the inequalities between social classes in China, ease tensions, and bolster stability. It seems quite likely that the weakened power of the education system, and the shrinking array of population control tools available to the government more generally, will force either a more responsive and service-oriented public policy or, failing that, a more fundamental reorientation of the relationship between ruler and ruled.

6

Housing: Home is where the wallet is

Few things in China are as affected by the convergence of demographic, economic, and political pressures as is its housing market. Rapid urbanization and income growth have made tens of millions of Chinese households into potential homeowners. That has taken place alongside the repression of the financial sector, redirecting savings from financial assets to real estate and inflating property prices in the process. And local governments that still rely on land-use fees from real estate developers to fund urban development have every incentive to support astronomical prices by keeping supply scarce.

The threat of a collapsing real estate bubble may preoccupy foreign observers and investors, but for the average urban Chinese family, that is neither here nor there. It's the pervasive sense of scarcity of affordable housing that remains a widespread and pressing concern. Nearly all middle-class Chinese, existing and aspiring, want to own property; it is a rite of passage into, and an entitlement of, middle-class status.

Understanding the Chinese housing market gets one a long way toward getting how the Chinese economy ticks. China's property sector is such a perfect microcosm of everything that makes the economy work that economics professors would have to invent it if it didn't already exist.

A quick historical detour is in order. After decades of property market underdevelopment during the planned economy, market reforms prompted a tremendous bull run in housing investment and prices during the Panda Boom. State sector liberalization turned investment in housing from a drain on state resources into a fabulous financial proposition for the firms able to participate in the market. The urban middle class was given a huge financial windfall in being allowed to purchase their homes from their work units at fire-sale prices. In fact, the way the government sold off China's existing housing stock to its residents contributed more to the creation of the urban middle class than any other policy of the previous era of stellar growth.

In addition to absorbing huge flows of excess savings from households and corporations, the real estate bull market has provided one of the few reliably profitable (at least so far) investment opportunities available to the typical Chinese saver. Household purchases of newly constructed real estate, in turn, flowed up the supply chain to enrich local governments and fund the social safety net's reconstruction. The housing market benefited from, and seemed to have contributed to, all of the Panda Boom's virtues, or vices, depending on whether you are a bull or bear. The housing cycle's peaks and troughs have inspired the most fervent apoplexy about both China's economic supremacy and its impending doom. China's real estate sector either put its economy on "a treadmill to hell" or was "the single most important sector in the entire global economy" or both.[1]

Not much has changed since then. Prospects for China's property market mirror those of the economy more generally. Growth of the property market seems likely to proceed over the next decade, but at a more measured pace than during the headiest years of the last decade, paralleling the deceleration of real GDP growth from double to single digits.

Similarly, housing sits at the nexus of the social constraints that are eclipsing economic growth as China's central preoccupation. The inflating housing prices that once cushioned urban household balance sheets against the hit they took during the layoffs of the earlier boom years now severely distress urbanites who want to buy new homes for their children. Sky-high real estate prices also fence off migrant-class families more firmly at the margins of city life. And the urban biases inherent in China's housing policies, as sharp and divisive as those felt in the education system, exacerbate tensions between the urban and migrant classes. Amid a revolution of rising expectations, the typical Chinese city dweller is unlikely to feel or see the reality of her life reflected in the steadily improving aggregate statistical measures of public welfare, which point to ever rising levels of economic development, higher incomes, and more plentiful living space. The most visceral sensation, instead, is anxiety about being left behind in an ever-accelerating and unwinnable race.

More affordable housing could help. But as with many other areas of public policy, the Chinese government is finding itself with much less appealing choices to improve housing affordability than those available when spurring the housing bull market was the central challenge. Although Chinese economists widely advocate property taxes to prevent a damaging bubble (by pushing investors' capital out of housing and into investment in other parts of the economy), housing's complex role in power politics and economic redistribution in China perennially stymie its execution.

Moreover, the most fundamental inequality of the urban housing market is also a contributor to scarcity. That is, the land for property development is taken from the rural households who use it—but do not own it—without reliable channels to obtain compensation. Unlawful land grabs have become increasingly untenable as rural peasants, who the government once had tools to adequately control, transform into geographically mobile, technologically interconnected, and difficult-to-manage migrant-class households.

The irony is that housing is more abundant in China today than ever before. Even so, the battle for limited supplies of this social and economic entitlement will rage on with ever more ferocity. That's because the China of tomorrow faces rising expectations, a changing population, longstanding institutional barriers, and the inescapable reality of the scarcity of easily inhabitable territory. The messy fight to stake a claim on this contested resource and store of economic value will convince everyone that it is scarce indeed.

Phat cribs and fatter wallets

Housing's economic role in the Panda Boom is well appreciated. China's recent accumulation of housing stock compensated for a long period of underinvestment in it. In the decades prior to skyrocketing growth, the below-cost provision of housing to urban workers had been a huge drag on state-owned enterprise (SOE) financial performance.[2] State workers received housing from their employers and usually paid only a nominal pittance in rent. Even if the land used for housing were free in a planned economy, rents were much less than would be required to compensate work units for the initial purchase (or construction costs) of workers' housing and its continued maintenance.

Housing subsidies stifled growth in many ways. For one, subsidies kept urban housing scarce. Low cash salaries for SOE workers meant that the market for real estate developers to sell housing directly to households was even more underdeveloped than China's overall economy. The few urban households who might have had enough money to buy homes on the private market would think twice before doing so if they might have a chance to get a heavily subsidized home from an employer instead. Although work units had political incentives to acquire housing, they were also dissuaded by the cost of doing so: Money spent on loss-making subsidies for workers' housing was money that was unavailable to reinvest in the business or return to the government as operating surplus. When housing is subsidized, its availability is limited to the availability of subsidies.

A transition to a private housing market at the launch of the Panda Boom, in the late 1990s and early 2000s, realigned these perverse incentives.[3] As part of their restructuring, SOEs transferred the housing stocks they owned to the employees living in them at deep discounts to their likely market value—admittedly a bit of a speculative proposition since no private market existed for these assets at the time. Everyone seemed to win: firms could focus their investments in assets useful to their core businesses, and urban households came into the possession of a highly valuable asset, cushioning the blow for many laid-off former SOE employees.

Privatization fundamentally reoriented the incentives of urban households participating in the housing market in ways that persisted through the boom years. Once granted firm ownership rights to their homes, urban Chinese entered a frenzy of redecorating, refurbishing, and otherwise renovating homes in ways that didn't make sense back when an SOE manager's whim could mean the loss of a home.[4] The unprecedented sense of stability and security that ownership rights conferred on homeowners, in other words, became the political foundation on which the housing market could prosper.

With higher net worth, many urban households made the same choice popular to people around the world when they come into a little money: they upgrade to nicer houses. Homes received during privatization served as collateral for loans that urban households took on to trade up and buy newer, fancier abodes. This worked particularly well because state-owned banks favored real assets (and particularly real estate) as loan collateral during the previous decades, for two reasons. One, they helped protect against loss in default; and two, they were easier to measure, monitor, and prove ownership of than less tangible types of collateral.

Collectively, this policy regime change amounted to an economist's dream: Improved microeconomic incentives translating into dramatically improved macroeconomic outcomes. From 2001 to 2011, real GDP growth in the construction and real estate sectors averaged 13.4% annually, while GDP growth in the rest of the economy averaged 10.2%. The Panda Boom would have been considerably less boomy—and less resource intensive—without the boost from real estate privatization (see Figure 6.1).

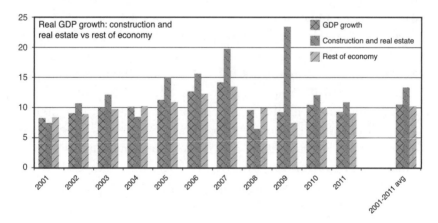

Figure 6.1   The property market takes off

Source: China Statistical Yearbook 2012,* Tables 2-4 to 2-8 and authors' calculations. *This figure assumes officially reported real GDP growth rates and composition of GDP are accurate.

The sizzling property market lifted growth directly, but also indirectly contributed to stronger demand for the products of related industries and for basic commodities. In 2007, when China's real estate boom was cresting, the housing and construction sectors accounted for 11% of Chinese GDP, close to the entire economic output of a smaller member of the G-20. On top of this, another tenth of all interindustry sales were made to the construction sector, meaning the total share of economic activity in the property supply chain, from the steelworkers smelting the reinforcing bars used to hold together concrete high rises to the advertisers distributing pamphlets on housing availability, was closer to a quarter of all economic activity.[5]

An urban middle class is born

Like its broader economic miracle, China's real estate success meant very different things to different people. For households holding urban household residency at the start of the last decade, real estate's privatization has meant a transformation of personal finances. Up until the late 1990s, almost all Chinese urban residents lived in heavily subsidized apartments owned and maintained by their work units. Their homes had all the characteristics typically associated with socialist housing. Living quarters were often cramped and shabby, but working-class families had the security of knowing they would have a place to live. While a minority of urban Chinese slowly moved into privately owned housing over the course of the decade, the majority of them still lived in their work-unit flats in early 1999 when the Chinese State Council abruptly instructed work units to privatize their housing stocks and sell them to their current residents. In merely a year, half of the urban housing stock was privatized, a massive and involved financial transaction with far-reaching implications for the economy and growth.[6]

Urban households received an implicit subsidy during the privatization process itself, since they were required to pay only a fraction of the likely "market value" of the home they inhabited—a price point that could only have been inferred more by art than science. And subsequently, urban households benefited from a tremendous increase in paper wealth as the housing they acquired appreciated in value. Housing prices do not always go up in China—Hainan (China's Hawaii), for example, saw a spectacular property bubble burst in the early 1990s, and needed about 20 years for prices to recover. So, too, did property prices in some parts of Shenzhen, Guangdong, fall some 30% to 40% in 2008 and 2009 from their 2007 peaks.[7]

But across most of the country, and in most years since the bull housing market began, the common experience has been that property appreciates faster than the increase in the average salary. The consensus among those seeking better stores of value for their hard-earned savings was that real estate ownership delivered much larger returns than financial assets like bank deposits, which on average, paid less than inflation in interest. Real estate ownership was also a more reliable investment than playing in the stock market, which was (and still is) widely perceived to be a gambling den rife with uninformed speculation, just as likely to plummet or jump by 50% in any given year. By 2012, surveys showed 85% of urban households owned at least one home, though this is likely defining *households* in a non-nuclear family sense.[8] Home ownership has played a crucial role in transforming China's urbanites from a working class—or, if you are a good Chinese communist, a proletariat—into a relatively well-off property-owning middle class.

Jobs all around

The migrant class, meanwhile, also benefited from the jobs created in the boiling property market. In 2010, construction supplied more than one in ten jobs for nonagricultural workers in China. And four-fifths of construction industry employment provided jobs for workers with less than a high school education who would otherwise have a hard time finding employment in factories or in any but the least skilled parts of the services sector (see Figure 6.2).

Employment in construction grew almost twice as fast as in other nonagricultural industries between 2000 and 2010, providing nearly one in six new jobs in nonagricultural sectors.[9] The explosion in the real estate market kept the old bogeyman—the fear of social unrest should real GDP growth drop beneath 8%—safely at bay. Migrant workers employed in urban areas earned modest salaries at their hard, sometimes dangerous jobs, but could at least cover minimum living expenses in the city because employers usually provided basic dormitory accommodation and meals.

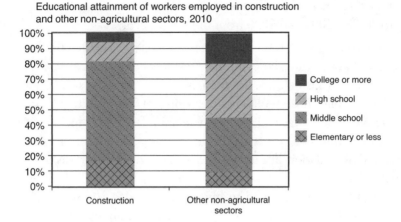

Educational attainment of workers employed in construction and other non-agricultural sectors, 2010

Figure 6.2   Without construction jobs, less-educated workers risk being left out of the modern economy

Source: National Bureau of Statistics sixth population census long form data, Table 4-6, and authors' calculations

True, China's housing prosperity was built on top of land that was regularly expropriated from under the homes and farmlands of rural Chinese. Much like the distribution of education opportunities, land policy in China is another stark example of urban bias.[10] Urban land in China is owned by the state, but land-use rights, giving their holders long-term control of the land and its development—typically 70 years for residential use—can be legally bought and sold. The existence of an active market in land-use rights provides a basis for their urban owners to claim compensation at a market value if the land rights are expropriated. By contrast, rural land is owned by peasant collectives that can assign the right to farm the land to members of the collective, but without the power to authorize legal construction on the property.

Urbanization has typically occurred as rural land became redesignated as urban, allowing local governments to sell land use rights to property developers. While governments are obligated to compensate peasants for the loss of their land, peasants have little recourse when governments fail to fulfill their pledges. When compensation is provided, it is usually calculated to offset peasants' lost income, not to give them some approximation of their land's value under urban use, usually much higher. Expropriations and disputes over the amount of compensation owed to displaced rural households were the most common cause of mass incidents in China until 2012, when environmental issues displaced them.[11] But restless peasants seemed a minute nuisance relative to the tremendous amount of growth and tax revenue generated by the property market, a nuisance that would be relatively easy to manage. Land ownership disputes are, by their definition, only of localized concern, meaning local government officials can usually suppress, wheedle, or co-opt their organizers into going along with development. And the huge windfall profits that local governments captured by converting land from less valuable agricultural use to more valuable urban use provided ample resources to clean up any mess caused along the way.

Fat pancakes from the sky: the rich man's boom

China's super elites, much like their middle-class compatriots, favored real estate investment as a store of wealth over much of the previous gilded decade of property development. By 2005, 10% of Chinese households owned a second property.[12] By 2011, market studies of Chinese "high net worth individuals" with investable assets over 10 million yuan (~$1.6 million), estimated that the wealthiest 590,000 Chinese households—that is, the wealthiest 0.1% of households—on average owned about 20 million yuan, or $2.5 million, of property each.[13] And real estate development itself contributed to much of their newfound wealth. For instance, 39 of the 100 wealthiest Chinese tycoons in 2012 made their fortunes at least in part in the property market's transition from a tool by which the state allocated land through fiat to one where market prices largely determined which consumers purchased newly developed real estate.[14] The rapid evolution from arbitrary pricing for land and real estate to higher market prices made many fortunes for influential officials, wealthy entrepreneurs, and SOE executives.

Rather than widening opportunities for an outsider entrepreneurial class, real estate marketization has overwhelmingly benefited insider developers, however. Perhaps real estate is an insider's game everywhere, but the cards seemed stacked particularly steeply to benefit insiders, government officials, and well-connected property tycoons in China, a consequence of the sector's incomplete transition to a competitive market. The prices that households pay for their homes may be market determined, but the land on which the condo is built must be purchased from a government monopoly. It was a particularly fertile institutional arrangement in which to incubate what political scientists call crony capitalism.

Indeed, the state's control of the supply of land, through each municipal and provincial office of the Ministry of Land and Natural Resources, as well as its authority to grant permission to build, means that local governments can easily profit off housing development. As the monopoly supplier of land for development, local governments have every incentive to keep the supply tight and prices high—and keep demand for their product stronger than its supply, encouraging developers to curry favor with the officials controlling land distribution. Often such actions are a necessity if local officials hope to keep their fiscal coffers plump to meet the numerous obligations they must spend on, from social welfare to education and keeping the peace.[15] Kickbacks and insider dealings are endemic, and often are paid in properties rather than cash—the same properties that palm-greasing made possible to develop. It seemed a virtuous cycle.

So happy together

Again, the impact on growth of China's incomplete transition to a truly competitive property market is generally understood, as are the indirect costs it has imposed. But less appreciated was the role housing played in maintaining social stability during the last 15 years. It was a period of social change that would've been tumultuous for any country, but change on a Chinese scale was mind-boggling—and housing privatization and the real estate boom offered a stake in the economy's success to urban elites, the working class, and rural farmers alike.

The smashing of the iron rice bowl dropped 25 million workers from SOE factories and assembly lines, most of whom had never looked for a job before. Indeed, because a worker's previous work unit had to agree before she could leave and take a new position, applying for a new job was not always encouraged or even possible. In the early years of the Panda Boom, Chinese parks and other public spaces were full of idle, able-bodied men and women in their early 50s who had been laid off from state-owned work units and essentially gave up job searches. Home ownership in part compensated displaced SOE workers for some of the wrenching loss of economic security they experienced during this period.

For rural Chinese, real estate privatization provided a livelihood. The housing explosion overlapped with the peak years of Chinese migration from the country to the city, with hundreds of millions moving off farms. Policymakers were also prepared to decriminalize immigration of rural Chinese to urban areas in the mid-2000s because the macroeconomic drivers of growth, principal among them real estate, were creating sufficiently strong job markets that the government no longer felt necessary to press rural workers to stay in the countryside.

At the same time, the real estate market effectively co-opted China's monied, college-educated elites, who a decade earlier may have seemed like a potential threat to the regime's stability. Many of the 20-something supporters and participants of the 1980s movement became wealthy entrepreneurs in the late 1990s and 2000s, benefiting from the economic dynamism that phenomenal and uninterrupted growth unleashed. Wild oats sowed, most of the former iconoclasts of the late 1980s are now firmly entrenched in the Chinese establishment. But the very possibility for these outsiders to become integrated into the mainstream was in part made possible by the opening of new sectors of the economy and the wealth accumulation in the housing market.

When virtues become flaws

Yet the housing market's role as a socioeconomic salve couldn't go on indefinitely; it would be naive to think otherwise. The change began in the late 2000s, as the housing market dynamics that previously buttressed social stability during the Panda Boom began to undermine it. Urban middle-class families who felt rich when rising housing prices made them paper yuan millionaires began to feel impossibly burdened by the obligation of providing a home to their marrying and unwed children. This is an even more intractable problem for migrant-class Chinese, many of whom have lived as *de facto* urban residents for many years, and who want to own a home where they live instead of where they are considered legal residents in the countryside.

What both of these groups share is an interest in housing afford-ability. However, the super elites, after benefiting from their role in the wheeling and dealing that made China's property market fizzle, are a powerful vested interest against policies that would tame hous-ing price inflation. Sliding housing prices might upset wealthy home-owners. Perhaps more important from the government's perspective, falling prices could make the vast stores of land owned by real estate developers uneconomical to develop. Developers, many of whom have close ties (sometimes blood ties) to local government officials, could experience steep financial losses; they might also suspend work on construction sites and lay off their workforces.

"I love you...after you've closed on that two-bedroom"

The average home price in China has hovered between 15 and 20 times the average urban income between 2008 and 2012.[16] Prices are considerably higher in first-tier markets such as Beijing and Shang-hai, where a typical 800 square foot (74 square meter) apartment cost $260,000 in 2013. Prices in centrally located neighborhoods in those cities were easily two to three times higher.[17] Chinese mortgage regu-lations are often tightened or loosened as a tool to manage the swings of the property market, but homebuyers are in general required to fork over at least a 30% down payment for a mortgage. To put that in context, a 30% down payment on a typical Beijing home that costs $80,000 is roughly the equivalent of 8 to 10 years' income for the typi-cal Beijing wage-earner, who takes home just under $10,000 a year.[18] Of course, most Chinese young men earn less than typical wage in their first few years in the workforce. In addition, housing prices and wages both rise rapidly, effectively shrinking the purchasing power of savings as it accumulates. A typical male urban dweller would have to save most of his income from the time of workforce entry to his early 30s to have a shot at simply putting a down payment on a home.[19]

For most young Chinese men, a down payment on a home realis-tically must come from a combined effort: his savings and often con-tributions from his parents as well as the grandparents to their only child's (and grandchild's) home. The property business has become a family business. But why is the family so preoccupied with such matters? To prevent the family from suffering the collective trauma of a middle-class young man's fancy of love turn into one of forlorn desperation because he wasn't marriage material enough.

Indeed, rising divorce rates, weakening traditional social ties, and anxiety about economic and social status have made property acquisition the preeminent criterion for choosing a spouse. Sadly, romance and sex have fallen victim to the economic demands of keeping up with the Joneses in urban China today. Housing once again serves a social function, but not the one many would've imagined—as an indispensable component of a transactional mating ritual.

The economics of contemporary Chinese marriage have become quite simple: to get a girl, a boy must buy a house for her to live in. A simple rationale justifies this demand from a young woman's perspective. Chinese regulation of the housing rental market offers little in the way of tenant protections from arbitrary rent hikes or evictions, and renters often do not qualify for "resident" status when enrolling their children in the local public schools. And more fundamentally, a Chinese husband is still expected to be a provider, and one of the things he should provide is a home for his family. In a rapidly changing society where expenses that didn't exist a generation ago are becoming essential to a middle-class lifestyle, how can a wife be confident that a man can provide economic security without first being able to provide its most basic component: shelter? Property ownership also provides a reassuring anchor in a culture only two or three generations removed from pre-communist rural agricultural life, where control of land could mean the difference between a life of relative economic security and one of privation.

Meeting the precondition of matrimony is difficult to execute, especially for men of average means. Here things become complicated. China remains a hierarchical society, where no one wants to marry down, and familial contributions to their children's future home are an easy measure of whether a prospective son- or daughter-in-law comes from a suitable background. Deng Xiaoping famously explained the transition from planned to market economy meant that "some people would get rich first;" now those people want their children to marry other children of their socioeconomic cohort.

The parents' role in subsidizing their children's lives has become so commonplace that it has even entered the popular vernacular as the phrase *kenlao,* literally "chewing on the aged." It refers to how dependent middle-class Chinese youth are on their elders to support the lifestyle that they expect, and which is expected of them. Kenlao is often presented as a sign of weak moral fiber among today's *balinghou* or *jiulinghou* (the post-80s and post-90s generations), who never suffered or struggled the way their parents did during the Cultural Revolution. But really, kenlao reflects societal expectations that young people adopt lifestyles, or often, that young men provide their young wives with lifestyles, that are unattainable without substantial support from the savings of their elders.

Judged by their financial or private material status, middle-class Chinese have never been wealthier and their standards of living have never been higher. Yet nostalgia for the halcyon planned economy days—when at least in idealized memory, urban households earned a pittance and needed just as little because the government provided for all—continues to strike a chord in Chinese hearts. With government fiat deciding who would and who would not get a home, scarcity was objectively much more severe than today, and individuals had little ability to influence where or how they lived. But at the same time, there was no role for the anxiety about being left behind or caught sideways in a rapidly transforming society that now pervades China. Today, the market offers a previously unimaginable array of choices. But with most of them beyond the means of the average consumer, many young Chinese men (and their parents) fear they are being left behind in a "winner take all" marriage market.

For Chinese just entering the middle class, the distress over housing's affordability is at its core an unspoken anxiety about class. After all, Chinese salaries keep going up every year, real output rises, and average urban floor space per capita does as well. Macroeconomic indicators point universally to rising standards of living in all areas, and housing is no exception. But the value of a Chinese person's home, symbolically and socially, is as a measure of his or her place in the world. And here the fixation over housing reveals a deeper psychological neurosis of a people who no longer know what lifestyle is enough to aspire to. How exactly is one to know whether you're marrying up or down, when salaries for white-collar workers in foreign-owned enterprises exploded during the 1990s and early 2000s, then those of SOE workers during the late 2000s, and now blue-collar workers' salaries are growing faster than white-collar salaries? Without firmly anchoring your place in the world, it's impossible to know what lifestyle a bride should be able to demand of her groom, and his family, throwing the marriage market into disarray. The perceived scarcity of affordable housing to a large extent reflects unmoored and abstract expectations about middle-class Chinese life as much as it does tangible and objective scarcity.

On the outside looking in

Such concerns over housing, marriage, and station in life are a world apart from what occupies the minds of the migrant class. The breakdown of the traditional migrant class lifecycle has transformed their cohort's attitudes and aspirations, with complex implications for China's housing supply.

Some background is necessary to explain why. The typical migrant's move from rural to urban China used to be understood to be temporary. Rural-born workers who take jobs in factories and cities are even today called the *floating population,* implying the fleeting nature and conditionality of their stay in the cities. The regimented lifestyle of migrant factory workers and the heavily accented regional dialects of Chinese they speak largely keep them physically and culturally isolated from the urban society where they live. In any case, most employers of migrant workers were uninterested in those laborers over the age of 30. Through the mid-2000s, public policy toward migrants largely focused on expelling them back to the countryside during periodic crackdowns. In more recent years, the focus shifted to monitoring a potentially volatile new social class and quelling unrest rather than integrating the migrants into civic life.

Policymakers assumed that migrants would be young and mostly unmarried, work for several years in urban areas, and eventually return "home" to the countryside to marry and start families. After all, that was how things had been for at least a decade. Only a funny thing happened: A growing legion of migrants never "floated" back.

True, migrant workers often did head home in their mid- to late-20s to marry a middle school sweetheart, or more likely a girl from the neighborhood vetted by their parents.

But their stay at home usually lasted only long enough for the wedding. Then they were back to the coasts and back to work. Factory workers would leave their children with their parents or siblings in the countryside, visiting once a year or even less often, but most of their time—most of their lives—was spent fashioning a life in cities. Other migrant workers, in particular those working as entrepreneurs, would even bring their children along with them to the city. They are familiar sights in major coastal cities, men and women draped in long green army coats huddled over roadside produce stands and trinket stalls. The parents are usually accompanied by small children bundled in many layers. And unlike their urban toddler counterparts who have upgraded to Pampers, migrant children still don open-bottomed pants used for potty training. Diapers are an unaffordable luxury.

Within this broader context, it is perhaps easier to see why public policy attached low priority to providing homes for migrant-class families in urban China. Chinese policymakers had relied on the migrant-class's marginalization in the cities, as well as their deep family and cultural roots linking them to their places of birth, to keep them socially and economically tethered to the countryside, mostly to serve as a social stabilizer in case of an economic downturn. Migrants could "always go back to farming" if factory work dried up. Their impermanent presence in cities and the fact that their children could not be enrolled in city schools, all served to nudge them back toward the countryside if the urban economy slowed. Chinese law has largely prohibited the sale of rural households' land-use rights precisely to maintain at least the possibility of migrants once again picking up their old plows and hoes if conditions demanded it. Moreover, almost all rural Chinese owned their homes in the countryside, another powerful economic anchor.[20]

The economic crisis of the late 2000s, however, brought the inadequacy of existing migrant policies into sharper relief. Extensive press coverage of laid-off migrant workers' journey home, and their inability to readjust to the rhythms of rural life—and in particular, the grueling agricultural work—perhaps caught policymakers off guard.[21]

Many migrant workers' description of their reluctance to return to farming life echoed the words of Canadian-American economist John Galbraith: "I was born and reared on a farm in Canada, and to this day I never awaken in the morning without a sense of satisfaction that I will not have to spend the next hours in that monotonous but richly commended toil."[22] Displaced migrants were only too eager to return "home" to work in urban areas as soon as growth revived in the second half of 2009. Many of them, however, sought jobs in inland second-tier cities, rather than coastal ones, leaving many factory employers in a lurch.

The tension between the migrant class's de jure temporary status in China's urban areas and their de facto lives in limbo is among one of the most pressing policy challenges in the country today. It is clearly a priority. After being appointed to the second-highest position in the Politburo Standing Committee in 2012, Premier Li Keqiang's first statement on public policy dealt with urbanization as the "huge engine" of economic growth.[23]

But meeting the challenge will mean addressing some of the most daunting scarcities built into Chinese economic institutions. If migrant-class Chinese are to become one of the key drivers of urbanization and economic growth, they will need a place to live in urban China. The dismal math of housing affordability for typical urban Chinese will simply not add up for members of the migrant class. But how can a government that struggles to build enough affordable housing for urban residents also provide it to an influx of migrants, too?

Socialist property rights with Chinese characteristics

Liberalization of household registration rules would mean that "rural" Chinese are officially permitted to relocate to cities and participate in public health, education, and pension schemes. But reforms to allow rural Chinese to use their largest source of wealth—the family plot of land—to finance their lives in the cities are progressing only in fits and starts. The market for rural land is very weak. It remains owned primarily by rural collectives, and the use rights granted to rural families to farm on it are usually half the length or less of the 70 years allowed for urban residential land-use rights.[24] Even more important, rural land-use rights are messy to monetize because farmers themselves are prohibited from converting agricultural land to industrial or residential use. In contrast, although the outright ownership of urban land in 2013 belongs to the state, the right to use it for development can be much more freely traded.

Converting rural land is within the exclusive domain of urban governments, who capture the huge difference in value created by the use of land in the modern economy rather than for agriculture. Without this gigantic piggybank, which for many local governments produces as much revenue as do all "on-budget" sources of income, China's local governments could suddenly find themselves hard pressed to pay for all the new social spending obligations that a more generous welfare state and growing elderly population will impose on them.[25]

Just as complex will be sanctioning the enfranchisement of the migrant class into urban China. Once the choice is made, it will obligate the government to shoulder the responsibility of ensuring that migrants have an adequate place to live, likely requiring a massive public housing campaign. In fact, perhaps in preparation of this eventuality, the Chinese government has made bringing online new supplies of "social housing" a priority. By 2015, Beijing has set out to build 36 million units of affordable housing.[26]

As of 2012, China surpassed its targets of starting 7 million units and completing the construction on 6 million units, at least according to official statistics.[27] But the process was anything but smooth. Local governments had to provide the land for affordable housing construction at no cost to developers, causing tax revenues from sales of land use rights to plummet in 2012 by 12.6% from 2011.[28] As a result, local governments scrambled to offset the loss in revenue by, among other things, selling off some of their municipal auto fleets, usually composed of high-end foreign imports.[29] Disgruntled local authorities who were accustomed to pulling in revenue from supporting high-end residential and commercial real estate likely complained to the central government about the affordable mandate. Pressure from local governments feeling financially put-upon may have been why the central government reduced low-income housing targets for

2013 to 6.3 million units started and 4.7 million basically completed.[30] The government's experience with affordable housing so far makes its ability to supply it for the tens of millions who want it a very open question.

The tribulations that migrant integration into urban life will cause, and the policy challenges it will present to the government, can be partially understood through the lives of college graduates from rural backgrounds who are starting lives in the cities. Members of this group lack the family wealth necessary to replicate Chinese middle-class lifestyles yet hold expectations, as highly educated elites, to ascend to such exalted status. This "middle-class package" usually includes owning a home and a car and sending their children to desirable city schools. But to obtain such a life is a grueling uphill slog for those unfortunate enough to be latecomers to urban China. Their struggle has spawned a new vocabulary to describe its unique poignancies: *luohun* (naked marriage)—describing a couple who marries without first buying a home or holding an extravagant wedding—and *fangnu* (house slave), describing 30-something yuppies who have mortgaged their lives and souls to their mortgage. They are China's most squeezed generation.

Revenge of the capitalists

China's exorbitant real estate prices demand a Chinese government policy response that seems obvious enough: Get the prices down. And for the past couple of years, the central government has been bent on containing the rise in prices. Results, mixed at best, have fallen short in large part because their implementation bumped up against the vested interests of China's most powerful groups: the wealthy ownership class and officialdom. As long as these domestic political fundamentals do not change, future efforts to curb housing prices can be expected to meet similar outcomes. It's not so much that China's elites have a direct interest in keeping housing prices high. But the policies that benefit them, like excessive credit supply that pushes the economy into overheating, raise real estate prices. Conversely, policies that could slow appreciation, like a more transparent system of property regulation, inspire fear among the elites of intrusive and unwelcome scrutiny of their personal wealth. At least so far, elite influence on housing market policy has prevented the government from taking steps that would bring China's real estate prices back to earth.

One of China's most important battlegrounds between the elites and the rest over the future of the property market takes place in the realm of monetary policy and bank prudential regulation. The capital-intensive real estate sector is one of the parts of an economy most sensitive to fluctuations in credit conditions and monetary policy. The groups who benefit most directly from a bull market—real estate moguls and local government officials—constitute a powerful interest group lobbying for the easy credit and low interest rates that keep investment projects funded and prices buoyant.[31]

Indeed, the pressure they exert on the policymaking process is intense. A Chinese central bank economist once quipped to the authors during the slowdown of 2012, "Of the people worried about growth [this year], some are genuinely worried, while others act worried because the good times begin when the stimulus starts flowing." The acknowledgments of many central government officials that economic growth will and should slow in the decade following the Panda Boom stands in fairly stark contrast to the annual GDP growth goals of local governments, invariably several percentage points higher than those set by the center. Elites favor a hot economy, fast growth, and ample credit—all of which contribute to stellar real estate markets and rising prices. A little inflation isn't going to crimp the pocketbooks of those who already can afford two or three homes in any event; in fact, it would help raise the value of their investments.

No taxation without representation...but with corruption

China's ownership class also plays a key role in confounding central government efforts to tax real estate. Property taxes are an obvious macroeconomic tool to control chronically overheated housing prices. They are also a common means by which many local governments around the world extract revenue from home and land owners. That revenue can be redirected into a slate of public services from education to infrastructure maintenance, among others, that China now sorely needs. In addition to raising public revenue, a property tax can increase the carrying costs to investors of using property as a store of value, encouraging investors to shift their money into other assets that aren't taxed heavily.

But the effect of a property tax would likely be much larger in China given the peculiarities of the local real estate market. Without property taxes, many Chinese properties have essentially zero carrying cost: Keep the power out and the faucet turned off, and the only real cost of ownership is a fee to the property management company for sweeping the halls. With the rental market underdeveloped and under-regulated, many property investors leave their units empty as a store of wealth. This has contributed to a huge overhang of properties across China that, while vacant, are not considered unsold. A rumor widely circulated in 2010 claimed that data from State Grid, China's monopoly power transmission company, showed 64.5 million apartment units that were connected to the grid but that did not incur any power use over a six-month period.[32]

An appropriately calibrated property tax would impose enough costs on "store of value" investors to encourage them to rent their units out, thereby expanding the effective supply of Chinese housing and likely lowering the cost of living in urban areas. The government began experimenting with just such a tax in 2011, limiting it to just two municipalities, Shanghai and Chongqing. But these taxes were very conservative, applying only to a small minority of houses within city limits. In Shanghai, a city of perhaps over 20 million residents, tax was collected on a mere 37,000 units in 2012.[33] In Chongqing, a megacity of roughly 30 million, it was collected on just 8,500.[34] In March 2013, the State Council also ordered local tax bureaus and divisions of the Ministry of Housing and Urban-Rural Development to begin collecting a 20% value-added tax on sales of secondhand property. But it remains to be seen whether this tax will be applied any more widely than previous taxes have been.[35]

Government caution on these types of taxes isn't without cause. The wealthy and ownership class have lobbied behind the scenes to slow implementation of a property tax system, not so much for financial reasons as for their own safety. There is a general public understanding that property ownership is a major store of value used by corrupt Chinese officials, which makes it an explosive issue for a middle class that is desperately yearning to ascend into the ownership league.

In fact, the property holdings of corrupt officials constitute their own genre of news coverage, in which reporters attempt to identify and expose the most venal local officials. The sprawling state news organization Xinhua reported in early 2013 that two corrupt officials in a mid-sized city in Guangdong were being investigated for corruption after it was revealed in an Internet chat room that they owned eight properties worth over 100 million yuan (\$16 million).[36] Among the commercial and private Chinese media outlets, there now seems to be implicit competition to excavate this type of corruption. And the more ill-begotten wealth uncovered the better, such as an early 2013 story about a corrupt official who lorded over 192 properties.[37] A property tax system, applying equally to all property-owners in China, would require records of who owns, who owes, and who paid. A "sunshine" rule for property ownership would make corrupt officials more vulnerable to being exposed. Why would they want to do that to themselves?

Perhaps it is for this reason that the Chinese middle class is so skeptical of property tax proposals. An informal poll on *weibo,* the Chinese version of Twitter, showed that more than 90% of respondents disapproved of the tax in 2012 (see Figure 6.3).[38]

Although this may be in part the same grumbling heard round the world when the tax man comes calling, digging further into middle class views on property taxes reveals some uniquely Chinese angles to it. Another online poll from Sina.com showed that just 36% believe the tax will curb property prices.[40] Few seem to be convinced of the government's argument that a property tax is meant to curtail housing asset speculation that drives up housing costs. Instead, they appear to be more convinced that it's merely another ploy to extract more rents from already constrained households—that instead of driving down the cost of housing, it would have no effect on prices because the property developers and the government are in cahoots. The mere suggestion of imposing a property tax by the Chinese government has prompted wide contempt and hostilities.

Q: Do you support a property tax?

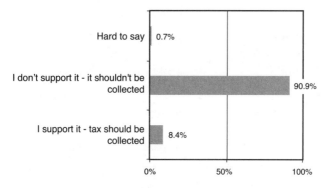

Figure 6.3   Weibo users are skeptical of property taxes
Source: NTD China Blog[39]

Squeezed

Popular commentary on China's property boom invariably vacillates between the macroeconomic data-driven story of its successes
and the periodic investigative reports exposing "ghost towns" without
residents, a house of cards waiting to collapse. But viewed through
the lens of scarcity, the central challenge of China's housing market is
not whether the government can deflate a housing bubble or prevent
the market from collapsing. It is rather how to address the social and
institutional scarcities that have both fed and grown on the back of
China's long housing bull market.

With housing affordability a relic of the past, and the migrant
class clamoring for a home in the cities, the imperative for increasing
the supply of affordable housing seems more overwhelming each day.
Without bringing new supply onto the market, who would be able to
afford to live in Chinese cities? What will become of the highly anticipated urbanization growth engine? In other East Asian economies
such as Japan, South Korea, and Taiwan that preceded China on the
road to development, astronomical housing costs priced the typical
middle-class lifestyle out of reach for the average wage earner and
contributed to a high cost of living that fostered some of the lowest
birthrates in the world. Given the deep imbalances already present in

Chinese demographics, this additional disincentive to potential parents is something that China would be wise to avoid.

Conversely, who will pay for public welfare if the real estate bonanza ends? If development slows, prices come under control, governments provide land for construction more generously, and commercially developed property is replaced by public housing as the preferred choice for new urban families, China's public finances could face a crisis. Local debt has already been estimated to be around 11 trillion yuan ($2 trillion), according to China's National Audit Office.[41] It is an open secret by now that local governments have become addicted to generating revenue via sales of long-term land-use rights over the course of the previous decade.

Kicking their habit cold turkey could prove devastating for public finances and regional property markets alike. Yet finding alternative sources of revenue may be an enormous long-term challenge for local governments. It should not be forgotten that the burden of providing low-cost housing to urbanites almost bankrupted the Chinese state in the late 1990s. How to prevent the repeat of a similar episode surely keeps the Ministry of Finance policy wonks awake at night. At this early stage of the new Chinese government, discussion is already under way to inaugurate a round of significant fiscal reforms to address a public finance system that has become wobbly and unsustainable.

The holy grail of Chinese housing policy seems to be a legitimate nationalized real estate tax, a policy twofer that replaces land sale revenue's contribution to public finance and keeps property prices in check. But in politics there is no free lunch; demand taxes from your constituency and you can suddenly find yourself beholden to their demands. Can the government credibly manage the inevitable demands that educated and empowered people will have on public spending once they are forced to pay property taxes?

Without a deeper reserve of political capital, the government may be unable to make the difficult but necessary choices to bring a runaway housing sector back to earth. The property market is still the ideal microcosm of what makes China's economy tick. But the tailwinds that made housing an indisputable boon to developers, investors, and tax collectors during the Panda Boom have now turned into headwinds that could hamper economic and social development. China's housing boom may not be going bust, but the profound social anxieties and inequalities tied up in housing may be just as daunting a challenge to address in the next decade as a conventional housing collapse would be.

Part III

Political Scarcity

7

Ideology: The unbearable lightness of the Yellow River Spirit

Have you heard of the Yellow River Spirit? Neither had the tens of thousands of aspiring Chinese civil servants who stared blankly at the final essay question of the 2011 civil service exam on the subject of "Carry Forward the Yellow River Spirit," to be exposited from an angle of their choice.[1] The test takers had studied Chinese Communist Party (CCP) history and ideology since childhood and could reflexively recite dozens of its slogans and dogmas. And yet writing a précis on the Yellow River Spirit had stumped them. Their bewilderment was no accident. *Yellow River Spirit* sounds indistinguishable in form or content from any number of CCP slogans—Harmonious Society, Scientific Outlook on Development, or Three Represents, for example—but in fact means, basically, nothing. That seemed precisely the point. The essay was designed to identify aspiring civil servants who could explicate, expound, and convincingly defend an ideological cipher.

If the CCP populated a single country, it would number the size of Germany. In the past decade alone, the CCP has recruited nearly 30 million new members, according to its "human resources office," the Organization Department.[2] At about 82 million strong, it represents 6% of the total Chinese population. The party's swelling ranks could be interpreted as a sign that the world's largest single political party is in good health. But such an impression belies the uncertainty beneath the surface: The party is mired in a profound identity crisis that could well affect its governance capacity and future resilience.

Ask a deceptively simple question: What specific ideology does the CCP stand for? No clear answers emerge. Communism? A search for traces of it in today's China leaves one highly disappointed. Capitalism? Sort of, but full-blown capitalism is not to be fully trusted either. Seeking out nascent democratic processes or archetype authoritarianism in the country would prove to be equally futile. About the only immutable notion that the CCP espouses is that it shares in the legacy of previous dynasties in wanting to shape a strong, respected, and modern China, whatever that may entail.

The CCP's ideological scarcity is a relatively recent development. Born in 1921, the CCP has evolved from a revolutionary, liberator, and nation-builder to an establishment elite over its 90-year lifespan. Along the way, it has adopted a panoply of ideologies and concepts, from Marxism-Leninism to market economics and even inklings of democracy, but always sifted through a sieve of Chinese characteristics. Whether led by Mao Zedong or today's leaders, the CCP's ideas have tended to be borrowed from Western political philosophies and then refashioned into derivative, sometimes radically different, Chinese versions. Since 1949, China has bounced from Mao Zedong Thought and Deng Xiaoping Theory to Three Represents and the Scientific Outlook on Development as guiding ideologies,[3] each championed by a succeeding generation of leaders. The language of Chinese political theory can seem obscure, but behind each slogan's "splendid bureaucratese" lies a stark progression from political and economic populism to elitism to seeming incoherence.

Each successive ideological philosophy resonated less with a Chinese public increasingly cynical about the gap between what the political system promises and what it is capable of delivering today. A CCP that still retains communism in its name has all but dismantled China's social safety net and public goods systems over the past two decades without putting a new one in place. A party that pursued opening and reform (Deng Xiaoping Theory) now appears to be losing momentum on, or unsure about, continuing reforms. A party that is supposed to represent the interests of the majority of society (Three Represents) has seen ever larger spoils accrue to the political elites. A party that pledged to reverse the startling social and economic inequalities in the country (Harmonious Society) instead saw a rising Gini coefficient and intensifying social unrest over the past decade.

Obvious hypocrisy undermines the party's credibility to govern and increases the risks of competing ideas and political movements gathering steam. Suppressing dissent, though practiced with some regularity, is a costly and unpopular business in a country that bases its model of economic growth on liberalizing state controls. Maintaining control of a complex and increasingly open society would be nearly impossible without the broad buy-in from the elites and at least grudging acquiescence from "Zhou six-pack."

What's more, the party's inability to state what interests or ideologies it represents, other than the narrow interest of preserving the status quo, is also problematic for its own members. Ideological work has always been central to the party's capacity to instill discipline, shared purpose, and strategic direction among its millions of members.

Yet keeping their own people's hearts and minds is becoming harder for a party that has become ideologically adrift. The fact that the CCP absorbed and tweaked different political ideas reflects a fundamental ideological promiscuity, which historically served the party well.[4] Finding a way to accommodate market economics in the 1980s allowed the party to rev up economic growth, strengthen its mandate, and defer the revolution of rising expectations that overwhelmed other communist bloc states. Since then, dialectical materialism has abandoned dialectics, leaving only materialism in its place, or so bemoan many Chinese. After many iterations of this process, today's China is now made up of such disparate ideological materials that they can no longer seriously be considered a coherent whole. A political party that demands the public's allegiance seems to have little in the way of deeper substance and beliefs to offer. The party's practice of ideological promiscuity, or pragmatic selection, has actually undermined and forfeited the very ideologies and values it sought to disseminate.

Incapable of defining its ideas in any meaningful way, the CCP's raison d'etre these days, at its most basic, appears to rest on the argument "our record has been quite good. And if not us, then who?" This applies to its own members as well as to the general public. For young cadres, for example, joining the party is primarily about career advancement rather than about a belief in a concrete set of principles. The party often warns that without its steady hand the country would fall into disarray. The prevailing mentality of national unity at all cost is made compelling by a Chinese history that all too often featured periods of state fracturing, when a nasty and brutish period of chaos followed the dissolution of a failing dynasty only to be followed by yet another "enlightened" emperor.

But could the political system's longevity rest on that simple justification alone? What if the Chinese people start to question the status quo and ask whether the CCP is capable of governing China's 21st century? It is an old question that requires a new answer. To remain relevant the CCP will need to convince its members, as well as the general public, that it stands for a compelling set of principles and philosophies that resonate in a transformed society, rather than rely on its usual vague and obscure sloganeering. In other words, its credibility and capacity to govern hinge on rewinning the hearts and minds of the Chinese people.

At home, the party seems to clearly recognize its own ideological malaise and that mere economic growth can no longer guarantee its resilience. In the past few years, it has looked to its recent and distant past in search of an enduring Chinese idea that it could herald as a new ideological renaissance and that the Chinese people would find compelling. For the moment, it has settled on the "Chinese Dream," yet another abstraction that waits to be filled with substance.

To the non-Chinese world, this soul searching is also intended to build a reserve of soft power to project abroad, an effort that Beijing increasingly prioritizes. That's because as the rulers of the greatest rising power of the 21st century, the CCP must grapple with how it can present its conception of China that attracts, rather than repels, the rest of the world. The challenge of defining a new ideology is daunting for a regime as committed to pragmatism as the CCP. President Xi Jinping may still call for "grasping for stones to cross the river" but can the Chinese public see the contours of the other side?

A young nation-state

The CCP has so much difficulty defining who it is and what it stands for in part because it spent the first 50 years of its existence tearing down the traditional China that came before it. The ancient Middle Kingdom is a latecomer to the Western conception of nation-states. In China scholar Lucian Pye's words, it is a "civiliza-tion pretending to be a nation-state."[5] When the Treaty of Westphalia was signed in 1648, creating the modern states system in Europe, the Manchus from northeastern China had barely begun ruling a Qing dynasty that would last more than 260 years, longer than the United States has been in existence.

Modernization wasn't particularly compelling for the Chinese; when the Manchus came to power, they still commanded one of the world's biggest economies. China had for two millennia become accustomed to being the most civilized part of the world and was largely uninterested in foreign innovations such as industrialization and military modernization. After all, what could the new world truly offer to an empire whose innovations include paper, printing, com-pass, and gun powder, the four major inventions that are taught to all Chinese school children? And China's flirtation with establishing a navy ended in the previous Ming dynasty in the early 1400s, when a Muslim eunuch named Zheng He led Columbus-esque voyages as far as eastern Africa. Historians bicker over the reasons why the naval program lost steam under the Ming, but China waited another six centuries before it again demonstrated ambitions to global maritime power by commissioning its first aircraft carrier in 2012.[6] Of course, China during the Qing was never as insular as it is often described. There were periods of reform to rejuvenate the state, such as the Self-Strengthening Movement, that included incorporating Western prac-tices and technologies into Chinese institutions.

These episodic searches for a new Chinese modernity tended to occur after disastrous defeats at the hands of foreign powers, when China felt it was particularly weak. With the Qing dynasty's collapse in 1912, arguably one of the weakest periods in modern Chinese history, the country once again grappled with defining what Chinese moder-nity would be and how to achieve it. In Europe, a similar process of searching for modern institutions and ideas had already begun with the enlightenment and renaissance in the 17th century, and continued in the United States and Japan in the 18th and 19th centuries. Yet for China, those centuries were more defined by the gradual decline of the dynastic empire and a forced transition to a modern republic that is strong, united, and created in China's own image. It was anything but peaceful. The last Manchu emperor's formal abdication of his throne in 1912 accelerated a wrenching unraveling of massive social and political dislocations that included internal rebellions, civil wars, foreign domination, and economic decline. China historian Jonathan Spence described the post-Qing descent into chaos thusly:

> There remained a crucial vacuum at the center of the Chinese state and no specially talented leaders able to fill it, only various groupings with rival ideologies and claims. The legacy of dynastic collapse was not a confident new republic, but a period of civil war and intellectual disorder that, tragically for the Chinese people, was even harsher than the period that had followed the fall of the Ming 268 years before.[7]

The dynasty had been crumbling since the mid-19th century, when China's encounters with foreign powers resulted in embarrassing and repeated defeats. The disintegration of dynastic rule was tortuously slow: Mainland Chinese historiography calls it the *Century of Humiliation*, the period between the Treaty of Nanjing in 1842 ending the first Opium War to the founding of the People's Republic of China in 1949. The Century of Humiliation was the terrible crucible in which mainland China's modernity was forged.[8] For many Chinese, it was a period of subjugation at the hands of foreigners, from the Western imposition of "treaty ports" on Chinese sovereignty to the Japanese annexation of Manchuria, which holds a unique position in the Chinese narrative of historical enmities.[9] Such humiliation was also exploited by domestic anti-Qing political forces that sought independence. The combination of domestic turbulence and foreign pressure proved too much for the Manchu dynasty, forcing the dowager empress to abdicate on behalf of the child-emperor Puyi.

The late Qing is not remembered kindly in modern China, but its fall did make two invaluable contributions to the development of ideas about government in mainland China. The first was exposing the weaknesses of the state and society relative to the foreign powers. As the Qing ceded control of territory to British, French, German, Japanese, and Russian control, foreign influence brought an influx of new ideas into a society that was again searching for rejuvenation. The second was the trauma of anarchy, which taught Chinese intellectuals to connect a strong state with the ability to fend off foreign intrusion and secure prosperity.

In this period of foreign intrusion and subjugation, Chinese intellectuals selectively picked through ideologies and intellectual capital from the vortex of foreign influences around them, searching for
a coherent Chinese modernity that could support a strong, modern
state. Few outside certain intellectual circles had ever heard of concepts such as democracy or communism in the turbulent years that
preceded the Qing's disintegration, let alone foreseen that a band of
communists would emerge triumphant.

E pluribus mishmash

Marxism-Leninism would have seemed a dubious candidate for
China's road to modernity before it became the official state ideology. In fact, it could have just as well been social democracy, whose
seeds were eventually planted in Taiwan rather than on the mainland.
Although a civil war proved the central battleground that determined
the future of China, the short history between the Qing collapse and
the creation of the modern Chinese republic was also one defined
by the battle of ideas. China was choosing among various currents of
modernity to rid itself of traditionalism and feudalism. Paradoxically,
in its search for modernity, China primarily defined itself as what it
is not—traditional—rather than settling on what it is. Yet aspects of
the imperial legacy managed to seep back into China, enabled by the
pragmatic mix of adopting a Western idea (Marxism), a formidable
bureaucracy, and traditions Mao used to reinforce his absolute rule
as something of a modern-day emperor. Since his death, China has
traversed a wide spectrum of ideologies, with each iteration weaker
than the previous, leaving a Chinese public yearning for a durable
ideological glue other than "strong China."

Karl Marx himself never thought the Soviet Union would be
the early adopter of his socioeconomic theories. He had predicted
that socialism would first take root in England, the birthplace of the
industrial revolution, where the accumulation of capital among a
small coterie of industrialists stood in stark contrast to the decrepit
working conditions of the average laborer. England seemed to him to
have all the ingredients ripe for fomenting major social and political
transformations. But socialism bypassed England and instead swept

into Moscow, rebranded as Leninism. The Bolshevik Revolution was triggered by many factors, but Vladimir Lenin's success at its core was uniting a post-czarist Russia amid civil war and severe social and economic malaise.

As the Soviet revolution progressed, intellectual ferment was peaking in post-Qing China as well. Fractured and dominated by various warlords, post-Qing China was a vacuous ideological orphan easily filled with Western ideas, which interacted with a volatile anti-imperialist and anti-establishment sentiment. This combustible mix exploded in the infamous student protests in 1919 that came to define the May Fourth Movement.[10]

Although the rallies were triggered by the Treaty of Versailles that ended World War I and awarded the German concession in Shandong Province to Japan, the May Fourth Movement had its genesis in what came to be known as the *new culture movement*.[11] Led by towering intellectual and dean of faculty at the prestigious Beijing University, Chen Duxiu, the movement sought to decisively break with the conservative and ancient traditions of dynastic China and to usher in a constitutional government that trumpeted science and democracy. As Chen argued passionately in his influential 1915 treatise "Call to Youth:"

> All men are equal. Each has his right to be independent, but absolutely no right to enslave others nor any obligations to make himself servile. By slavery we mean that in ancient times the ignorant and the weak lost their right to freedom, which was savagely usurped by tyrants... Emancipation means freeing oneself from the bondage of slavery achieving a completely and independent and free personality... Now our country still has not awakened from its long dream and isolates itself by going down the same rut... All our traditional ethics, law, scholarship, rites, and customs are survivals of feudalism.[12]

Well-versed in the Western philosophical canon and its political ideas, Chen and his intellectual conspirators thought that reviving a weak and disintegrated China meant the country had to part with its past and abandon feudalism, however broadly construed. In its place would be established a new consensus on modernity, largely based on freedom and equality, providing the ideological force to return China to a position of strength. Eventually, Chen was to discover that sense of modernity embodied in Marxist thought, prompting him to found the Communist Party in 1921. An equally important intellectual at the time, Li Dazhao, was heavily influenced by the success of the Bolshevik Revolution in the Soviet Union. As the May Fourth Movement fizzled out, Li became more convinced of Bolshevism as a possible model for China.

Along the way, these two men became intellectual mentors and influential teachers to a charismatic and thoughtful 20-something Chinese man who had been accumulating his own revolutionary zeal. Like Chen, Mao's intellectual foundation lacked a demonstrable bias toward communism. As a young man, he worked in the Beijing University library and digested quintessential Western liberalism from the likes of Smith and Rousseau as much as traditional Chinese thought. However, Mao also became a close associate of Li's while enrolled in Beijing University and as an early member of the CCP. These formative experiences likely provided the foundation for Mao's eventual brand of radicalism.

The fervent days of the nascent 20th century perfectly suited the rise of countercultural scholars like Chen and Li. If any era could be called the Chinese enlightenment, the heady decade following the Qing disintegration would be a strong qualifier. But they didn't have a monopoly on ideas; another equally, if not more important intellectual named Lu Xun captured the public's imagination. To be sure, Lu Xun was a different kind of intellectual, a tenacious and harsh public critic of the political and social milieu. Every generation produces literary voices that capture the zeitgeist and relentlessly challenge the prevailing paradigm. Lu Xun served that role for his generation. He was among that elite class of unique social and political critics who savagely disparaged the Confucian legacies of China as the dominant ill of the time.[13]

In their search for that elusive modernity, Chen, Li, and Lu captured their era's common conviction that traditional Chinese thought and culture had to be uprooted for China to catapult into the ranks of modern nation-states, even as various thinkers promoted different strategies to reach the end game.

Although he was influenced by both Li and Chen, Mao parted company with his mentors philosophically during the CCP's early existence, long before he became the founder of a republic. Mao shifted his focus to fomenting revolution among the peasantry, which was particularly at odds with the focus of Chen and most of the other CCP leadership on revolution starting from the cities. Chen's more orthodox view of Marxism also did not see eye to eye with Mao's radicalization on land policy. The philosophical disagreement turned into a lasting split between the once teacher and student relationship. At their core, Mao and Chen differed because the former saw communism as the tool to achieve national unity; the latter, meanwhile, continued to believe that democratic institutions were necessary to achieve modernity.

The eventual triumph of Mao's brand of communism was far from preordained, however. Before Mao, there was Dr. Sun Yat-Sen, widely considered the founding father of the Chinese republican government. Educated in the West, Sun was greatly influenced by men such as Lincoln, as well as by aspects of socialism and Leninism. He synthesized Western political thought into three core elements of a political philosophy he called Three Principles of the People (*san min*). Divided into *minzu* (nationalism), *minquan* (governance by the people), and *minsheng* (livelihood/social welfare), Sun envisioned a constitutional government to rule the young republic. Like all other intellectual titans of that tumultuous era, Sun fundamentally wanted to effect a Chinese renaissance and drive out the foreigners.

Sun's lasting political legacy was the creation of the Kuomintang (KMT) in 1912, or Nationalist Party, that became the ruling political party in Taiwan when it fled the mainland after World War II. But what became a political rivalry was once an alliance of convenience, when Mao's CCP and Chiang Kai-shek's KMT set aside a bloody civil war to combine forces and repel Japanese aggression. No sooner did they succeed in defeating the Japanese did the tenuous alliance begin fraying, and the temporary truce gave way to continued battle for control of China. Mao and his communists eventually triumphed, formally establishing the People's Republic of China on October 1, 1949.[14]

But that historical outcome was probably more of a toss up than most imagine now. A counterfactual recounting of that period could have conceived a KMT eking out a military victory—perhaps with stronger support from the United States—and the current Taiwanese government may have sat in Beijing, eventually realizing Sun's principles and ideas. (To be fair, the KMT under Chiang was until the 1980s arguably nearly as authoritarian as the mainland government.) Indeed, Mao and Chiang in principle were both aligned with Sun's emphasis on a people's government, but they were only able to truly agree on the interpretation of nationalism (minzu). In essence, the unifying objective, whether it was Mao's socialism or Sun's republican government, concerned first and foremost with ending foreign domination and building a strong China after a century of relative weakness.

To the victor go the spoils: Mao won the war and with it the battle of ideas. China came to be dominated by a communist party, and Mao earnestly believed that China should be shaped in a socialist image, though his plan to achieve that goal was still quite different from what Marx himself imagined. Over time, it appeared that whatever puritanical beliefs in the socialist cause Mao may have held gave way to a utilitarian view of an ideology that could be transmuted and repackaged to maintain political power. In fact, Mao was hardly a proponent of thoroughly exterminating traditional Chinese thought and culture. He seemed to believe that governance of China required distinct Chinese characteristics, reportedly quipping that to govern China requires "Marxism plus Emperor Qin."[15] For Mao, the specific ideology didn't matter so much. These concepts, which were not indigenous to China in the first place, were merely tools for articulating the single immutable ideology that has dominated the last century: Chinese nationalism.[16]

What comes after a revolution?

From the dynastic collapse, it took 37 years for mainland China to be reunited into a republic, a realization that immediately imbued Mao with unrivaled founding father status. His era unified China under a coherent ideological framework: equality, struggle of the peasant and working classes against the landowning and capitalist elites, and a powerful state reshaping society into a socialist utopia. Yet for roughly half of the 27 years that Mao presided over China, the country regressed, either wrecked by manmade famines or plunged into political turmoil. By the end of his rule, the Chinese modernity project was left in tatters. The CCP seemed more ruthless than communitarian and more retrograde than progressive. Mao's revolutionary ideology, so compelling to a humiliated nation dominated by foreign powers, became a traumatizing and disillusioning basis for nation building after the foreign enemies were driven out. At the end of the Maoist era, China found itself nowhere near the great nation that its leaders had envisioned. With its Great Helmsman looking not so great, the CCP turned toward another of its founding leaders to craft China's future.

Forging the Deng Xiaoping consensus

Deng Xiaoping understood the complexity of the state of the nation he assumed control of in 1978. More important, he realized that the CCP was facing its biggest identity crisis since its founding. The CCP ideology was bankrupt, and once the public awoke from the nightmarish decade of the Cultural Revolution that had just concluded, there could be pervasive disillusion. The political system itself would be destabilized and potentially collapse. From that assessment Deng arrived at three key and interrelated conclusions: 1. Stability is absolutely necessary to proceed with nation building; 2. To ensure that stability, the CCP must remain in control and guide the nation; 3. To remain in control, the CCP must rejuvenate itself and stand for *something*.[17] Deng seemed to believe that an economic base matters in ensuring that a socialist system would endure.

Deng immediately went to work on task three, a precondition that needed to be met before the first two could be realized. Removing the perverse ideological straitjacket that the CCP wore at the time proved a Herculean task. In setting aside incessant political revolution to focus on economic production, Deng would be indirectly rendering a verdict on the Mao era as being spectacularly wrong. But Deng saw little choice; the CCP had to revisit the past before it could pivot to the future. According to a former high-ranking CCP official who recalled that period of uncertainty:

> Finally, they were able to debate the rights and wrongs of Mao Zedong, and to put the case of the ordinary Chinese people without fear or shame. This was where the true creativity and life-force of the Third Plenum lay! This was how it differed utterly from previous meetings—those scripted presentations upon which the deadening of spirit lay so heavy. Finally, they had forced Deng Xiaoping to go along with this new turn of events and adapt to the change that was in the air...
>
> So Deng tossed aside the old script that had been written for him by Hu Qiaomu and asked Hu Yaobang and Yu Guangyuan to write new scripts titled "The Liberation of Our Thought" and "Making Full Use of Democracy," and he sat up and took notice.[18]

Deng's transformational reform and opening up (*gaige kaifang*) policy, unveiled at the now famous Third Plenum of the 11th CCP Congress in 1978, proved instrumental in turning China into the country that it is today.[19] But Deng's accomplishment was not simply advocating reform. His particular ingenuity was rebranding a formerly communist regime into one that could accept market capitalism. Destructive class struggle took a backseat to a new pragmatism that was focused on development and nation building, encapsulated in Deng's oft-cited aphorism that it "doesn't matter whether it's a white or black cat, so long as it catches mice then it's a good cat."[20] Capitalism, socialism, and any other -*isms* could be adapted insofar that they contributed to economic dynamism.

That phrase came to embody the central tenet of the Deng Xiaoping theory, which eventually assumed the pithy moniker *socialism with Chinese characteristics*. With 20/20 hindsight, it is apparent how radical a departure Deng Xiaoping theory marked from Maoism. The latter advocated a permanent struggle of the huddled masses against intellectuals and owners of capital. Deng, in contrast, didn't explicitly disavow the class struggle promoted by extreme leftists during the Cultural Revolution, but effectively ended it by shifting the focus of political life to economic growth rather than never-ending struggle for an elusive egalitarianism. Where Maoism encouraged state control of

economic production, Deng Xiaoping theory happily encouraged policymakers to devolve decision making onto individual firms and their
managers. Where Maoism advocated economic autarky and independence from the international capitalist system, Deng opened the door
for foreign multinationals to bring advanced technology and management techniques into China's backward and inefficient economy. In
essence, where Maoism prized orthodoxy and ideologically pure commitment to a radicalized, utopian Marxism, Deng Xiaoping theory
prized pragmatism and results.

Such a drastic ideological shift was a tricky proposition. After all,
as a matter of political orthodoxy, a *communist* party couldn't just
abandon collective ownership on a whim, and conservatives (communist true believers) within the CCP stood ready to challenge a dramatic shift in direction from revolutionary to pecuniary zeal. Deng
and his allies had to ensure that the political solidarity of the party
held and allowed his agenda to move forward—and were happy to
couch economic reforms under the banner of socialism to do it.

In essence, Deng depoliticized the reform process so that economics took precedence over the sanctity of ideology. But in doing
so, the CCP's official ideology went from heterodoxy under Mao to, if
not quite nihilism, at least a much less-coherent vision of the society
its seismic economic transformation was making China into. Deng's
CCP got away with it because China was rehabilitating itself after
the psychological trauma of the Cultural Revolution and stability was
powerfully appealing. Furthermore, the turn toward market economics that Deng fostered created rapidly increasing prosperity that
salved the conscience of reluctant adherents. That was the political
consensus Deng forged and fought to maintain.

And fight he did, particularly after the Deng consensus came
under its greatest duress after the student demonstrations in 1989.
Although many at the time had considered those protests part of a
wave of democratization reaching Chinese shores, it is probably more
apt to interpret it as a referendum on the first decade of economic
reforms. The late 1980s saw mass unemployment and untamed inflation, vast uncertainties caused by discombobulating social and economic changes, and political uncertainty at the top. Transitioning from
a closed economic system to a more open one carries with it inherent

risks and has proved destabilizing elsewhere in the world. This period of relative openness, in which Chinese citizens could absorb foreign ideas and see how far behind the country remained, witnessed pervasive dissatisfaction. Deng Xiaoping theory attached the party's claim on legitimacy to delivering economic growth and rising standards of living. But when inflation overheated and unemployment rose in the late 1980s, dissatisfaction with the CCP turned into near revolt.

The 1989 student movement, taking a chapter from the May Fourth Movement, struck at the heart of CCP legitimacy and was only subdued when Deng ordered the army to suppress it.[21] That such instability had rocked the political system gave ample openings for the conservatives to indict Deng's policies as entirely erroneous. Intense political wrangling was inevitable after the political crisis, and it took Deng's considerable political capital and skills to hold his line. It wasn't until 1992, when the then-octogenarian Deng embarked on a tour of southern China to tout the continuation of reform and opening up, that it became clear the opposition had been defeated. The Deng consensus prevailed, China continued to grow, and the practical progress of growth re-anchored the CCP's claim on power. But new ideological underpinnings were nowhere to be found.

New slogans, same consensus

One reason why Deng is often celebrated as a visionary is because he understood, from the outset, that development would require longer than his lifetime. So to ensure that the reform consensus did not get derailed, the perspicacious elder statesman determined that he needed a deep bench to carry forward the unfinished business of nation building. With a grand political stroke, Deng selected two generations of successors—Jiang Zemin and Hu Jintao—to pave the way for another 20 years of basic continuity with the Deng consensus policies, without which the Panda Boom would've been impossible.

When Jiang secured power in 1992, China remained a relative backwater nursing its wounds from the tumult that closed the previous decade. But China was about to undergo major transformations, as the Jiang administration laid the groundwork for one of the most enduring investment and infrastructure bull cycles the world has seen. His capable and market-oriented premier, Zhu Rongji, also began dismantling pillars of the socialist economy: state-owned enterprises. Such action would've been unthinkable under the ideological strictures of the CCP of yesteryear. But Jiang and Zhu held fast to the Deng consensus and unleashed a Chinese economic dynamism that attracted global attention. Meanwhile, Jiang also performed an important facelift to the party that would remold it into the CCP of today.

Since the days of Mao and Deng, each successive leader has wanted to leave his theoretical and ideological mark on the political system, much like how some U.S. presidents are associated with a particular "doctrine." For Jiang, his theoretical magnum opus was formalized at the 16th CCP Congress in 2002 under the official name Three Represents:

> An important conclusion can be reached from reviewing our Party's history over the past 70-odd years; that is, the reason our Party enjoys the people's support is that throughout the historical periods of revolution, construction and reform, it has always represented the development trend of China's advanced productive forces, the orientation of China's advanced culture, and the fundamental interests of the overwhelming majority of the Chinese people. With the formulation of the correct line, principles and policies, the Party has untiringly worked for the fundamental interests of the country and the people. Under the new conditions of historic significance, how our Party can better translate the Three Represents into action constitutes a major issue that all Party members, especially senior officials, must ponder deeply.[22]

Did you catch that? Neither did most Chinese people. The Three Represents have been mocked endlessly by average Chinese for the term's obscure indecipherability. But its vagueness serves a purpose; it's the equivalent of a Chinese "big tent" policy. The first thing the CCP must represent, "the development trend of China's advanced productive forces," is the needs of China's rising capitalist class, the same group the CCP crushed or drove beyond the mainland's borders as it rose to power. The second thing, "the orientation of China's advanced culture," is the mindset of China's educated political class. The final "represent" emphasizes that the CCP now represents the interests of all Chinese citizens—including the wealthy and the latte-sipping elites—rather than exclusively the downtrodden masses on whose behalf the original dictatorship of the proletariat was designed.

Although couched in turgid communist jargon, the central idea was to enfranchise those who would normally be considered capitalists and intellectuals—businessmen, private entrepreneurs, academics, among others—and who were once anathema to the CCP. The Three Represents served as a clarion call for the party to refashion itself into an elite governing institution and shed its former identity as a revolution maker. The logic was rather simple: If the CCP were to remain relevant and capable of economic stewardship, it must become friendly to the individual elements that are facilitating economic growth. And so the "red capitalists" were born, as Jiang took the Deng consensus even further by indisputably branding the CCP as the party of economic growth.

The second identity crisis

By the time Hu Jintao stepped into the office of the CCP chairman in 2002, the *communist* in the party's name seemed entirely anachronistic. China had already entered the World Trade Organization, and globalization became the buzzword of the Chinese media, like it was elsewhere in the world. The only residual communist legacies remaining in the economy were periodic interventions in the prices of inputs like energy, prohibition on private land ownership, and some macroeconomic planning. Although state assets loomed large in certain parts of the economy, even those assets were driven by the Growth Imperative to ensure profitability and healthy bottom lines.

Jiang's rebranding of the CCP proved consequential: The party itself became not only an enabler of profiteering but also an active participant in sharing in the economic spoils. The red capitalists, it turned out, were merely the bridge that fortified the relationship between politics and business—the political class and business class became much more deeply intertwined. It was an appealing gambit for those who belonged to that class of establishment elites, be they politicians, state company CEOs, or private sector moguls. For a political party nominally premised on a classless society and peasant mobilization to have deliberately absorbed an emerging ruling class is nothing short of remarkable.

As the party co-opted newly sprouted private enterpreneurs, its politics became increasingly interest driven with little concern for ideology. With its political monopoly, the CCP was well positioned to be the ultimate vanguard of the status quo, serving the interests of the elite class and neglecting or excluding much of the urban working class and rural Chinese. Dialectical materialism was abandoned in favor of rabid materialism, generating a perverse kind of social Darwinism in which individual behavior was dictated by few moral scruples and competition is zero-sum. Those with political access climbed rapidly and in turn showered patronage on those in familiar circles. In an environment in which institutions were weak or nonexistent and rule of law more farce than enforced, upward mobility became increasingly dependent on discrete networks and elbowing into the elite strata of the political establishment. Indeed, defending the CCP is the equivalent of defending the status quo. Arguably at no time in recent memory has the status quo been so profitable or power so infused with money.[23]

Even in the absence of a unifying ideology, the party could sustain its governing mandate as long as the Growth Imperative lifted all boats. Yet several years into Hu's term, it became apparent that while those with authority and political patronage moved up to yachts, too many Chinese seemed incapable of moving beyond wooden canoes. The issue wasn't so much whether the country was growing wealthier overall; average income continued to rise as the economy barreled ahead like a freight train. Instead, the public began taking notice that opportunity for advancement for the average Chinese in "the middle class" became scarcer. The playing field was no longer even and was tilted heavily toward a certain set of people—those who belonged to or fell within the orbit of the party.[24]

Inequality isn't unique to China. In fact, the level of inequality in the United States is comparable to China's, at least when measured by their respective Gini coefficients.[25] But a crucial difference is that the majority of Americans generally still believe in the capacity of the existing system to eventually correct the unfairness. Or at the very least, there is faith in current institutions, particularly legal channels, to constrain the worst excesses of the system. Consequently, Americans for the most part continue to accept that the political system guarantees equal protection before the law and does not egregiously obstruct social and economic opportunities.

In China, however, such high levels of inequality, and the perception that it is growing, can become considerably more destabilizing. Not only do many Chinese feel the system is rigged against them, the political party that helms the system is having a difficult time convincing the public it is primarily serving their interests. The legitimizing potency of the Growth Imperative is weakening, quickly being replaced by widespread skepticism. These sentiments are hardened as the Chinese public watches the CCP's behavior drift further from its rhetoric of "serving the people."

Broadly speaking, political parties have three tools at their disposal to command loyalty: The material benefits they channel to their supporters, the charisma of their leaders, and the appeal of their policy and ideology.[26] Perhaps recognizing the weakening influence of material incentives on Chinese citizens, then-President Hu set out to conquer the CCP's ideological vacuity with his Scientific Development Concept and Harmonious Society campaigns.[27] In addition to putting his distinct mark on CCP doctrinal legacy, Hu seemed earnest in attempting to formulate a response to the myriad challenges of inequality, social change, and weak institutions. At its core, his ideas sought to moderate the focus of Chinese politics on the Growth Imperative and reorient toward more sustainable and comprehensive development. Although Hu began floating his idea soon after he assumed power, it wasn't until the 17th CCP Congress in 2007 that it became formalized as the newly accepted Hu doctrine.[28]

But his attempt at ideological renewal failed to overcome the status quo. For scientific development to succeed, it would've meant sacrificing growth for social equality and environmental sustainability, directly undermining the interests of the red capitalists and entrepreneur officials who had become, to use an old-fashioned term, the party's vanguard.[29] A cautious consensus-builder, Hu inserted his doctrine into the CCP constitution revisions during the final plenum of the 17th Party Congress in early November 2012, but ultimately was powerless to turn his concept into reality. The political system would grant Hu a token ideological legacy, but it would not deviate from its fundamental configuration for growth and moneymaking. Despite Hu and his administration's good intentions, they were not going to reprogram the system.

After Hu, the CCP finds itself caught in ideological doldrums, unable to retake the moral and ethical high ground that it once commanded. It is a looming normative crisis, and all the more so for a party that is no longer the sole dispenser of truths for its people. Deng could rely on the near-divine authority imbued in CCP propaganda when he remade the country's vision of itself. In his day, religion, superstition, and independent media were banned, leaving the CCP's leaders as the sole and ultimate arbiters of right and wrong. In earlier eras, the CCP's ideological suppleness and moral disposition facilitated its continued "enlightened rule" over a changing society, despite the lack of the kinds of democratic institutions championed in Western countries. Now, in the absence of a binding ideology, the ruled are starting to notice that some of the rulers have no clothes. Or clothes that have strange labels with Gucci and Louis Vuitton embroidered on them.

Nationalism to the rescue (sort of)

Finding the Hu doctrine unable to provide a new ideological compass, the CCP has admirably improvised stopgap measures to rally the people to its rule. Nationalist pride in the country's tangible achievements remains a time-honored and serviceable "gap filler." The CCP continued to deliver on growth and tout the country's economic strength. In a matter of a few years, China successively leapt over Germany and Japan to become the world's number-two economy in 2010. Symbolic political set pieces also served as emotionally stirring distractions. For Hu, his crowning achievement in boosting patriotic fervor was of course the successful execution of the Beijing

Olympics. China's deployment of the first Chinese woman in its first space-docking mission is a close second.[30] Finally, under his watch, Hu commissioned the country's first aircraft carrier, a reengineered Soviet Varyag that has come to symbolize the rekindling of China's global maritime ambitions since the days of Admiral Zheng the eunuch. These grandiose projects imbued the CCP with momentary purpose, illustrating its ability to revive national greatness.[31]

Moreover, China's rising international stature can easily be harnessed to validate the CCP's mandate and mode of governance. This was especially true after the 2008–2009 financial crisis, when China sprinted out of economic catastrophe barely scratched and the United States lumbered along with no recovery in sight. For many outside observers, China evinced an aura of invincibility and dominance.

Yet within China, the CCP has been troubled by increasing social unrest and a ballooning credibility gap with its own people. Chinese nationalism, which can be manipulated for rebooting the CCP brand, is a volatile and unpredictable stand-in for ideology. Chinese leaders understand well that nationalism can easily mutate into an anti-state movement that brings down the regime. All too often in Chinese history, a collusion of nationalists and anti-establishmentarians have led to disastrous outcomes for whoever held power at the time.

Stoking the nationalist fire has delayed an existential challenge, but the CCP nevertheless remains strategically flummoxed and ideologically directionless. Advocates of political and social reforms that could accommodate the tremendous changes shouldered by Chinese society over the past decade have been largely ignored, including former Premier Wen Jiabao.[32] Political liberalization encompassing transparency and legal constraints would risk exposing just how deeply some members of the party have embedded themselves in the most lucrative corners of the economy at the expense of the "average Zhou." Moreover, so many people have skin in the growth game that dramatically altering the status quo could upset vested interests so powerful that social stability itself might be threatened. That disastrous scenario must be avoided.[33] Consequently, instead of redefining itself through reform during the last administration, the CCP began looking for ideological rebirth in its history: something distinctly Chinese but also capable of anchoring its authority.

Virtue is as virtuous does

If Socrates is remembered as the progenitor of Western political philosophy and Jesus Christ the fountainhead of Christian values in the West, then Confucius, at different times, arguably occupies both positions for China.[34] The great sage from Shandong not only developed his own political philosophy, he was also as peripatetic as Jesus, roaming the ancient Middle Kingdom to spread his teachings. Confucian ideas became the foundation of a Chinese system of political and moral philosophy named in his honor. Confucianism never exactly rose to the status of a religion akin to Judaism, Islam, or Christianity, although the boundaries between the sacred and the profane were fuzzier in China than in the West. Confucianism primarily resided in the secular world, divining influential concepts of social ethics and morality and the code of conduct between the rulers and the governed.

Confucianism was designated a state ideology in the Han dynasty around 200 B.C. The hierarchy, prioritization of social harmony over individual rights, and the conservatism it embodied came to define Chinese political philosophy over the subsequent two millennia. The communist revolution marked a sea change, when Mao expelled Confucianism as "feudal," hierarchical, and unsuitable for the kind of modernity China needed. During the second great wave of the Cultural Revolution in the early 1970s, Confucius became something of a state enemy, along with Lin Biao, the once confidant and heir to Mao who was rebranded as traitor. One of Confucius's supposed sins was that he advocated reviving old political families that at the time could have threatened Mao's grip on power:

> Lin was a reactionary parallel to Confucius, in that Lin had opposed Mao just as Confucius had stood against the politically centralizing and economically progressive policies of the emerging feudal and anti-aristocratic states of the fifth century B.C. By a similar historical leap, Mao Zedong could be compared to the third-century B.C. Emperor Qin Shi Huangdi, who had done so much to unify China.[35]

That such accusations were illogical and twisted, like much of what transpired during the Cultural Revolution, made them no less fervent. As far as the Great Helmsman was concerned, Confucianism could not compete with Maoism, the only prophetic ideology to which unquestionable allegiance was owed. More than 30 years after Mao's death, however, the same CCP that had sent Confucius into intellectual exile is now haltingly rehabilitating the bearded sage as the latest prescription for ideological morbidity.[36] Like so much else in early 21st century China, ideas once considered despicable by pious communists are now being co-opted by a party seeking new tools to maintain the status quo. It doesn't hurt that, like most philosophical systems that have been around for millennia, Confucianism contains sufficient multitudes to support almost any point of view. "It's such a big basket you can select whatever you want. They will ask people to behave appropriately, not too aggressive, not use violence and don't pursue revolution," according to Cheng Li of the Brookings Institution.[37]

Confucian themes began to reenter Chinese political discourse through Hu's Harmonious Society campaign, tinged with emphases on balance and order. The Confucian concern for public well-being is also an appealing counterbalance to the party's elite image. The ideal Confucian ruler is imbued with a deep sense of benevolence and virtue, a flattering self image for the ruling class, who regularly assign blame for corruption and "indiscipline" within the party to lower, less-virtuous apparatchiks. Moreover, Confucianism is the philosophical system legitimizing the Chinese civil service exam, which survived the collapse of the Qing and conflict with the Nationalists to remain the basis by which the CCP chooses and promotes its cadres. The Confucian emphasis on merit can help combat the perception that officials are appointed because of relationships, not talent. It also provides a rhetorical retort to the long-honed Western criticisms of the flaws of undemocratic, unrepresentative, unresponsive governments. In the words of Tsinghua University professor and Canadian national Daniel Bell, a proponent of the Confucian meritocratic system of governance:

> Reformist Confucians put forward political ideals that are meant to work better than Western-style democracy in terms of securing the interests of all those affected by the policies of the government, including future generations and foreigners.

Their ideal is not a world where everybody is treated as an equal but one where the interests of non-voters would be taken more seriously than in most nation-centered democracies. And the key value for realizing global political ideals is meritocracy, meaning equality of opportunity in education and government, with positions of leadership being distributed to the most virtuous and qualified members of the community. The idea is that everyone has the potential to become morally exemplary, but, in real life, the capacity to make competent and morally justifiable political judgments varies among people, and an important task of the political system is to identify those with above-average ability.[38]

The CCP generally seems to believe that it knows better than the Chinese public what is the best course for the country. It is no surprise that Bell's description essentially comports with the political orthodoxy of the moment. These tempting synergies have convinced some within the party establishment to begin selectively adopting Confucian precepts as part of a new indigenous model of governance that can potentially be an alternative to Western-style electoral democracy.

As was only fitting for a party that historically excelled at creating cults of personality, the CCP's recent embrace of Confucius was naturally announced by a concerted publicity campaign. The sage who Mao dragged through the dirt was featured prominently in the opening ceremony of the 2008 Beijing Olympics, in which Confucianism and nationalism mixed. Later, in 2010, a state film company recruited famous Hong Kong film star Chow Yun-Fat to star in a Confucius biopic. Film and media are longstanding tools of the Propaganda Department for shaping public psychology, often to startling effect. State-sponsored Confucianization seemed to have culminated in early 2011, when a towering 30-foot bronze sculpture of Confucius unexpectedly appeared in Tiananmen Square.[39] Standing opposite the iconic Mao portrait in the square, the sage's mysterious appearance seemed pregnant with symbolism—representing among other things a possible threat to the patriarch of modern China and his radical ideology. Was this a warning that the once ubiquitous Mao statues across the country would be systematically replaced?[40]

Figure 7.1   Now you see Confucius...now you don't

Source: Ministry of Tofu

Yet as mysteriously as the statue was erected, it disappeared from the square one spring night a few months later in similarly unannounced fashion.[41] With no official explanation, those outside the party's inner circle can only speculate at the significance of these actions. At the very least, Confucius's quiet retreat emphasized the persistence of support for Mao among the party's rank and file and, more importantly, the public revival of the Great Helmsman. Mao nostalgia has reportedly grown in parts of the country, borne out of a halcyon recollection that the days under Mao were more equal.[42] Viewed from another perspective, harnessing Mao seemed to be a criticism emanating from certain "new leftist'" circles in China that the CCP of today has strayed from the chairman's purported goal of social equality. Burying Mao remains too politically sensitive. In the contest of state iconography and ideological symbolism, Confucius appeared to have lost this round.

What's more, Confucius as domestic cultural icon seemed to have little appeal for the average Chinese, as demonstrated by the terrible showing of the state-backed Confucius film. Even with the star power of Chow Yun-Fat, the film's opening was thoroughly upstaged by James Cameron's *Avatar,* one of just a couple dozen foreign films allowed into the China market in a year. Chinese audiences voted with their feet and movie tickets, and blue aliens trumped Confucius at the box office, causing considerable embarrassment to the state film authorities.[43] They even took the uncharacteristic action of pulling *Avatar* showings from theaters earlier than planned, in the hopes of drawing audiences to Confucius. It didn't work. Even so, that hasn't stopped the authorities from promoting Confucius as the face of China's overseas charm offensive.

Confucius as cultural export

Although Mao was immortalized as the subject of Andy Warhol's pop art in America, the Chinese ruler's repellant image in the West spans a narrow range from murderous tyrant to ruthless autocrat to wild-eyed utopian. For Chinese propagandists increasingly preoccupied with cosmopolitanism and global appeal, or soft power, Mao understandably seems unsuitable as the enduring face that is associated with the country. Confucius, however, is innocuous and inviting enough; his worst offense is being too easy a target for "Confucius says" jokes in the West.

Lukewarm success in promoting Confucius at home hasn't discouraged Beijing from taking him abroad.[44] Long a quiet bystander to the global market of peddling cultural values and exporting ideologies, China has lately taken a decidedly more proactive posture. China's now overflowing foreign reserves and cash, allowing Beijing to pursue soft power endeavors overseas that were previously unthinkable, undoubtedly played a role. And so the Confucius Institute was born, a government-backed educational and cultural entity modeled after the likes of Spain's Cervantes Institute and Germany's Goethe Institut.[45] The expansion of the institutes has not been without controversy, especially in the United States, where concerns over political influence and indoctrination in these institutes percolate beneath the surface. Despite these fears, the Chinese government reports that about 320 institutes have been established in some 90 different countries around the world.[46] According to *Hanban*, the central office within the Ministry of Education overseeing the program, the government hopes to set up 1,000 institutes by 2020. Spreading Confucius Institutes around the world is no trivial matter. During Hu's last major state visit to the United States as Chinese president in 2009, he made sure to visit a large Confucius Institute in Chicago.

But back home, Hu's Confucian-esque harmonious society has not galvanized the sort of ideological renaissance that was initially hoped. Fittingly, the idea's lasting legacy for the Chinese public may be the co-opting of the term *harmonize* to subversively describe Internet censorship—a false and superficial harmony imposed from above.[47] The party itself, in any case, remains bereft of an ideological anchor that can either strengthen its credibility with its own people or offer a compelling set of ideas that other nations can emulate. The Middle Kingdom is once again grasping at ideological straws.

Searching for a distinctly Chinese paradigm?

Over the next decade, the party will need to overcome its core ideological scarcity: defining who and what it stands for if not the proletariat and peasant classes or communist revolution. The inherent conflicts between the interests of the owners of capital, the interests of intellectuals, and interests of industrial and agricultural labor, whose land is appropriated for urbanization and real estate development and whose labor protections and cushy jobs are stripped away to make Chinese industry globally competitive, are too complex and real for the political establishment to confront head on.

But it is also precisely because of China's economic success that the CCP has so far been able to avoid fully confronting its identity crisis, both ideological and moral. This is largely a consequence of substituting the Growth Imperative for ideology. But as the grand bargain of accepting economic growth and increasing personal wealth in exchange for political allegiance breaks down, the CCP has yet to formulate a plan B to reboot its ideological appeal. It has, deliberately or not, become an ideological chameleon—an extreme version of pragmatism bereft of core principles and ethics grounding its claim to political authority. It is capable of abandoning ideologies as fast as championing them—from Maoism to capitalism to Confucianism—viewing all as utilitarian instruments aimed at maintaining the status quo.

In many ways, the CCP has become a victim of its own enormous success. Incredible economic development has begotten a more contentious public that's less desperate for material progress, one less prone to be affected by facile and empty political slogans. Put another way, changes in Chinese society have moved faster and ahead of the country's governance and political ideas.

Indeed, not only does the party's lack of unifying ideas lead to an increasingly cynical public, it also inclines observers in the outside world to be skeptical about the country's true intentions. Not all the skepticism is entirely fair, but reactionary elements in the Chinese political class do not help matters when they excoriate most foreign slights as ideological warfare conducted by Westerners. This is in part because the party is not entirely confident in the strength of its own persuasion and fears being overwhelmed by compelling ideologies from the outside, just as China experienced a century earlier at the Qing dynasty's collapse.

Take, for example, the recent Nobel Peace Prize brouhaha. When the Nobel committee awarded its coveted prize to Chinese political dissident Liu Xiaobo in 2010, Beijing was indignant. From a country that always held the Nobel as the epitome of prestige and global recognition, the vitriol leveled against the award in the wake of the Liu episode was striking. As the always "fair and balanced" official newspaper *Global Times* opined:[48]

> In 1989, the Dalai Lama, a separatist, won the prize. Liu Xiaobo, the new winner, wants to copy Western political systems in China.
>
> There are many different perspectives to view these two people, but neither of the two are among those who made constructive contributions to China's peace and growth in recent decades...

They have reason to question whether the Nobel Peace Prize has been degraded to a political tool that serves an anti-China purpose. It seems that instead of peace and unity in China, the Nobel committee would like to see the country split by an ideological rift, or better yet, collapse like the Soviet Union.[49]

While the op-ed's tone bordered on the conspiratorial, its suspicions of a politically motivated ploy to undermine Beijing's authority aren't so far removed from the thinking within certain party circles. In response, China unveiled its own Confucius Peace Prize in the same year, which was first awarded to an unknown Taiwanese politician and then given to Russia's Vladimir Putin in 2011.[50] The award was widely considered a meaningless farce, even prompting the Ministry of Education to distance itself from the spectacle. That the Confucius prize was created merely as a counter to an award that is the product of a "Western paradigm" reflects a larger truth about China's internal concern of losing the battle over ideological legitimacy. It is a long-standing existential fear that has intensified under a political system unsure about its own ideological roots.

Yet herein lies the silver lining. As a great civilization and powerful state, the Middle Kingdom *should* have ideas and wisdom to offer the world. The CCP is fully aware of its current ideological conundrum and has begun to upgrade its ideological "software" and boost soft power both at home and abroad. This is partly why the CCP has lately been searching deep into history for something uniquely Chinese that will resonate with its own people and the outside world. Just as America claims exceptionalism as part of its own creation myth, many Chinese ardently believe that China is entitled to its own exceptionalism as well. In fact, there are clear and objective factors that make China a "unique" power: its unrivaled scale, its dual identity as both an "old" empire and a modern state, and its economic dynamism, among others. But as the soon-to-be-largest economy in the world, it will be insufficient to simply rest on the size of the Chinese economy as its contribution to the global good. As seasoned China hand Orville Schell observed:

> China's leaders...will continue to feel a certain gnawing, inchoate sense of deficiency and incompleteness in their quest for global respect until they find the strength to begin addressing

the crucial, but elusive, issue of making China an ethical, as well as an economic and military, power.[51]

The CCP undoubtedly wants to be the agent that catalyzes another ideological and ethical rebirth so that China can stand on its own, apart and distinct from the rest. But along the way, it will face setbacks, particularly in reviving the party's appeal to its own people. The task's urgency makes further delay or avoidance a non-option. Whether the CCP can lead China to become that exceptional and respected power will have to be left to tomorrow's history books.

8

Values: What would Confucius do?

In the spring of 1964, a New Yorker named Catherine "Kitty" Genovese was randomly raped and stabbed to death by a roaming lunatic. Although specific facts of the event remain controversial, it was clear that witnesses were present as the gruesome murder unfolded in front of Genovese's home, but all chose inaction. A devastating *New York Times* investigative report published two weeks after the tragedy claimed that as many as 38 bystanders did absolutely nothing to help Genovese.[1] The case, and the media circus surrounding it, inflamed public passions over a growing American social apathy, sparking a sociological dissection of the Genovese syndrome and debate of public morality.

Forty-seven years later on the other side of the world in southern China, another tragic event stirred similar passions about the state of Chinese moral decay and values. In the fall of 2011, a two-year-old toddler named Yue Yue was run over twice by trucks and left on the street of an outdoor market suffering critical trauma.[2] More than a dozen passersby ignored the small, motionless body strewn on the pavement. In this digital age, a security camera's recording of the entire episode went viral on the Internet, dramatically amplifying the visceral impact of the tragedy in a way that would have been impossible in Genovese's day. Outrage and shame swept the Chinese public as baby Yue Yue became one of the most discussed topics in Chinese social media.[3]

This horrific incident in and of itself would've been collectively traumatic to any society. But it was magnitudes more disconcerting in China because it crystallized a palpable social malaise with which many Chinese were already grappling. A new generation who matured in the 1980s and 1990s, many of whom belong to the burgeoning urban middle class, feels morally unanchored in a miasma of nonsensical ideologies and questionable social values. They have been raised on economic growth and steadily advancing prosperity, but with scant thought to their intense alienation from their fellow citizens, or even their own families. Participation in the growth miracle has required compromises and adjustments to values: the competition is cutthroat, only allowing each man to skim off his share of a small pie by remaining an inch ahead of the next. In China's social Darwinism, everyone must play the game, and few have time to reflect on the consequences of an eroding set of normative values.

The "each man for his own" mentality is manifest to anyone who has ventured to ride one of China's overcrowded subways in Beijing or Shanghai. Even before passengers disgorge from the train, a rush of new passengers scurry in with a sort of practiced efficiency to secure a seat for themselves. If they do not act fast, someone else will swoop in and take it. The crush of people eager to win one of the few prized seats heightens the tension and incentivizes the competitors toward self-centered callousness. Seemingly trivial, these behavioral "norms" are in many ways deeply connected to the growing concern about a low-ethics society, or what the Chinese regularly refer to as *suzhi*. The Chinese have seen what ethical depravity has wrought in the recent past—the perverted and often violent social warfare of Mao Zedong's Cultural Revolution pitted neighbor against neighbor, breeding widespread suspicion.[4] Many Chinese still fear the kind of havoc a return to that dark period's pervasive mob mentality could wreak on society. In fact, during the Bo Xilai crisis of 2012, then-Premier Wen Jiabao sternly warned against a return to the Cultural Revolution, a reference that needed no elaboration for Chinese of his generation.

After 35 years of a prolonged growth marathon, many Chinese are awakening to the fact that their country's economic transition has not been accompanied by a comparable social transition that could have developed values and norms to make the socioeconomic changes tolerable and less discomfiting. While China's growth spurt engenders a mixture of fear and awe in outside observers, the intellectual and moral foundation it has grown out of has been deliberately neglected and as a result, severely weakened. The post-material aspirations of a growing share of middle class Chinese, and the demand for dignity of the migrant class, are needs unmet by China's sociopolitical status quo. For now, elite opinion makers seem to prefer attacking Western, universal values to a clearly articulated alternative. It is easier and safer to take a stand on what China is against than on what it is for.

In spite of the expansion of collective wealth, Chinese society has become more brittle and individuals more disillusioned with their station in life. In the rush to seek those glorious riches, material well-being has warped personal relationships, for example, stripping marriage of its nontransactional value. Surviving today's Chinese society requires embracing the corrosive nature of unbridled competition for limited supplies of everything—from housing to healthcare to jobs to education. Patient-doctor relationships have degenerated into violence; property developers and home buyers warily eye each other; local officials and rural residents have toxic relations. Younger Chinese individuals, who are perhaps an emerging lost generation, are profoundly confused in a sea of malleable and ad hoc values as they grapple with what they want to do and who they want to be. Without anchoring these dizzying changes in a clear and compelling system of values, Chinese society seems to be teetering at the edge of a psychological crisis.

The effects are twofold. For individuals unsure of what their decades of hard work were for, social pressures feel ever weightier. Having checked the boxes next to apartment and car, middle-class Chinese are contemplating the sort of society they want to live in. And rural Chinese and migrant laborers, no longer desperately poor, are growing increasingly dissatisfied with a society that prioritizes economic growth above their dignity and equality. For the political system that governs them, a shifting consensus on the legitimate aspirations of Chinese people is deeply confounding and potentially destabilizing. More progressive elements within the government are moving to accommodate changing values. Establishment intellectuals are fortifying the Chinese Communist Party's (CCP) philosophical defenses against the values, alternately referred to as universal or Western, that weave through the common social fabric of other middle-class societies. In the coming ten years, as environmental degradation, social equality, and happiness displace economic scarcity as the Chinese public's chief concerns, the contest between different visions of Chinese values can only intensify.

Qu nar (or where to)?

The civilization that created the compass is at a loss for finding its own way forward. The brewing debate over what kind of life or country the Chinese people are collectively trying to construct is arguably even more crucial than the better publicized bickering over how to rebalance the economy. For two generations since World War II, the CCP has demanded unimaginable sacrifice from its people in the name of nation building. After the sacrifice, the rewards are supposed to be forthcoming. The United States, for example, saw its greatest expansion of the middle class in the 30 years after WWII. But those three decades of economic change were also accompanied by bouts of social turmoil as the middle class fought, sometimes violently, to shape a nation predicated on social progress and tolerance. This period's economic prosperity was inseparable from the social enfranchisement of American women, African Americans, and immigrants from near and far.

In a democracy, political discontinuity is the accepted cost of managing social instability, a feature built into the system. But even without formal avenues to explore it, the Chinese public too is wrestling with similar questions of social change and the kind of nation their sacrifices have wrought. Many Chinese are deeply dissatisfied with what they find. With more information available to them and public discourse more vibrant than ever before, the Chinese middle class is being pushed to grapple with post-material definitions of happiness and fulfillment while simultaneously being pulled toward an enduring and resilient Chinese culture. Migrant workers and rural Chinese, too, are struggling with what society they wish to belong to, although their ability to affect public discourse is more limited.

Reconciling the old and the new is a perplexing and delicate challenge that the governing elite needs to resolve, about as urgently as it must sustain economic growth. It is a high-stakes game. If the political system's top-down engineering is unable to shape the country into the version that the public demands, then social change may be catalyzed by bottom-up forces that the current political system is incapable of managing. What's more, if the political establishment cannot offer a compelling vision for what China, the aspiring global power, ought to be, it leaves a vacuum to be filled by (*gulp*) Western values. Even to this day, the reductive lesson that the CCP apparatchiks took from the collapse of the Soviet bloc is that Western ideas, especially insidious ones like toppling regimes, infected the people. The Cold War was fought on many battlegrounds, but the Soviets lost it and the west emerged victorious on the front of values.

Instead of lying prostrate and being overtaken by Western values, the CCP and its intellectual allies have decided to lean forward and promote Chinese values. But such an effort requires them first and foremost to settle on what those Chinese values actually are and mean. Such a precondition is far from being met. The scarcity of enduring values and a complicated relationship with universal values leaves a Chinese society searching desperately for what it means to be a *Chinese* citizen. And it leaves the country struggling with what type of global power it intends to be. That both are taking place simultaneously generates a level of sociopolitical uncertainty unprecedented since China's opening to the outside world in the late 1970s.

Software upgrades

China has built up a vast reserve of hard capital in an impossibly short period of time, but it has also simultaneously neglected its social capital. The Chinese tend to describe the conundrum as a "hardware versus software" problem. The loss of social capital is especially jarring in a culture that traditionally emphasized personal relationships rather than impersonal institutions and for a political system that was ideologically socialist. But like the ideological waywardness of the political system, social norms and values that ensure smooth functioning of an unwieldy society, such as Good Samaritans, public kindness, and mutual trust, are increasingly scarce. The situation invites occasional, uncomfortable comparisons with weakened post-modern societies elsewhere around the world. In *Bowling Alone,* social scientist Robert Putnam diagnosed a dearth of social capital in contemporary

America that combined a decline of trust, communities, and civic engagement—which Putnam warned could lead to an erosion of the political system.[5]

Putnam's assessment of contemporary America may be debatable, but the lack of a clear and generally accepted values system seems to be gnawing at a Chinese culture fertilized by moralistic philosophizing, from Mencius to Confucius. Ancient rulers were at least nominally bound by strict moral codes of conduct and the practice of virtuous values: benevolence, humaneness, and harmony. Indeed, these are supposed to be the uniquely Chinese values that define the civilization's aspirations, as distinct from universal values of freedom, democracy, and human rights, borne out of the Western Judeo-Christian tradition. A focal point of recent contention, the Chinese values versus universal values debate sits at the heart of the country's latest soft power project to promote an equal if distinct Chinese values system.

The values dilemma has collided with the wide penetration of Internet communication to become a public values debate. The diversification of discourse in China today, a relatively new phenomenon that is in part a symptom of the information age, limits the political class's ability to dictate the terms of debate. As latercomers to a freer public sphere, the Chinese public is preoccupied with airing views and voices because it is so novel and efficiently enabled by technology. A surfeit of ideas propounded by party hacks, state-sponsored theorists, independent bloviators, and pseudo public intellectuals all vie for influence and gin up competing definitions of what kind of Chinese society ought to be fashioned. Defining the Chinese idea and an attendant values system has never been more complex.

Beijing has two unappetizing choices as the values debate bubbles over in coming years: Confront it, or be confronted by it. That the political system's grand bargain with the Chinese people was solely about delivering economic growth in exchange for stability was always something of a canard. The state also has an implicit social contract with its people to shape a decent society, one in which individuals can be moral and humane citizens. But China's economic transition to a middle-income society has accelerated a moral transition to a society based on post-materialist values, which could well imply a dramatic reordering of national priorities. It is far from certain that the current system, as it is, can keep up with these changes.

Pursuit of happiness

Without unfettered and wider participation in public discourse and regular opinion polls, it's hard to nail down the Chinese public's true range of views on values. But soul searching is nevertheless noticeable in the air. Take, for example, the striking and growing public interest in that most un-Chinese of health treatments, psychotherapy. It is an interest that, at least among the middle class, reflects a maladjusted and restless public seeking sustenance in the abstract realm of morality and values. Much like the Chinese government's insistence on noninterference in its internal affairs, private thoughts and psychological issues aren't to be intruded upon by a stranger in a swivel chair. Seeking professional support has long been widely seen as a culturally unacceptable admission of mental weakness. Mental health issues were to be endured with a large helping of stoicism, only publicly visible when their degeneration trickled out in one of three ways: by metastasizing into a breakdown, suicide, or a violent outburst of anger. In fact, all have been reported with increasing frequency lately. As Evan Osnos of the *New Yorker* reports:

> If the suicides [Foxconn] revealed cracks in the world of migrant labor, another macabre phenomenon exposed the stresses mounting in one more demographic: in a series of murderous attacks over the summer, middle-aged men in financial or psychological trouble set upon young children in their classrooms or near the schools. The killers all had grievances against landlords, neighbors, or others. China has strict gun controls, so the attackers used cleavers and hammers, and the killings terrified a public that, because of the one-child policy, is uniquely sensitive to school violence.[6]

In fact, Chinese gallows humor regularly dwells on how a U.S.-style second amendment would be absolutely disastrous for China—that legalized firearms cannot coexist in such a high-strung society.

The middle-class turn toward Freud and therapeutic outlets could suggest worsening individual discontent, or it could be that priorities have simply changed and motivated an urgent collective search for new answers. Indeed, *happiness* has caught on fire across China over the past few years, with some Chinese economists even proposing the creation of a Gross Happiness Index.[7] The latest obsession over happiness isn't borne out of thin air; some recent evidence suggests that the focus is necessary. According to University of Southern California economist Richard Easterlin's recent study of Chinese life satisfaction, long-term surveys suggest life satisfaction among Chinese over the past 15 to 20 years lagged far behind the fourfold increase in per capita consumption (see Figure 8.1).[8] The level of Chinese life satisfaction, he argues, is similar to those in central and eastern European states. What's more, even happiness is unequally distributed, as Easterlin demonstrates the difference among income groups.

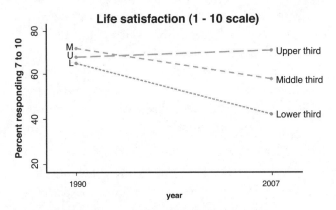

Figure 8.1   Chinese life satisfaction since 1990

Source: Easterlin, "China's life satisfaction, 1990-2010."

At the 2011 national legislature meeting, then-Premier Wen Jiabao launched a widespread discussion about happiness by declaring that it is the CCP's job to "let people live more happily and with more dignity."[9] His remarks left the nation rather confused over what happiness is, exactly, and how to achieve it. When China's central television took on the issue of happiness in a "man on the street" interview segment in October 2012, it found cynicism, suspicion, confusion, and an interviewee who wouldn't participate in the interview unless he was paid, claiming that more renminbis make him happy.[10] The segment affirmed precisely the metastasizing social problem that Wen had identified.

The Chinese government has at the very least begun to recognize the increasingly untenable nature of legitimizing authority based on economic growth. China's stagnating collective happiness, despite rising standards of living, fits into a pattern typical of countries emerging from poverty. Ronald Inglehart of the University of Michigan, a pioneer in identifying the correlation between economic growth and happiness, argues that there is typically a transition to post-materialist values at a certain stage of economic development and industrialization. As the founder of the World Values Survey, Inglehart's work claims a positive correlation between rising wealth and well-being in the "growth-intensive" phase of development. But once per capita income approaches a certain level, the correlation begins to weaken or break down:

> Inglehart places the boundary between these two stages at income of US$5,000 (32,877 yuan), at 1995 purchasing power parity (PPP). In 2009, that was equivalent to US$7,038 (46,277 yuan), and in 2010 China's per-capita GDP is thought to have passed that level. And so China has, by these figures, already entered the second of Inglehart's stages, where well-being is insensitive to economic growth. This means that policies designed to increase well-being cannot focus on GDP alone. For this reason, research into national happiness will be an important factor in China's public-policy decisions as the nation reaches middle-income levels.[11]

In fact, at the heart of the Panda Boom was the economic exploitation of China's most abundant input: labor. It was people, cheaper than machines, who powered the economy ahead, toiling away on small farms or assembling widgets in coastal factories. The supply of humans was so great that individuals were essentially viewed as instruments of economic growth, hardly distinguishable or entitled to treatment as individuals. Wages were meager, and survival was paramount. Individual well-being and happiness were quaint afterthoughts that seemed rather meaningless during the heady days of rapid growth. According to the World Values Survey's data, Chinese happiness has declined since the mid-1980s, coinciding with the period of hypergrowth (see Figure 8.2).[12] That type of labor-intensive and no-holds-barred growth had a decisive impact on shaping social values, which also became instrumentalist and concerned foremost with achieving financial and material ends. If economic prosperity continues to beget social discontent, then the old formula appears broken and a new equation is needed.

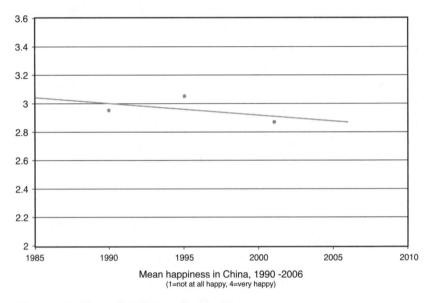

Mean happiness in China, 1990 -2006
(1=not at all happy, 4=very happy)

Figure 8.2   Measuring Chinese happiness

Source: Inglehart, World Values Survey

Nature abhors a vacuum. Cambridge, Massachusetts, would seem an unlikely place to supply the Chinese with doses of moral certitude given their government's uneasy relationship with Western values. Yet well-known Harvard moral philosopher Michael J. Sandel has become a hero, a modern-day American Confucius, whose lectures on justice and what's "right" are making waves in college classrooms in Beijing. Already considered an intellectual celebrity in Japan, Sandel's simple but thought-provoking seminars on ethics and social morality strike a particular chord with middle class, young, and educated Chinese. His emphasis on fairness and the value of public goods resonates with a Chinese public who achingly feel the inadequacy of both. And his

latest book on the moral limits of markets perfectly captures a pervasive feeling among a healthy fraction of the Chinese public: Society
has become as transactional as the market, and perverse materialism
has trumped all other intrinsic values in dictating social relationships.
When discussing his book, Sandel has argued:

> In recent years, seemingly technical economic questions have
> crowded out questions of justice and the common good. I
> think there is a growing sense, in many societies, that G.D.P.
> and market values do not by themselves produce happiness,
> or a good society.[13]

Many middle-class Chinese, in particular those of the one-child
generation who have enjoyed material plentitude disproportionate to
what would be expected in a developing country, see little reason to
turn exclusively to economic progress to provide improved quality of
life or personal fulfillment. As they reach maturity, they are seeking a
new moral compass that is currently nowhere to be found.

Separate but unequal

In the spectacular Chinese documentary "Last Train Home,"
the unspoken but obvious inequality in China is given an intimately
human face.[14] The depiction of the life of a Chinese migrant family,
embarking on the annual harrowing slow-train journey to reunite with
family in their hometown, offers a powerful and effective portrayal of
the severe social dislocations that growth has wrought. The story isn't
particularly new. But it aptly captures the deep and profound erosion
of family values and the sense of equality, once bedrocks of Chinese
society, wrought by what has been called the greatest internal migration in human history.

Rather than the communitarian, classless society once envisioned
by Mao, China is now a society with more than 200 million second-
class citizens. They are aliens within their own country, entitled to
a fraction of the prosperity that they were instrumental in creating.
They built Shanghai's skyline and now the world's fastest-growing
bullet train network, but they are forced to retreat to the outskirts

of the urban oasis, enviously eyeing the life of the rich and richer. China's migrant worker population has long been marginalized. No wonder they are probably the least happy cohort based on Easterlin's findings. Now many of them seem to have had enough: They want what the urban elites have.

Migrants are already voting with their feet, refusing to return to the coast and preferring to take their chances closer to home. This is likely in part retaliation against the discrimination they face in the largest coastal cities, where equal access to urban elite entitlements such as education, healthcare, and pensions is far from reality. In some ways resembling undocumented immigrants in the United States, Chinese migrants are deliberately excluded from the country's prosperity through both economic marginalization and political fiat.

This inequality is especially grating for the post-1990s generation of migrants (i.e. those born after 1990) who are treated as outsiders in the same cities where their parents worked for decades. The aspirations of these migrants, who have witnessed but never been within reach of the Chinese middle-class lifestyle, stretch higher with the rise of each skyscraper they build. Their parents aspire for them to attain the education and economically secure lifestyle that was impossible for migrants a generation earlier, who set out for the assembly line when they were 18 or even younger. Meanwhile, today's migrant-youth want to obtain the Starbucks-sipping, iPhone-wielding yuppie glory that is second nature to their urbane contemporaries.

The political obstacles to their attaining equality are daunting. From the vantage point of the urban elites who dominate policymaking, enfranchising 200 million-plus migrants and potentially a future influx of rural emigrants would put new demands on already limited resources and opportunities, particularly on the dispensation of public goods.[15] Like in many other countries, enfranchising a previously marginalized population is a politically charged decision that often encounters strong elite resistance. To practice the value of equality would require urban elites to willfully undermine their own interests. Why would they do that so easily?

The migrant class's growing frustration with a dual-track society and China's tattered social fabric was captured with brutal and heart-rending honesty in a 2011 essay by a migrant who had "made it" in the rarified world of the Chinese elite class. Entitled "I fought for 18 years to have a cup of coffee with you," the post was an immediate sensation in the Chinese Internet:

> Here's a question I pose for my white-collar friends: what if I never graduated from middle school, and had become a migrant worker? Would you sit down for a cup of coffee with me at Starbucks? The answer, unequivocally, is that you wouldn't. That is simply not a possibility. If we compared our experiences growing up, you will find that for the things that you take for granted, I have sacrificed and exerted huge amounts of efforts to acquire.
>
> From the moment I was born, our life's path swerved away from each other. I was given a rural resident card while you got a city one. If I grew up keeping my rural residence, I wouldn't be able to work in the city today. I would also be denied social security, and proper medical care...
>
> Finally, I graduated. Finding a job in Shanghai was hard, but going back to the village was not an option. The average salary for our class was 2000RMB per month. Perhaps you think that 2000RMB is an adequate salary, but I still needed to pay for rent, to pay for utilities, to pay back my student loans, and to send money home to put my brother and sister through school. What was left, I used for food. After all of this, I still couldn't join you for a coffee at Starbucks!
>
> Since that time I've earned a master's degree, and currently live in Shanghai where my annual salary is 80,000RMB. I fought for eighteen years, and can finally sit down with you for a cup of coffee... I didn't write this to complain. The terrifying thing isn't that justice is relative. The terrifying thing is to witness injustice and to act as if one sees nothing...
>
> During a macro-economics class, a classmate attacked blue collar workers who'd been laid off, and unemployed high school dropouts: "80% of them are where they are because they don't work hard. They chose not to specialize in

something when they were young, so they can't get jobs now! Those kids are perfectly capable of studying and working. I've heard that a lot of students use their holidays to make thousands to pay their tuition." You can't find a person who knows less about the struggles of rural China than this classmate of mine.[16]

These words crystallized an image of a society not deliberately cruel, but indifferent, enormously stratified, and self-interested. It is little wonder that American moral philosopher Sandel's wisdom has such resonance in today's China. In contrast to the other notable Harvard moral philosopher John Rawls, whose notion of justice is predicated on the concept of veil of ignorance,[17] Sandel builds a framework for justice that accepts that *a priori* conditions of perfect equality are impossible. It is a moral system for human beings born into different stations in life and therefore unable to be ignorant of their lot and positions in a particular society. This is China's moral dilemma: The *hukou*, or residence permit system, is the most powerful political instrument that discriminates at the outset of a Chinese lifetime. The geography of birth automatically puts a Chinese on a path that for his or her whole life will determine opportunities and outcomes. For a Chinese migrant or rural resident, inequality begins at birth.[18]

A relic of the planned economy era in which Chinese leaders wanted to prevent mass population movements and overcrowded cities, the hukou has become less a tool of social management and more a symbol of systemic inequality.[19] Economic pressure to adjust the system is growing, as the Chinese government repeatedly trumpets rapid urbanization as the prescription for sustaining future growth and consumption. Today, barely 50% urbanized, China has ample room to bring its rural population into the cities to reach the roughly 70% to 80% rate of developed countries. Economically, such a policy makes sense. But its success will also depend on how the migrant issue is addressed. Migrant slums are already starting to encircle major cities, and the improper handling of their absorption into urban society with equal treatment risks unanticipated social instability.

Without broader awareness of the values of equality and social responsibility, the urban elite can be expected to defend its turf and disrupt the rural-urban integration process. Despite Chinese academics and some policymakers proposing a change to the current class divisions, in an undemocratic polity, it will be up to the Chinese leadership to decide whether it wants to adopt enlightened policies. A change in values seems likely to lag economic and social realities, a common situation in rapidly developing economies. Closing that gap, however, may require a significant, and possibly volatile, social catalyst before the government's hand is forced. If the American civil rights movement is instructive in any way, enfranchising a society's marginalized populations is a politically toxic and costly guarantee of periodic social clashes.

Governing post-materialist China: The "what have you done for me lately" problem

The CCP, the government it controls, and the intellectual elite whose interests are aligned with it are attacking the problem of values for a new China from many angles. Provincial governments are experimenting with ways to prioritize happiness along with economic progress, and China's public intellectuals are searching for value systems that can resonate with the Chinese public and perpetuate and justify the status quo. The state is also simultaneously proffering uninspiring idols and role models such as Lei Feng to inspire public morality and ethics—an effort that was aborted nearly as fast as it was trotted out.[20] Even official Chinese press couldn't quite contain its puzzlement in how to sell an anachronistic icon so detached from contemporary Chinese life.

These state and pseudo-state elements collectively face the incredibly frustrating problem fundamental to politics in a rapidly developing country: having delivered material prosperity to an unprecedented proportion of the Chinese population, the government must satisfy a set of public concerns fast moving into new territory. It must respond to a public no longer so enthused by the promise of fast, steady economic growth.

It's (mostly) sunny in Canton

It is apt that Guangdong Province, ground zero of the launch of China's labor-intensive manufacturing model, is taking charge of ensuring that its citizens are not simply materially prosperous but also psychologically happy.[21] Reprising its role as a progressive province—after all, it was the genesis of China's economic reform experiment in the 1980s—Guangdong is now again pioneering not economic but social experiments that could alleviate bottom-up social pressures. The province has not only constructed its own happiness index, it has relaxed the one-child policy, better accommodated social protests, and even encouraged improved sex lives for Guangdongers.[22] Given its proximity to Hong Kong and Taiwan, the Guangdong cultural DNA resembles more that of its liberal cousins rather than the stodgier Chinese capital. A large portion of Guangdong's media and entertainment takes its cues from those two outposts of Chinese democracy and press freedom. Like California in the United States, Guangdong tends to lead China in adopting relatively progressive elements.

The now-famous Wukan protest of 2011, in which an entire village confronted and protested against local officials over corrupt land seizures, was not resolved with police batons but rather with a surprising ouster of the local party secretary and the election of a new one.[23] China had flirted with nationalizing local-level elections for years, but never seriously executed it. The conclusion of the Wukan episode prompted expectations that a new "Guangdong model" of humane and transparent governance would proliferate across the country. It was the kind of change in social governance with which Guangdong denizens could get on board.

It didn't meet such exalted expectations, however. China was on the eve of a major political transition, and the appetite in Beijing for tweaking the political system was weak. Renewed hope for substantive changes again swept the southern province as new President Xi Jinping made an effort to visit Guangdong as one of the first stops after securing power. Such hopes may again evaporate: the province's flagship liberal newspaper was subsequently engulfed in a political tiff over freedom of press and speech with the propaganda department.[24] Once again, Guangdong is center stage in another battle over what values the country should espouse.

Swatting flies

While many middle-class Chinese yearn for values that aren't far apart from those generally accepted in the West, elements within the Chinese leadership and some elites find these values rather odious. Their preoccupation with the power of Western values is not new. From the time of Mao, there were those in the party-state that felt the West, which essentially meant the United States, was bent on toppling the Chinese regime not at the barrel of a gun but by winning the hearts and minds of the Chinese people. The issue became particularly salient after former Secretary of State John Foster Dulles unveiled the concept of "peaceful evolution." The Chinese leadership was extraordinarily concerned about the effects of peaceful evolution:

> Therefore, imperialist countries are inclined to adopt a "soft" method in addition to employing "hard" policies. In January 1953, U.S. Secretary of States Dulles emphasized the strategy of "peaceful evolution." He pointed out that "the enslaved people" of socialist countries should be "liberated," and become "free people," and that "liberation can be achieved through means other than war," and "the means ought to be and can be peaceful." He displayed satisfaction with the "liberalization-demanding forces" which had emerged in some socialist countries and placed his hope on the third and fourth generations within socialist countries, contending that if the leader of a socialist regime "continues wanting to have children and these children will produce their children, then the leader's offspring will obtain freedom."[25]

The end of the Cold War would have reinforced the perennially paranoid chairman's paranoia had he lived to see it. From where the CCP sat, the collapse of the Soviet Union reeked of a peaceful evolution instigated by Washington. After all, the USSR fell with no direct military engagement with the United States. The ensuing "color revolutions" that fanned across eastern Europe, and the democratic triumphalism in the West epitomized by Francis Fukuyama's *End of History*,[26] did nothing to assuage Beijing's suspicions. Vigilance against the onslaught of Western values and ideas has been a hallmark of Chinese government policy, even if in practice it has proved mostly futile. When Deng launched reform and opening up, he was well aware that it was impossible to both adopt Western economic practices and prevent Western values from seeping into China. He likened those ideas and values to pernicious "flies" that will inevitably blow into an open window.[27]

To control the fly population, the Chinese government has in place longstanding restrictions on the import of Western cultural products. For instance, under the World Trade Organization, China imposes an import quota on Hollywood films so that only 20 make it into the China market each year (though restrictions have been modestly loosened).[28] Politically sensitive foreign books are regularly banned and Western media is either systematically delegitimized by official Chinese media or blocked entirely during politically sensitive periods like the annual meetings of the National People's Congress and its less-exciting cousin the Chinese People's Political Consultative Conference. Yet these efforts are proving to be less effective in an Internet age when borders are porous and information will leak into China despite the government's sophisticated censoring technology. Beijing may still officially stick to the import quota on U.S. films, but the proliferation of the pirated DVD industry and web videos renders such a quota almost meaningless. Many Chinese have access to new Hollywood releases before most Americans have seen the film.

Moreover, opening up the Chinese economy and normalizing relations with the United States in the late 1970s meant a dramatic uptick in people-to-people exchanges, particularly in the education realm. Chinese students arrived in America and Canada in droves, with 200,000 entering North American universities in 2011, up nearly a quarter from the previous year.[29] Over the past three decades, countless Chinese have intimately experienced the U.S. education system and been immersed in its values. Many have returned, the so-called sea turtles (*haigui*), bringing back economic policy prescriptions and business practices that are helping to shape the Chinese political economy.

Yet the outcome would likely surprise Dulles as much as it would Mao. As the Chinese returnees are absorbed back into the fold, they have by and large not been at the forefront of reshaping Chinese values or seriously advocating on behalf of Western political institutions. In some ways, a newer generation of returnees may be opting for the reverse: defending Chinese values because their close encounters with the United States have led to the conclusion that it is a highly imperfect country, not necessarily the "beautiful nation" (*mei guo*) of their imaginations. These attitudinal changes were likely also reinforced by the decade-long Iraq War and the devastating financial crisis of 2008. Instead of the idealized conception of the United States that some Chinese may have once held, it has become more of a "normal" country, with both strengths and warts and all.

The squandering of American soft power over the past decade has also invited many in the Chinese political system to exploit these wounds to the American idea and change tactics. Accustomed to reacting to the overwhelming influence of U.S. values, the Chinese government has decided to lean forward with a cultural and values proposition in the past few years. It has enlisted scholars and wealthy Chinese elites to propose a distinct set of Chinese values that are anything but universal.[30] At the heart of this effort is not only a genuine belief that China should not be made in America's image but also worsening insecurity over what value propositions China stands for, both to its own people and to the world.[31]

China pushes back on values

The debate over universal values began after the tragic Sichuan earthquake in 2008 and has intensified since.[32] Commenting on the quake recovery efforts, the liberal newspaper *Southern Weekend* commended the top leaders' rapid response as upholding the universal values of human rights, rule of law, and democracy.[33] The piece triggered a response from influential and left-leaning blogger Sima Nan who dismissed the concept of universal values as a fantasy that's unsuitable for China. In an interview over his fiery response, Nan launched into a diatribe against the supposed imposition of universal values:

> They [the West] argue that so long as we honor the pledge to uphold universal values, then we'll achieve national reconciliation at home and reconciliation with the world. So this implies that today's China does not have cultural/national

reconciliation and that other countries have not reconciled with us; that all the responsibility is on us because we have not met the bottom line precondition of universal values, and that makes the "foreign bosses" displeased. What absurd logic! This is outrageous social critique![34]

These sentiments do not stand far apart from what is being argued by elements within the government, many of whom have begun to adopt the idea that China's particular historical and cultural roots mean that it cannot fit under the rubric of universal values.[35] Put another way, it is unique and exceptional, not universal. The underlying motives are primarily political.

First, strengthening the CCP's governance credibility has become a great challenge in a values and ideological vacuum. The core values of socialism have vanished—if they were practiced at all—and in their place are corruption, wanton use of power, and materialism. A new distinct Chinese values system could rejuvenate the political system and provide the party with a stronger popular mandate. Second, the Chinese government seems to believe that the predominance of the universal values paradigm needs to be challenged precisely because it is already so deeply embedded and accepted as the natural state of affairs. Whether consciously or not, former Premier Wen's invocation of living "happily and with more dignity" echoes universal values enshrined, among other places, in the U.S. Declaration of Independence, precisely the kind of American value that China officially rejects. Of course, from the government's standpoint, it could simply argue that happiness as a value also comports with the traditional Chinese notion of harmony, and therefore ideologically aligns with former President Hu's harmonious society.

Rather than accepting Western values wholesale, Beijing is putting financial and political muscle behind advocating Chinese concepts and values. It is in part a recognition that as the potential economic leader of the world, Chinese influence in the world of ideas remains quite limited. China likely is not interested in revising universal values; it simply wants its ideas legitimated in a way that has equal relevance in the world's eye. An influential CCP political journal characterizes it thusly:

After the Cold War, Western developed countries always leveraged their economic and scientific strength to conduct thought and cultural infiltration among developing countries, marketing Western values and models of governance. It attempts to build a unified western values and social system in the world. However, those developing countries that have accepted western values and social systems have experienced political unrest and economic recessions, causing the western system to be severely criticized. This was especially so after the financial crisis, which further prompted a global aversion to the western governance model. But the west continues to monopolize global public opinion, having long advocated western ideologies that created a stubborn global public opinion bias. As Chinese society has opened itself to the outside and as western leadership of global opinion continues, western capitalism and culture's impact within China is growing by the day.[36]

As conspiratorial as it may sound, the passage reflects the sentiment that in the battle of ideas, China increasingly believes it needs to be on the offensive. But therein lies the problem: If none of the Chinese values are universally applicable, and no other country is able to adopt them, then how does China increase the market share of its values? To use a technology analogy, if a new system or software is incompatible with the existing ecosystem, consumers will still prefer to adopt an existing system that functions relatively well and is low cost to adopt. By actively focusing on the particularity of Chineseness, the values stemming from it can only apply to those who ascribe to such identification or share some cultural and ethnic affinities.

Indeed, the Chinese values on offer are excavated from ancient China and are derivatives of vague Confucian ideals on morality and norms of governance. Just as Confucianism has been trotted out as a possible palliative to the CCP's ideological vacuity, it is also being repackaged into a code of conduct for Chinese policies abroad. A leading proponent of a Confucian-based foreign policy is Chinese scholar Yan Xuetong of Tsinghua University.[37] Often described in the West as a nationalist or Chinese hawk, Yan considers himself a realist and articulates a set of Chinese principles and values that he believes are capable of competing with the Western model of governance. He draws heavily from pre-dynastic China when the Warring States period is, in his view, analogous to today's multipolar world. The central idea is the Confucian principle of moral leadership and humane authority as values that should be adopted for both domestic governance and the projection of Chinese soft power.[38] He believes that moral leadership, more than economic or military might, is the source of political power and the value most crucial in strengthening China's standing in the world. The other element is meritocracy, where leaders are supposed to be selected based on virtue and wisdom, rather than mere competence, to ensure humane authority. In a provocatively titled *New York Times* op-ed "How China Can Defeat America," Yan writes:

> China's quest to enhance its world leadership status and America's effort to maintain its present position is a zero-sum game. It is the battle for people's hearts and minds that will determine who eventually prevails. And, as China's ancient philosophers predicted, the country that displays more humane authority will win.[39]

Drawing upon the political inspirations of ancient China for modern purposes is not particularly surprising. Prominent Americans such as Henry Kissinger, a historian by training, have also speculated that China was more likely to turn to its historical traditions for intellectual justifications of its conduct, behavior, and norms.[40] Although Yan correctly assesses that soft power springs from the perception of domestic strength, meaning moral leadership has to address domestic issues first, it is entirely unclear how moral leadership is practiced in reality. Even Beijing's diplomacy tends to veer toward the transactional, tethered to money and not a set of values. It has won Beijing some fast but hardly enduring friends, leading China scholar Minxin Pei to describe it as the "loneliest superpower."[41]

Humane authority, too, is not the equivalent of human rights; that would depend too much on individual agency. It is about an enlightened and virtuous leadership that will properly arrange the sociopolitical system in a way that would solve social inequality, weed out corruption, and raise China's global profile as a benign power that takes the moral high ground. The prescription is almost entirely supply side rather than demand side driven—as long as a leader can supply the proper type of governance, there will be no need for bottom-up demand for a different system.

On the tail of a year of political scandals and corruption crises in 2012, epitomized by the fall of Bo Xilai, moral leadership may be a tough sell to the Chinese public. Humane authority also presupposes an impossibly disciplined human nature to do the "right" thing that simply does not seem to exist. In fact, upholding moral leadership requires the same kind of definitive values that Yan and his allies have failed to articulate. Are the criteria for humane authority entirely different from common notions of equality, fairness, and freedom? And who decides a particular leader has sufficient moral certitude to lead the country?

These questions are left unanswered, and likely intentionally so. The empirical evidence for whether such an ancient set of political and social values can function well in today's China is nonexistent. More evidence suggests that China remains a long way from realizing the exalted aspirations of a moral leadership, particularly as the credibility gap between the government and the governed widens daily. For the average Chinese, endemic corruption also weakens the claim to an exemplary leadership that can maintain the full confidence of its people.

But these inconvenient caveats have not dissuaded proponents of such ideas. Among these appear to be a rising cohort of younger, white-collar Chinese elites who, once convinced of Westernization as the only path to development, no longer equates modernization with Westernization. One such circle of like-minded individuals was described by Anand Giridharadas in his book *Chinese Dreams*, in which a collective fervor over Western ideas and values gave way to doubt and disillusion over what they perceived as wholesale Westernization of China:

> They had each come to believe that the society had gone too far in embracing foreign philosophies and frameworks, from European Marxist ideology to American capitalist ideology. They wanted now to be part of the invention of an indigenous, modern school of thought to carry the country forward on ideas of its own.[42]

One of the leaders of this cohort is a Stanford-educated Chinese returnee, Eric X. Li.[43] Having spent most of his formative years in the United States, Li is among those whose intimate interaction with the West has apparently led to a more critical, or at least nuanced, view of it. Perhaps it is because the imperfect democracy that is America has exposed the obvious and open secret that it is far from an idealized nation and parts of it are nearly as unequal as China is now. At least America is transparent about its inequality.[44] Just take a look around the perimeters of the two most prestigious symbols of American might: the White House and Harvard University. The homeless openly dot Lafayette Park, a stone's throw from the fortified gates of the U.S. president's residence. And Harvard Square, where a minestrone of personalities and social classes mix, sits just outside the sanctified gates of elite American pedagogy.

Whatever the reason, personal or calculated, Li and his compatriots have adopted a dimmer view of the realities of America and the value system that created those realities. Instead, they champion a form of Chinese exceptionalism and are working assiduously to present a Chinese values and ideas system that is more or less Confucian in nature. Having accumulated considerable wealth as a successful venture capitalist, Li has the luxury of pouring some of his wealth into think tanks, business schools, and other intellectual endeavors both in China and in America to promote his ideas.[45] The core of the Chinese values system he presents, to the extent it is discernable, involve an emphasis on meritocracy and rejection of Western democracy. Like many others who hold similar views, the main purpose of Chinese values, as articulated so far, is to stand in opposition of universal values without elaborating on why precisely such values cannot apply to China. The usual, and only, explanation is simply that the uniqueness of Chinese history and traditions means that it is unfit or uninterested in political and social institutions that were determined by the evolution of Western historical circumstances.

China the exceptional?

After the financial crisis—and the latest string of tragic gun violence in the United States—the moral standing of the West has been eroded in the eyes of many Chinese, a sentiment to which the Chinese exceptionalism school readily attaches itself. Even champions of American neoliberal values such as former Federal Reserve Chair Alan Greenspan admitted to an intellectual faux pas. During a congressional testimony amid the crisis, Greenspan revealed that "I've found a flaw [in my thinking]. I don't know how significant or permanent it is... This modern risk-management paradigm held sway for decades. The whole intellectual edifice, however, collapsed in the summer of last year."[46] The crumbling of that intellectual edifice, no matter how fleeting, gave some in the Chinese government a ready gift of delegitimizing an already demoralized United States as the perennial beacon of universal values. Justifying the Chinese way or Chinese values, whatever they may be, became a whole lot easier in the face of American troubles.

There was a time when delegitimizing the American idea was much more difficult and ineffective. Whenever the United States issued a human rights report on China, the Chinese government responded with its own human rights white paper on America that criticized the prevalence of racism and violence, as if those elements are absent from Chinese society. It mattered little whether the Chinese public was convinced of America's "tainted" human rights record; it was merely a political charade intended to demonstrate that the Chinese government was a better steward of its society than the American democrats of theirs. But no longer. The West has now faltered in its moral leadership, wreaking financial havoc across the globe. Or at least the official Chinese press made sure that was the message contained in nearly every op-ed that splashed across the pages of the *People's Daily*. Beijing can now argue, convincingly or not, that its governing mandate has no need for universal values—insisting as it always had that its value of human rights meant clothing, feeding, and sheltering its people, all of which revolved around materialism.

But now many millions of Chinese are fed well, fashionably clothed, and reside in swanky apartments. Their unprecedented access to a fire hose of information allows them to effortlessly compare the values and actions of people beyond their borders with their own leaders and fellow citizens. It is true that they do not approve of every conduct of the West or uncritically accept established Western norms, yet they are even more frustrated by how certain Chinese officials have obtained so much wealth and how ordinary children can be senselessly left for dead with no claims to responsibility. Or how Chinese school buses collapse like origami upon impact and American school buses are built like fortified Humvees.[47] Isn't protecting their children the government's moral obligation?

Something else they have discovered is that China *is* rather different from the United States, where the American people seem to genuinely believe in and are invested in the system and the processes that make the system function. They find human agency, and an abiding belief in a shared set of values that is a stabilizing force across an extraordinarily diverse American society. That contrast is stark for a growing number of Chinese who are seriously examining the state of their own society, seemingly adrift from a sense of purpose and close-knit kinship. As the country grows into the preeminent global economic power, it has given few hints about what the nation has to offer. This is hardly a surprise since its own people seem incapable of defining the Chinese idea, at least so far.

Soft power always begins at home, a central truth that seems to consistently elude some of the more conservative voices in the Chinese government. While indulging in *schadenfreude* of American economic and political dysfunction, the Chinese government has neglected to clearly articulate a set of values that is appropriately suited to the country's current economic and social conditions. Chinese society appears to be in need of a binding agent to prevent the moral and value vacuum from degenerating into a more severe social cancer. Perhaps as one of the children of the Cultural Revolution, President Xi seems especially sensitive to social and moral decay and has chosen to promote the Chinese Dream.[48]

Such China revival rhetoric has been well received by the Chinese public so far, suggesting that the government understands how crucial addressing the scarcity of social values is. But its actualization depends on defining the Chinese idea with an underlying intellectual and values foundation. Yet in some respects, the government's idea may still stand apart from the numerous versions that society has imagined: For *Southern Weekend*, the Chinese dream is constitutionalism and rule of law; for migrant parents, theirs is a secondary education for their children and equality; for the middle class, it's humane governance and freedom of expression.

And such is the central paradox that will confound Chinese politics over the next decade: In spite of China's impressive economic achievements, Chinese society has ironically grown shakier because for all its newfound wealth, it has preciously little to grasp on to.

9

Freedom: Keep on rockin' in the firewalled world

To call a golden retriever ugly is tantamount to blasphemy in the United States. Not so in Harbin, the frigid northeastern capital of Heilongjiang Province. In spring 2012, the city's officials issued a regulation that demanded that dog owners dispose of "large-sized and ugly and scary dogs," including golden and Labrador retrievers, chow chows, and mastiffs, among 45 other breeds.[1] The authority's justification was preposterous, simply stating that while the dogs do not bite, they seem to "frighten" citizens. Once given up, the dogs were most likely to be handed over to a shadowy network of canine traffickers and destined for the slaughterhouse. At least that's what many residents believed.

Harbin dog owners were apoplectic, instantly organizing street protests and petition campaigns to prevent the inhumane law from becoming reality. The public outcry was fierce and emotionally charged, demonstrating a unity against an irrational public policy that even official Chinese media couldn't ignore. One online plea from Harbin in particular reverberated through the Chinese-speaking Internet:

> Harbin doggies today will be our pet dogs tomorrow!!! Please forward this message! Please put aside what you are working on right now and dial the telephone number at the end of the article and fight for our beloved dogs' right to live, okay?

All people who love dogs, please click the share button. This seemingly insignificant gesture may be able to save lives of hundreds and thousands of doggies.

Please don't think it is troublesome. Please don't think it doesn't concern you. Don't think Harbin is too far away.

This time it is Harbin. Next time, it might be Shanghai, Beijing, and Hangzhou.[2]

Protestors deliberately hinted at a "dog slaughter contagion" to enlist national sympathies for this grassroots cause. It wasn't hard, as media coverage regularly showed grandfathers and grandmothers with heartrending outpourings of their attachment to their pets. One silver-haired grandmother pleaded that her Samoyed was her only companion now that she lives alone. Another elderly gentleman, with tears streaming down his face, gave this testimony:

I have diabetes, cardiac disease and arteriosclerosis. My wife is not in good health either. Ever since I started to keep this golden retriever in 2010, it had been taking me outdoors to exercise, and my health got much better. My golden retriever was never a disturbance to the neighborhood. I always cleaned up its poop when I walked it. I live on the highest floor. A resident on the third floor often pilfers things. My golden is an early bird. It wakes me up at 4 or 5 every morning. I saw him steal things, so he often filed complaints against me. It is the fifth time. When I go upstairs, the golden uses its strength to pull me upstairs, otherwise I can't go upstairs on my own. If it is killed, *how am I going to live?*

In a country such as the United States, it is easy to envision a Supreme Court showdown titled *Dog Owners United v. Harbin* swiftly materializing, its outcome virtually assured (spoiler: dog owners win). Yet in China, even given the strident public outrage against such an illiberal and extreme policy, the government may still get its way. No court or legal parameters will obstruct its actions. A sense of helplessness seems to have blanketed a Harbin public that has little recourse against the authorities other than insistent persuasion.

The Harbin saga reflects twin coexisting and contradictory realities in China: It is both a much freer and perversely prohibitive country than most imagine. That the citizens demonstrated and paraded on Harbin streets without immediate suppression indicates the freer aspects of Chinese politics. But the freedom to own dogs longer than 27.5 inches (70 centimeters) without state intrusion, that is too much to ask.

To be sure, the range of economic and social freedoms in China today would have been unimaginable for earlier generations. Along nearly every dimension, China is arguably a freer country than two decades ago. But the existing range is no longer sufficient. In particular, social and political freedoms have not progressed in tandem with economic growth along the typical trajectory of development. If anything, the quiet curtailing of individual freedoms has been papered over by an outstanding economic record. Yet having accumulated wealth during the economic boom, millions of Chinese, many of whom consider themselves middle class, appear to be undertaking a collective psychological shift on the *type* of life to lead.

That type of middle-class life increasingly counts as essential a set of general freedoms recognizable in many parts of the world: information, speech, legal protection, and a sense of ownership. Few Chinese seriously demand the sort of electoral democracy that defines a core feature of the Western system. What they increasingly expect instead is to have the right to own dogs, for example, without the fear of having to arbitrarily relinquish them to the doggy-knackers. Or the right to access unadulterated and safe food, the freedom to breathe clean air, and the freedom to pursue whatever version of Chinese happiness befits their imaginations.

The paradox of rising middle-class expectations is that economic prosperity begets sociopolitical transformations and shifting priorities at the individual level. Even as the vast majority of Chinese have become economically better off, they appear to be less satisfied with the current state of domestic affairs. The latest Pew Global Attitudes survey affirms the growing public discontent that stems from what can be broadly described as the "costs of growth" (see Figure 9.1).[3] Economic growth is absent from the list, and only one issue of concern rose in prominence to 50%: corrupt officials. This encapsulates the fundamental mismatch between rising middle class expectations and a government that has fallen short of bolstering individual freedoms by neglecting social problems. Another piece of evidence comes from the latest Gallup opinion poll, which surprisingly revealed that nearly 60% of the Chinese participants believe that environment should be prioritized over economic growth.[4]

Percentage of Chinese rating public issue "a serious problem"

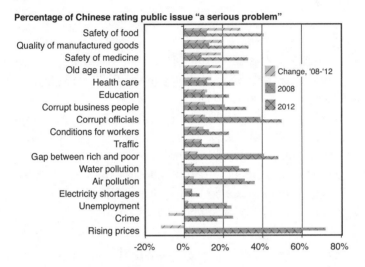

Figure 9.1   Public concern over corruption has risen

Source: Pew Global Attitudes Project 2012[5]

For decades, the Chinese government has relied on delivering rapid growth, employment opportunities, and improving livelihoods to its citizens in exchange for maintaining authority, or the mandate to govern. Indeed, the *Growth Imperative* is essentially the grand bargain struck between the ruling class and the Chinese people: As long as the government is competent at expanding the economic pie and lifting all boats, then the public should generally steer clear of politics and avoid making unnecessary demands on their rulers.

But that was then. For the first time in many decades, the governing elite is no longer able to ignore the public's demands for more individual rights and freedoms, and a burgeoning middle class is increasingly dissatisfied with simply material well-being. To accommodate these new demands will require loosening aspects of political control that the political system has so far been very cautious to nudge. This is in large part because of the rise of internal corruption as a central concern of the average Chinese, affecting everything from social welfare provisions to sustaining a fair education system. The incentives for those with political access and power are generally skewed toward preserving their considerable privileges rather than enfranchising the majority of Chinese. In the first decade of the 21st century in particular, the balance of the distribution of wealth has tilted toward those in or closely associated with the political class. It is a sufficiently pervasive and apparent problem that, as the public opinion polls reflect, it has become a focal point of popular resentment. The outgrowth of this phenomenon is that the state, over the last several years, decided to extend and intensify its controls over society to prevent major fissures that could result from this sense of growing political and social inequality.

Yet the more the state doubles down on maintaining stability, the more the public bristles at its intrusion into private life, as the past several years of rising protests and other types of collective action across China demonstrate. The proliferation of bottom-up demands has been aided by the arrival of the information age in China. Never before in China's recent history has the state been so challenged to maintain its credibility and trust as today, when it faces a public equipped with social media tools and information technology. Whether the public is right or wrong on any given issue is irrelevant, government response is nonetheless tested. Government actions and statements must now pass a rigorous bullshit test in the court of public opinion or be subject to mockery or even outright hostility.

These new developments are forcing the government to respond more effectively and to allow for a degree of individual freedoms that a control-obsessed political apparatus has historically been loath to dispense. Underlying its resistance is the fear of the unknown if certain actions were taken: If society outgrows the state and functions more autonomously, what sort of role will be reserved for the state? For a political system that has long been accustomed to dictating social freedoms and monopolizing the flow of information, it is understandable that the growing pluralism of society presents clear risks to the functioning of the existing system.

The examples of China's Asian neighbors are also instructive. Japan, South Korea, and Taiwan all confronted similar governance challenges during their periods of modernization, as rising standards of living, a better educated population, and a more complex urban economy made single-party rule increasingly untenable. Compounding the governance challenge is the relentlessness of instant information—a factor that none of China's Asian Tiger forebears had to manage during their transitions from relatively authoritarian regimes to more open and transparent ones. Whether the Chinese government can still maintain its resilience and adapt in the brave new world of social pluralism hinges, paradoxically, on its capacity to tolerate a freer society.

A decade of harmony?

If China's former President Hu Jintao had a doctrine, it would arguably be harmonious society (*hexie shehui*), a concept that is so wide ranging and vague that its meaning is difficult to pin down. In its simplest sense, the doctrine is meant to narrow the cleavages in Chinese society, particularly growing inequality, and engineer more sustainable growth. It channels a longstanding notion in ancient Chinese thought, harmony, and adapts it to the contemporary need to clean up the detritus of breakneck development. The intention was that an all-encompassing doctrine would spawn a set of policies that address environmental degradation, wasteful energy consumption, income inequality, social protection, and government accountability. All of these were factors that, if left to fester, could shake the political system.

But fester they did. The decade of the Panda Boom following harmonious society's introduction in 2002, when Hu officially rose to power, was characterized by runaway GDP growth, hitting a jaw-dropping peak of 13% in 2007. It was also a decade that saw widening income inequality, rising energy intensity (the amount of energy it takes to produce one unit of GDP), China eclipsing the United States as the world's leading emitter of greenhouse gases, rising incidence of air pollution-induced lung disease cases, severe water pollution,[6] and the extinction of the Yangtze freshwater dolphin the *Baiji*.[7] The litany of uncomfortable facts goes on, and few seem to comport with the harmonious society agenda.

To be fair, the Hu administration had attempted to realize its version of harmony. Its foremost efforts were encapsulated in the 11th Five-Year Plan, released just ahead of Hu's second term in 2006. This economic blueprint emphasized balancing economic development with resource and environmental considerations and more equally dividing the spoils of economic wealth. Beyond the plan, attempts were also made to establish a measure of "green GDP," incorporating the environmental costs of growth into GDP calculations and linking local politicians' performance to achieving sustainability.

But when the environment ministry published a report that claimed environmental costs factored in China's green GDP amounted to 3% of the economy or more, it immediately triggered a political firestorm. A large swath of data in China is deemed politically sensitive, and this one, so potentially damaging for local politicians' prospects of promotions during a key political transition period in 2007, was especially so.[8] Generating growth was one of the most important criteria for determining promotions and future political prospects, and a new metric that lowers measured growth was a guaranteed mortal enemy of the nomenklatura. In other words, the built-in political incentives simply reinforced the Growth Imperative at each level of government. It was too powerful a force to stop, and too many benefited from the existing paradigm to allow the politics to be derailed.

Since then, talk of a green GDP has disappeared. And just like green GDP, many of the 11th Five-Year Plan's other well-intentioned and relatively bold initiatives were essentially dead on arrival. When a global financial crisis inconveniently intervened in China's growth trajectory in 2008, any lingering concerns about sustainability were readily abandoned as the entire ship of state steered toward full-throttled growth.

The Pavlovian default reversion to growth-focused policy did not occur in a vacuum, of course. It had serious ramifications for the public's social and political freedoms, in large part because the existing economic model did not address one of the central aspects of Hu's agenda—recalibrating social equality.[9] In fact, society became even less harmonious under Hu's watch, forcing the state to adjust and deliver harmony by other means.

Stability Inc.

Alongside the Growth Imperative sits the *Stability Mandate*, the only other criterion that counts nearly as much as growth in determining a CCP cadre's political prospects. Stability is a tall order in today's China: The promotion of growth has engendered social discontent, undermining rather than strengthening stability. The government has apparently taken notice of this paradox. Since the financial crisis, not only has there been a noticeable uptick in official language directing attention to stability maintenance (*weiwen*), the words have been backed by action and resources from the authorities.[10]

In 2011, China allocated 624 billion yuan ($100 billion) for domestic public security, a 14% increase from the previous year and over 6% of total public spending, higher than healthcare spending. By contrast, China's reported defense budget in the same year was 601 billion yuan (less than $100 billion).[11] Spending on domestic security and national defense was projected to hit $111 billion and $106 billion in 2012, respectively.[12] Of the $100 billion public security budget, about 70% went to domestic police and the paramilitary force, the People's Armed Police (PAP), while the courts and judicial functions received a much smaller fraction. On matters of law and order, there isn't much competition—order wins by a wide margin, at least in terms of resource allocation.

Such an emphasis on order trickles down all the way from the top. To get a sense of just how seriously the CCP takes weiwen, one need look no further than the powerful Political and Legal Affairs Committee (PLAC) of the Central Committee, which has control of the entire internal security apparatus. An official order from the central government in the early 1990s granted the PLAC authority over social management (*shehui guanli*) and weiwen. Since then, the central organ has grown very influential, even as its actions and how it truly functions remain opaque.

Meng Jianzhu, the Politburo member who now sits atop its helm, is one of China's two dozen or so most powerful leaders (his predecessor in the post, Zhou Yongkang, was even a Politburo Standing

Committee member, one of the nine men at the top of the last administration). It could be argued that the government of Xi Jinping has downgraded the status of public security by "only" appointing a Politburo member to head the PLAC, signaling a moderation in the security apparatus's influence. But even so, the weiwen system has grown so large, so complex, so embedded into every level of government operations that it cannot be easily taken out of the fabric of the political system. A broad political consensus ensures the existence of the weiwen system in China, a situation that perhaps parallels the rise of the Department of Homeland Security in the United States. Given China's scale and population movements, some form of domestic security is inevitable, especially as the sort of "rightful resistance"[13] among Chinese citizens continues to grow into thematically related, yet independently organized sporadic outbursts of violence.

In fact, it is precisely to contain these outbursts that China has poured more resources behind the PAP. After 1989, it was decided that the People's Liberation Army (PLA) should not be mobilized for handling domestic riots or rebellions, particularly as the handling of the student demonstrations severely tarnished its reputation. Since then, even as the CCP has methodically erased that episode from national memory, it has sought to separate the functions of national security, with the PLA engaging almost exclusively in national defense and foreign adventurism and the PAP taking the lead on internal security. To be sure, the PAP has other mandates such as disaster relief and countering domestic terrorism. But ultimately, its role as domestic peacekeeper has become its predominant function. Estimated to be more than 1 million strong, the PAP is probably now roughly half the size of the PLA and is dispatched around the country. PAP presence can seem ubiquitous, especially in major cities like Beijing. Their general mode of transportation is a government-issued SUV or an ostentatious luxury import bearing the plates of WJ (*wujing*) in red, followed by a series of black numbers.[14]

But the weiwen program reaches far beyond the PAP, comprising a sprawling network of central and local functionaries. A patchwork of central government agencies is involved in stability maintenance, including the ministries of public security, railway, and justice. The budgetary spoils are divided among these various agencies, but it is impossible to know what the actual divisions are. This is of course deliberate. It is meant to blur the lines between general public security and weiwen and prevents observers outside China's leadership from tracking down just how much is being spent. The system also has cells down the political hierarchy to the local counties and townships. Its reach is perhaps as impressive as it is intimidating.[15]

The preservation of stability usually does not involve overt force, at least not anymore. In fact, it is as much about "soft" coercion as it is about forceful repression.[16] Myriad tactics (other than overt force) are now employed to intimidate and suppress, including house arrests, detaining selective "activists," and neutralizing cross-provincial linkages of organizations and networks that could be politically destabilizing. If local authorities can preempt protests or petitioners by buying off the right people, they will do so. If not, the leaders of protests are often arrested and made examples of to prevent future action. Less understood and perhaps more disconcerting is the practice of outsourcing stability maintenance to local "private" entities—thugs or henchmen—who operate far beyond legal boundaries. Some of the behaviors are not so dissimilar from how elements of a mafia or banana republic would operate, an approach that risks further alienating the governed from the government. It is clearly a highly flawed system that is more about whack a mole than addressing underlying causes of social discontent.

Whether the huge amount of resources invested in weiwen is yielding results is questionable. One measure that the government used as a rough gauge of social discontent is the *mass incidents* metric. Another term without a concrete definition, mass incidents are usually interpreted as localized public disturbances, including protests, riots, or other acts of collective action involving 100 or more people. The last year in which China released official figures was in 2005, when 87,000 such incidents took place, up significantly from fewer than 9,000 a decade earlier.[17]

For the past several years, the Ministry of Public Security has apparently declined to publish the figures. Occasional information slipping into the public domain, though, reinforces the popular perception that mass incidents have increased. In 2011, for example, a sociologist from China's prestigious Tsinghua University, Sun Liping, publicly estimated that such incidents may have risen to 180,000 in

2010, or nearly 500 a day.[18] The central government's own silence on the issue, as well as its spending priorities, also fuel speculation that the problem has worsened.

While the central government largely foots the bill for supporting the PAP, it is still the local governments that dole out most of the funds for the overall weiwen system (see Tables 9.1 and 9.2).[19] In fact, provincial governments outspent the central government on stability measures to the tune of three to one in 2011. In some localities, such as Jiangyin City in southern Jiangsu Province, special funds have been set up to support a discrete weiwen office within the local public security bureau. In another district in Guangdong Province, of the 6,700 employees on the local government's payroll, about 25% were employed in some form of stability maintenance. Local authorities' preoccupation with stability again reflects the political incentives folded into a system that ensures the weiwen agenda receives priority.

Table 9.1   Central spending on public security

	2010 (yuan)	2011 projected (yuan)	+/– %
Central government	87.5 billion	102.4 billion	+17.1
Fiscal transfer to local government	60 billion	59.3 billion	–1.2
Total spending	147.5 billion	161.7 billion	+9.6

Table 9.2   Local spending on public security

	2010 (yuan)	2011 projected (yuan)	+/– %
PAP	23.5 billion	26.2 billion	+11.3
Police	273 billion	311.5 billion	+14
Court system	53.2 billion	60.2 billion	+13
Legal administration	15.7 billion	17.4 billion	+11
Anti-smuggling police	3 million	3 million	0
Other spending	6.4 billion	7 billion	+9.5

Source: *Caijing*, May 2011

The fiscal cost of maintaining such a system is readily apparent. Tsinghua's Sun, who incidentally was purportedly an academic advisor to future-President Xi Jinping during his doctoral studies, has railed repeatedly against the elevation of weiwen, arguing that it could be fiscally crippling. He cited that as early as 2007, Guangzhou, the capital of Guangdong Province, was already spending 4.4 billion yuan ($700 million) on stability, surpassing its social welfare funding that year of 3.5 billion yuan ($556 million).[20] Another expert at the Chinese Academy of Social Sciences, a leading state think tank, seems to agree:

> In many cases, local governments spent a lot of money under pressure to maintain stability. Although there are no authoritative statistics on nationwide cost of maintaining stability, we can get an idea by looking at some regions where fiscal funding for stability maintenance has exceeded public spending aimed at improving the people's livelihood. Such phenomena have become commonplace. It is especially worth noting that some malpractices, including public humiliation, which date back to the Cultural Revolution, have been revived. The maintenance of stability has not only created rent-seeking opportunities for some government officials and departments, but also served as a [sic] leverage for local governments to bargain with the central government for more resources.[21]

In the battle for limited fiscal resources, weiwen has won out over social welfare lately, hampering Beijing's ability to make good on its pledge to increase spending on the latter. Yet just as long-term central spending on healthcare and pensions will be unsustainable in a country the size of China, so too will endless spending for the Chinese version of homeland security.

The recent turn toward more coercive means to impose social stability is as much a reflection of the state's formidable powers as its underlying insecurity. For all the changes to Chinese politics, the political system fundamentally remains one that distrusts the broad mobilization of its own people. Judging by its recent behaviors, one may conclude that such fears have deepened. A more stifling internal security approach has been pursued to treat, often harshly, what the state perceives as various symptoms of social instability.[22] It systematically and efficiently metes out punishment to those deemed anti-state elements. Even as the state turns the screws tighter on society, it is also becoming apparent that such a reactive approach is unsustainable and combustible.

This is because the state and the party appear to be engaged in a protracted battle against an emerging social consciousness of rights and individual freedoms. These social attitudes are solidifying into demands and expectations faster than the political system can keep up. While true libertarians are hard to come by in China, many Chinese now expect a basic level of freedom for their speech, property, and civic participation. A revolution in communication technology, particularly social media, has allowed millions of Chinese to broadcast views and vote with their virtual feet. In essence, the government is increasingly in a contest with society over competing "truths." It is no surprise then that a central mandate of the weiwen project is to control information and curtail the Internet. But a growing proportion of the Chinese public is not following orders.

The "average Zhou" pushes back

The Arab Spring of 2010-2011 was a political contagion like few others—an organic virus transmitted via social media technology, infecting populations from Tunisia to Cairo at an exponential rate. As events unfolded thousands of miles away in the Middle East, leaders in Beijing were jittery. It wasn't because they saw mirror images of China in the social paroxysms enveloping the Arab world. After all, China was a development and growth wunderkind compared to Egypt or Yemen. The average Chinese had a higher income and has lived most of her life in an era of rising prosperity. What's more, few Chinese demand an actual alternative to the existing political system.

But the Arab uprising contained two elements that Beijing easily recognized. The first was the street vendor setting himself on fire on the streets of Tunisia. That single catalyst of the subsequent political cataclysm starkly reminded Beijing of the growing number of self-immolation cases among ethnic Tibetans as well as Han Chinese.

The second and more important source of Chinese leaders' anxieties was the remarkable power of communication technology and social media to foment large-scale, unpredictable social movements on display in the Arab Spring. Like some authoritarian countries of the Middle East, China has seen an explosion of both protest and social media over the past decade. The statistics regarding the latter are particularly dizzying: nearly 1 billion mobile phone users, about half a billion Internet users, and roughly 300 million users of Sina *weibo*, the Chinese Twitter.[23] Sina's microblogging service, which barely existed four years ago, now claims a user base that is the size of the entire United States:

Internet users: 538 million as of mid-2012, expanded 867 times over the past 15 years. Penetration rate is 40%.

Rural Internet users: 146 million.

Mobile device-based Internet users: 388 million, surpassing traditional desktop-based Internet access for the first time. More people are also using mobile devices to watch videos and TV, up by a third from 2011.

Average time spent on Internet per week: 19.9 hours, up from 18.7 in 2011 (see Figures 9.2 and 9.3).[24]

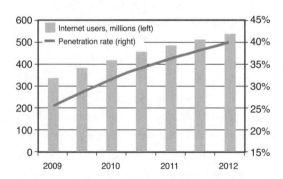

Figure 9.2   Total Internet users and Internet penetration rate

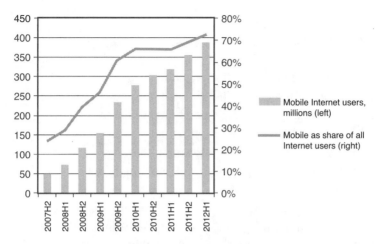

Figure 9.3   Internet users on mobile devices

Source: China Internet Network Information Center (CNNIC)

The staggering growth of the Internet and social media platforms caught most by surprise, including the Chinese government. From the outset, the government clearly understood that allowing the Internet to proliferate was good economics, but politically it was a major gamble. Their plan was to keep the Internet functional and useful while restricting it and somehow neutralizing its impact on society. This was the genesis of the infamous "Great Firewall" and a sophisticated censorship system doggedly working overtime to keep sensitive information away from the public.[25]

Even under these conditions, the scale and pace of Internet and telecommunications growth meant that efforts to prohibit and restrict access are often undermined. Propaganda officials looking over the shoulders of newspaper editors can keep a tight grip on traditional media, but are much less effective when over 500 million people have the potential power to make themselves heard directly and simultaneously. Short of completely shutting down the network infrastructure, the government has had to tolerate the fact that its censorship system, although first rate, was nonetheless porous. What's more, a small minority of tech-savvy Chinese regularly navigate their way around the system, or "scale the wall" in Chinese Internet colloquialism, to gain access to a world of information not available within China's borders.

From the politicians' perspective, concerns over digital technology are entirely legitimate and necessary. Even before the recent upheavals in the Middle East, Beijing already got a hint of the potential power of the burgeoning communication revolution. It was manifested during the unprecedented and deadly ethnic riots in Urumqi, Xinjiang in 2009, when clashes between the Han majority and Uighur minority bloodied the streets of the provincial capital.[26] The events that unfolded in the western hinterland commanded such attention that then-President Hu unexpectedly cut short his trip to a G8 summit, rushing home to orchestrate an emergency response. Naturally, the PAP was dispatched and put down the unrest, albeit only after days of intense standoff and killings. When some semblance of peace was restored and officials took stock of what happened, some 150 lay dead and thousands had been injured, according to reports. The tragic violence also claimed a political casualty: the iron-fisted party chief of Xinjiang was axed.

How the riots were sparked in the first place was as shocking as the violence itself. From a factory brawl between Han and Uighur migrant workers in southern Guangdong, China's manufacturing belt, text messages traversed thousands of miles to bring the news to compatriots in Xinjiang, sparking an uproar within days. Word soon spread across the Internet and further inflamed the situation. Amid the intensifying violence, one of the first actions authorities took was to cut off the Internet, isolating Xinjiang so that little information could flow in or out.[27] The government was clearly afraid of the potential for uprisings to ripple across other parts of the country, becoming uncontainable. What if latent ethnic nationalism were to boil to the surface and Han Chinese sought revenge in other parts of China? Given that cell phones and the Internet can transmit a call to arms in only minutes, the unthinkable could happen faster than the government could contain it. For the security state, this could have easily become a spiraling crisis. The choice was simple: The government had to resolutely and swiftly pull the plug.

The underlying fear of communication technology and the Internet had always been centered around their potential and real capacity to facilitate organized collective action. While the Chinese government is usually (and surprisingly, to foreign observers) tolerant of domestic online criticism and complaints, lately even encouraging it, a disgruntled citizen who moves from rhetoric to organized action steps across that "red line" of permissibility and into the arms of the weiwen system. Likewise, efforts to create the kind of civil society that could contend with the state, especially with its ability to manipulate information, are verboten. From the regime's perspective, the penetration of social media has distressingly blurred the boundaries between common grumbling, passive dissent, subversion, and proactive organized action. In the case of the Xinjiang riots, the Internet could have transmitted and exacerbated a "separatist" cause or ethnic vengeance.

That concern was also at the heart of how the Chinese state reacted to the calls for "Jasmine" revolution during the height of the Arab Spring. The rumors of an organized homemade Jasmine revolution, spread on the Internet in early 2011, sounded like advocacy of regime change and obviously could not be tolerated. The security apparatus was rattled, with police force showing up in areas in Beijing where rallies were supposed to be held. Keywords such as *jasmine,* and in fact many types of flower names, readily disappeared from search engines.

Instead, very little happened. At the appointed time, the only unusual crowds at the designated protest sites were of foreign journalists taking pictures of each other being harassed by swarms of plainclothes police officers. The intense foreign media attention again fueled the suspicion among some Chinese intellectuals that the Americans were really behind the Arab Spring. In a stroke of irony, then-U.S. Ambassador Jon Huntsman was incidentally caught on camera amid the crowds; he happened to be wearing a leather bomber jacket with a large American flag decal stitched on the sleeve. The video went viral, and so did the interpretation of his presence among the Chinese.[28]

Ultimately, nothing like the Arab Spring took place in China. But the intensity and resources dedicated to suppressing it reflect a sense of acute unease from the top towards a less-predictable, less-controllable public. That's because the Chinese government, particularly the security components, knows all too well that it now confronts the unprecedented and unsettling prospect of an era of social media.

From 100 flowers to 100 million weibos

As of this writing, at least, we are unaware of a rigorous and systematic study of the extent of the power and influence of Chinese social media on Chinese politics and society. But it is plain to see that social media has, at the very least, dramatically expanded the scope and boldness of speech in China. Outspoken speech and criticism of the government, once a treacherous rhetorical terrain, has now been trampled by hundreds of millions of tweets. The success and proliferation of social media in China is not because it is technologically novel or sophisticated per se, but because it fills a public need that previously had been denied Chinese citizens: the latitude and freedom to spout opinions and lodge serious critiques of society and the state. Weibo's political salience is in its powerful ability to shift the power of information and its dissemination into the hands of the public. In other words, it is the most potent propaganda and official-speak neutralizing agent the government has ever faced. Propaganda has never been as difficult as it is in this environment. The government senses, rightly, that its credibility is being eroded.

Scale also matters. Although China so far has punched below its weight in terms of groundbreaking technological innovation, it excels at digesting existing technology. Social media are no exception. Chinese social media platforms such as RenRen and Tencent's QQ are widely popular, in large part because they are incubated domestically and sheltered from competitors like Facebook and Google. Both reportedly count more than 100 million users as their members. But the organization most emblematic of how social media is shaping the political economy of China is Sina Corp., whose Twitter-like service weibo and its 300 million-plus users have become a free-for-all marketplace of commentary, an oblique and subversive challenger to official rhetoric, and amazingly, even an occasional shaper of public policy.

The formidable controls the state imposes on Chinese social media make a "weibo revolution" akin to what swept through the Levant highly unlikely. But social media's ability to hold the government accountable and answerable for its actions is still a tectonic change. In a December 2011 piece in the *Atlantic Monthly*, we observed that although the Chinese government averted the "anti-incumbent contagion" then sweeping the non-democratic world from the Middle East to Russia, the government was clearly facing real bottom-up pressures:

> 2011 was arguably the year in which the Chinese Twitterati found a voice and flashed its teeth, not to overtly challenge the state's legitimacy, but to hold it more accountable than it prefers. In the absence of a robust legal system, the government is now being forced to answer [for] itself in the court of public opinion.[29]

In many ways, the Chinese public, or at least the urban elites, are voting with their digital fingers, 140 Chinese characters at a time. On issues of public safety and environmental concerns, in particular, the weight of public opinion is increasingly acknowledged and even accommodated by officials determining policy.

Fast and furious...and deadly

The story of China's flagship high-speed rail (HSR) program sits at the nexus of the Growth Imperative, technological ambition, and bureaucratic and political interests.[30] The economic justification behind the project seemed convincing at face value. China had a shortage of rail capacity, and with urbanization projected to continue full throttle, rising population density meant that HSR could be economically competitive with flights along many routes. At the same time, fielding a state-of-the-art HSR system would elevate China into a league of select, elite nations that have the technological and managerial prowess to run such a system. For the environmentally minded, electrified public transport appealed as an alternative to burning jet fuel. The fundamentals were exciting and potentially highly rewarding.

Even more so, the politics were overwhelming. The charismatic party secretary of the railway ministry, Liu Zhijun, had a personal vested interest in seeing the project through because he could provide patronage and win political allies by awarding contracts to those in his network. It so happened that he ran the railway ministry, one of China's most powerful bureaucracies, one that behaved more like an independent fiefdom than a state apparatus subject to political checks and balances. Although other officials similarly pushed boundaries to expand their own political and bureaucratic turf, Liu's ambition was of a different scale. If successful, the project would enrich him personally and politically, as the godfather of China's first HSR.[31]

But it wasn't enough that the project was getting done, it also had to be done fast. When Liu took office in the mid-2000s, he decided that developing HSR technology indigenously was moving too slowly. He promptly switched tactics and decided to acquire foreign technology from the German, Japanese, and Canadian industry leaders, who were willing to risk transferring intellectual property in exchange for access to China's enormously lucrative market.[32] Starting in 2006, the ministry spent billions of dollars, some of which came directly from the State Council, on technology transfer fees and buying up whole trains intact so that they could be tweaked and reverse engineered. Over the next four and a half years, rail was laid at a furious pace to be ready for the slick bullet trains' arrival in 2010. That year alone the railway ministry spent over $1 billion on the project.

China had targets to meet. In its 2008 revision to the Medium- to Long-Term Plan on Rail Networks, Beijing by 2020 wanted a total of 75,000 miles (120,000 kilometers) of rail and raised its goal for passenger-dedicated lines from 7,500 miles (12,000 kilometers) to 10,000 miles (16,000 kilometers), the majority of which would be high-speed, defined as reaching speeds of 200km/h or above.[33] The global financial crisis of 2008 was a windfall for Liu, who convinced the top leadership that colossal shovel-ready infrastructure projects like the HSR should be expedited to boost growth. As a result, the target for the rail network was raised to 16,000 kilometers (see Figure 9.4). Backroom deals to award the bonanza of contracts meant that Liu and his affiliates could pocket massive kickbacks.

The 350km/h bullet trains, all named Harmony Express, captivated the attention of the world when they went into service in early 2010. In the United States, the contrast to America's decrepit and aging infrastructure and Amtrak's creaky, crawling service was especially stark. Coming at a time when the U.S. economy was flat on its back, and much of its financial system partly nationalized, the Chinese trains inevitably invited turtle-and-hare comparisons, spawning gushing approval in column after column in the U.S. media.[34]

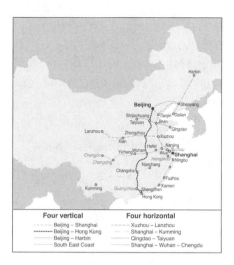

Figure 9.4   High-speed rail route map

Source: Marketwatch

Just when it looked as if Liu had scored a huge personal political victory while elevating China's global status, the high came crashing down, literally. One bullet train fatally rear-ended another that was idling on the track because of a signal malfunction on a rainy July night in southern China. At least 40 passengers were killed and hundreds more critically injured. The once shiny symbol of China's technological progress became a pile of corrugated steel and iron dangling precariously off of its track, taking on an ominous new meaning. The aftermath of the accident received extraordinary coverage both domestically and from the foreign press. Even though Minister Liu had been sacked for corruption earlier that year, his legacy of mismanagement and crony capitalism was clearly implicated in the fatalities (the Chinese court recently handed Liu a "suspended death sentence").[35]

That political corruption and hasty execution led to such a tragedy isn't surprising. What was unexpected was the public reaction that seemed, for the first time, to force accountability on a government unaccustomed to providing convincing answers. Domestic furor was initially in reaction to the crash recovery, which was bungled from the start when the Ministry of Railways apparently ordered one of the trains and other mangled parts to be buried, leading to widespread suspicions of what was not being told to the public. Some of the liberal, independent press defied government censorship and ran cover stories of the tragedy. One stirring op-ed from the highly respected *Economic Observer* captured the zeitgeist of the moment by directly confronting state propaganda, which was then touting the rescue of a two-year-old named Yiyi:

> Yiyi, when you've grown up and started to understand this world, how should we explain to you everything that happened on July 23, 2011? That train that would never arrive, it took away 40 lives that loved and were loved, including your parents. When you're grown, will we and this country we live in be able to honestly tell you about all the love and suffering, anger and doubts around us?

> ...Now, Yiyi, on behalf of you lying there on that sickbed and those lives buried in the ground, people are refusing to give up on finding the truth. Truth cannot be buried—no one plans to give up the inquiry. We know that anything we take lightly today might lead to our rights being violated and our lives being ignored again tomorrow. We reap what we sow. If every fact we seek becomes a secret, we'll never know the truth...

> To live—to live with dignity—is that rainbow you get to see only after suffering through the wind and the rain. Yiyi, when you're older maybe you'll realize that dark night of July 23 was when things started to change. After that day, we won't simply complain, but instead learn how to advocate and act. We understand that we have rights, we respect these rights and will spare no effort to protect them.[36]

The publication of such transparently critical sentiment in traditional media was only possible because of the many who, armed with mobile technology, had already knocked the state off balance with unsparing criticism in the weibo-verse. From celebrity blogger and race car sensation Han Han to ordinary citizens with a Sina app, instant photos and commentary spread like wildfire, fully undermining the initial official story of a weather-related incident. If that were true, why were authorities in a hurry to bury the marred trains? Were they getting rid of evidence? A particularly acerbic critique from Han Han took the government to task:

They think: "During the Qing dynasty, no one had television. Now everyone has a television. Progress!"

They think: "We're building you all this stuff, what do you care what happens in the process? Why should you care who it's really for, so long as you get to use it? The train from Shanghai to Beijing used to take a whole day. Now you're there in five hours (as long as there's no lightning). Why aren't you grateful? What's with all the questions?

"Every now and then, there's an accident. The top leaders all show how worried they are... Why do you want us to apologize when we haven't done anything wrong? It's the price of development...

A friend in the state apparatus told me, "You're all too greedy. Forty years ago, writers like you would've been shot. So you tell me, have things gotten better, or have they gotten worse?" I said, "No, you're all too greedy. Ninety years ago, that kind of thinking would have gotten you laughed out of the room. So you tell me: after all that, have things gotten better, or have they gotten worse?"[37]

The Crash of Wenzhou, or what has since been dubbed the "7.23 incident," became an awakening of sorts. For many Chinese, the accident symbolized something larger: That for all the breathless economic development speeding along at bullet train pace, the public continues to feel that it is being left behind. The Chinese economic miracle that has captured the world's attention is no longer so compelling to a large portion of Chinese. For more than a generation, Chinese society has been propelled forward by economic inertia, constantly adjusting to discombobulating change. Few had paused to seriously consider what those changes meant for the very fabric of society or how they have altered the individual. Call it the "rapid development malaise." The 7.23 incident crystallized an unarticulated sentiment being felt across the country. It became a political watershed because individuals' feelings were amplified and multiplied through a medium that was not available before.

The impact was tremendous. It was the first time that the public truly realized the transformative power such a communication tool could have on public discourse. It was also when the government woke up to the fact that it had underestimated weibo's sociopoliti-cal effects. After it became clear that the railway ministry botched its post-disaster recovery, Beijing sent top leaders including former Premier Wen Jiabao himself to appear in Wenzhou, assuage public concern, and pledge transparent disclosure of what went wrong.

Shortly thereafter, the central government announced that it is slowing down HSR investment, a public concession to popular pres-sure. But the damage to the government's credibility was already done. Even the official CCTV, usually guarded and conservative in its commentary, dared to weigh in with politically charged words that went viral. They underscored a shifting social paradigm that will increasingly come to define the central challenge facing the political system:

> If nobody can be safe, do we still want this speed? Can we drink a glass of milk that's safe? Can we stay in an apartment that will not fall? Can the roads we travel on in our cities not collapse? Can we travel in safe trains? And if and when a major accident does happen, can we not be in a hurry to bury the trains? Can we afford the people a basic sense of security? China, please slow down. If you're too fast, you may leave the souls of your people behind.[38]

Give me PM 2.5 or give me death

Beijing is a bellwether of China's future. With a GDP of about $250 billion and per capita GDP of nearly $13,000, Beijing is a quint-essential middle-class Chinese metropolis. It has all the trappings and luxuries to accommodate an increasingly cosmopolitan and status-conscious population. Replete with art districts, underground punk rockers, boutique cafes, and an overeducated citizenry, the city's residents would find more in common with New Yorkers or Washing-tonians than with their Chinese brethren in Guizhou. The city never stopped after the 2008 Olympics; it kept on demolishing, building, and racing forward, each new facade unrecognizable to any visitor who stayed away longer than six months.

Despite incessant changes, one element remained stubbornly the same: the haze that perennially envelops the city. Beijing's air is notoriously fetid. Trapped between the hills surrounding the city, the atmosphere hangs still and vacillates between a yellowish and grayish hue. Occasionally, rain or a northern air front descending from Mongolia will allow the sun to poke through. Some Beijing residents wear facemasks to cope with the noxious air. But all have noticed that their city's sky rarely matched the deep azure of photographs. By most accounts, the conditions have deteriorated in recent years.

Beijing urbanized in a hurry, adding millions of cars to its already traffic-choked ring roads during the Panda Boom. The municipal environmental bureau still insisted in 2011 that Beijing achieved 274 "blue sky" days—a statistic that was completely at odds with the public's empirical observations.[39] According to the city's environmental officials, the amount of PM 10, or tiny particulate matter smaller than 10 micrometers, declined and the city had three weeks of grade I air quality. In other words, a bang-up job by the government in cleaning up the environment.

But Beijingers weren't buying it, not only because the sky's color was a constant reminder of the government's false claims, but also because many had turned to a source that they found more credible on air quality. That was the U.S. embassy, which since 2009 had installed an air monitoring system that tracked PM 2.5, a much smaller and more hazardous air pollutant, broadcasting daily results on its Twitter feed ostensibly to help its own diplomats protect their health. (As of June 2013, the embassy's air quality Twitter feed had over 34,000 followers.) The PM 2.5 results were usually much worse than the official PM 10 readings. In fact, there were several occasions in which the air pollution was so off the charts that the embassy's tweeter undiplomatically described it as "crazy bad" (maybe someone put the intern in charge of the account that day).[40]

Although an undiplomatic stunt for the U.S. embassy, it was the Chinese government who was more flummoxed. Beijing dealt with the unintended discrediting of its public health propaganda with a timeless tactic: blasting U.S. interference in its domestic affairs and violation of Chinese laws.[41] Indeed, a spokesperson for the environmental ministry insisted that the U.S. embassy stop publishing its PM 2.5 data. That this seemingly innocuous issue unexpectedly escalated into a minor diplomatic kerfuffle reflects, on some level, the Chinese government's sensitivity and awareness of the growing credibility gap with its own people. It could no longer persuade its public of the reliability of its metric. And worse of all, it was being undermined by the Americans, one tweet at a time.

Indeed, adding to the frustration was precisely the fact that the more the government criticized the U.S. data, the more curious Chinese netizens and weibo-ers sought out the information. Much like the bullet train incident, Chinese Internet users and the Twitterati began questioning why the Beijing government's own PM 2.5 data wasn't released. Was it afraid that if released, the data would be so horrific that Beijing couldn't risk the public backlash? The public had reasons to be suspicious, as it turned out that the Beijing and Shanghai governments had already begun privately monitoring PM 2.5 but were not releasing the data publicly. The explanation, according to *Guangzhou Daily,* was that the "time wasn't ripe," implying that the data would not sit well with the public.[42]

From the vantage point of the Chinese government, it seemed as if the Chinese public wasn't mature enough to handle accurate statistics that reflected the inevitable consequences of unbridled growth, which after all had made their relatively pampered lifestyles possible. Unfortunately for the government, such self-willed opacity is no longer acceptable to a middle class with alternative sources of information and higher expectations for governance. Ultimately, the government caved. In early 2012, then-Premier Wen announced at a meeting of the State Council, China's cabinet, that the government would begin tracking PM 2.5, even as the majority of Chinese provinces cannot hope to meet the standard. Whether the government will enforce compliance in meeting PM 2.5 standards and dutifully report the data remains to be seen. But the announcement marks at least a partial victory for the public in the contest of dictating the terms of public policy.

The PM 2.5 case wasn't the only victory the people scored against the government regarding environmental rights. A Chinese version of NIMBYism (not in my backyard) appears to be on the rise. A former Ministry of Environmental Protection official recently revealed that since 1996, environment-related mass incidents have increased at an average rate of 29% a year. Since 2005, the environment ministry had received 927 cases, and the number of cases in 2011 shot up 120% over the previous year.[43] As this trend continues, in large part because China's legal system cannot adequately handle these cases, the era of unhinged industrialization will be forced to adjust to more challenges from citizens in the streets.

In mid-2012, a representative protest took place in Shifang, a city in southwestern Sichuan Province that lies close to Wenchuan, the site of a devastating earthquake in 2008. While such a case wasn't particularly unique—in fact, similar protests in Xiamen and Dalian preceded it—Shifang grabbed attention because 10,000 people reportedly amassed to protest over *environmental rights,* an issue that until then had rarely inspired collective action in China. Shifang residents were railing against a new copper plant that was being planned by a major Chinese company. It would've uprooted thousands of peasants, and even more concerning, put the area's water system at high risk of metal pollution.

With banners inscribed with "Give us back our community," the protest was live-tweeted on weibo with photos and videos instantly uploaded showing protesters injured at the rough hands of the riot police.[44] After a couple days of standing their ground, the people of Shifang triumphed as the local party secretary announced that the plant was not to go forward. Throughout the ordeal, Shifang had many sympathizers and supporters, one of whom was Han Han. In his characteristic biting prose, Han again set the tone for criticizing the inadequacies of the local government:

> People's requests for improving their environment must be respected. You leaders change every few years. You take on environmental destruction with nice-looking certificates of achievement. If you do well you get promoted, if you don't you get jail. The best of you emigrate, the worst of you are shot. But none of you actually live in the pollution. Only ordinary people live there. Even though you already stopped the plan to mine molybdenum copper, I think the pent-up public anger this project released comes from a deep-rooted animus that's about more than molybdenum copper. The proposed plant started it, but now it has become a mass incident.[45]

Shifang seemed to set a precedent. Just months after its protests were quelled, demonstrations sprung up in the wealthy coastal city of Ningbo over the planned expansion of a refinery owned by one of China's oil giant Sinopec.[46] Although the number of protesters was a fraction of those in Shifang, the rally still turned violent as angry Ning-boers engaged with the police. As with Shifang, photos quickly zipped across the Internet, portraying tense scenes of riot police facing down protesters.[47] In addition, the authorities seemed to have learned the lesson from previous incidents and ordered Sina to prevent photos from being uploaded on weibo. But it didn't take long before netizens started spreading the word about how to circumvent the technological restrictions.[48]

Coloring outside the lines

The Crash of Wenzhou was followed by the dramatic collapse of a stretch of new highway in Heilongjiang Province. The environmental activism of Shifang and Ningbo and the PM 2.5 incident appear to herald a new era of seriously questioning the longstanding Growth Imperative. Collectively, they reflect something greater than the sum of their parts. They sit at the intersection of a sociopolitical shift, abetted by technology, that will test the adaptability of the Chinese political system like never before.

A Chinese middle class, though still not even half of the country's population, already numbers in the hundreds of millions, most of whom are located along the coastal belt of wealthy China. As with middle classes in other countries, they tend to be agents of change. In China's case, its middle class is maturing amid a communication technology boom that previous middle class formations in the United States and elsewhere were not exposed to. This confluence could accelerate the emergence of a collective middle class consciousness that tests the governance model of a state that has always been at the forefront of constraining society. In some sense, China's middle-class denizens are following a textbook pattern found elsewhere in their demands and expectations of what ought to be considered "rights" and "freedoms." For instance, the much-hypothesized and controversial economic correlation between rising incomes and environmental consciousness—the so-called environmental Kuznets curve—may be arcing its course through China (see Figure 9.5).[49]

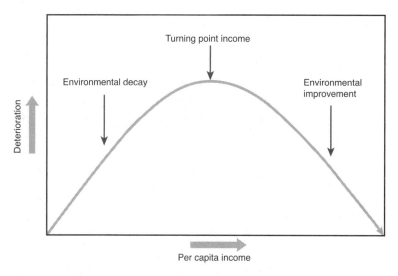

Figure 9.5 Environmental Kuznets curve

Source: Yandle, Vijayaraghavan, and Battarai, May 2002

The growth of society will prove disquieting for the state, especially its local authorities. Very few local officials have gotten the memo that their governance must adapt to rapidly changing public expectations. Instead, they continue to insist on the Stability Mandate and Growth Imperative. But in the weibo and Internet age, the underbelly of this state-society bargain is being exposed.[50] The tech-savvy middle class, broadcasting its discontent and criticism over web 2.0, is making protests and social incidents much harder to localize, embarrassing the authorities and possibly ruining their chances for career advancement. This is particularly disconcerting for a political system whose time-honored tactic of isolating collective action to prevent sweeping movements is now less effective.

Moreover, perhaps the most powerful effect of social media on China's politics is the corrosion of government credibility. Put another way, the weibo phenomenon has created a culture of cynicism and skepticism, which directly challenges the pro forma official-speak that is meant to shape public opinion. It has become embedded as a way of life, as the go-to platform for public debates, wild opinions, and what many believe to be more trustworthy information. It is a repository of what may have once been considered marginal voices, who are now discovering for the first time that like-minded sympathizers exist across the country.

The Shifang and Ningbo demonstrations, for example, were not the work of fringe environmental activists, but of ordinary members of the public who found approval even in an official Chinese media editorial. And finally, the fact that weibo is viewed as uniquely and indigenously Chinese, observed Internet rabble-rouser, blogger, and former Harvard Nieman Fellow Michael Anti, makes Chinese government claims of nefarious Western forces trying to split China ring hollow.[51] As one Chinese friend told the authors, "When people are bored or have a moment, they just check weibo to see what's going on. It is virtually second-nature now, people can't imagine what it would be like without it." Indeed, being able to use weibo provides a "core sense of security" to a large swath of the Chinese public, argues the *New Yorker*'s Evan Osnos.[52]

Is weibo too big to fail? Surely, the Chinese government can pull the plug if it chooses, just as it did during the Xinjiang fiasco. But that is the wrong question to pose in the first place. Social media is but a vessel that carries the expectations of the Chinese public efficiently and rapidly across a network of audiences who share similar concerns and grievances. Fundamentally, it is the new expectations of the governed that the government must now accommodate, not a new technology. The old grand bargain of delivering continued economic growth and expanding the pie to win fealty is fracturing. A significant and growing number of Chinese citizens appear to be waiting for a new social contract, one that prioritizes individual dignity and freedoms that have thus far been scarcely and haltingly dispensed.

In many instances, these demands are modest and seemingly trivial, such as the freedom to keep their golden retrievers. Yet when a government cannot even bend to these innocuous lifestyle freedoms, it is difficult to see how it can avoid a growing and unpleasant set of social pressures over the next decade. Whether it can relieve these pressures will be central to how the CCP can rebuild its credibility and sustain the popular mandate of a 21st century open Chinese society.

Conclusion

All your (economic) base are belong to us

China's political leaders have engineered a tremendously successful transition from a planned to a market-oriented economy, transforming from poor and predominantly rural to an at least half urban middle-income country along the way. But the unintended consequence of urbanization and liberalization of market forces on Chinese society is that it is being unrelentingly nudged in a more open and less-predictable direction. Karl Marx once postulated that a country's economic base determines its political superstructure. It is hard to imagine how the same old superstructure can stay firmly balanced on top of a new and somewhat wobbly base.

So, um, what's going to happen?

We conclude the book by sticking our necks out, gazing into the crystal ball of China's future in an attempt to describe the inevitable destination at the end of the road of reform and development that China's leaders have set out upon. Well, sort of.

Luckily for us, many forecasters have tread this treacherous path before. Unfortunately for us, virtually all have floundered. One prominent example was Gordon Chang's provocative *The Coming Collapse of China,* in which he cogently, if unapologetically one-sided, identified the myriad problems facing the country 12 years ago at the turn of the century:

> Peer beneath the veneer of modernization since Mao's death, and the symptoms of decay are everywhere: Deflation grips the economy, state-owned enterprises are failing, banks are

hopelessly insolvent, foreign investment continues to decline, and Communist party corruption eats away at the fabric of society...Beijing's cautious reforms have left the country stuck midway between communism and capitalism...[1]

Like in Chang's day, China today is confronted by seemingly intractable economic woes, a changing role in the world, and the uncertainty of managing it all with ostensibly inflexible and inadequate institutions. These incongruities are quickly apparent to new visitors and are brought into even sharper relief for those returning after a long absence.

At first glance, the Middle Kingdom is easy to mistake for the future. Its latest techno-wizardry and shiny high-tech toys are now regularly invoked as a reflection of the United States' own deficiencies. In U.S. President Barack Obama's 2013 State of the Union address, the sparse references to what China *is* doing (that is, renewable energy) were made exclusively to underscore what America *is not*. Scratch beneath China's surface, though, and much of the futuristic facade turns out to be quite thin.

For instance, the day after the Western world celebrated Christmas in 2012, China commenced the operation of the longest high-speed rail (HSR) route in the world, a 1,400 mile journey that snakes from arid Beijing to sultry Guangzhou.[2] A trip that took nearly 24 hours to complete on a standard train was cut to one-third the time. The trains do not symbolize breakthrough Chinese innovation or ingenuity per se (their technology was pioneered and commercialized long ago in the west), but rather a nation that is moving forward with purpose and ambition. One hundred years after Dr. Sun Yat-sen formed the first Chinese republic, China has marked another occasion in its steady return to global preeminence.

Once the spectacle ceases to dazzle, however, the social dislocation and inequality laid bare by China's showcase projects begin to illustrate how incomplete and imperfect the progress of its society and institutions are. The bullet trains are a perfect example. Unable to afford the fares, migrant workers on their infamous annual trek home for the Chinese New Year avoided the showy bullet trains in 2013, by and large tolerating the grueling journey on the old, overcrowded regular trains. Even the exceptions, like Gao Changliang and his family, proved the rule.[3]

The Gaos paid double the normal price for their HSR tickets because they were on a very special trip—the first return from Guangzhou to their native Henan Province in four years, and one that would mark the beginning of a long separation. Gao himself would be returning to Guangzhou after the holidays, where he would continue to work as a cab driver; his family would not because they still could not take part in urban life and the advantages it conferred. They hoped for a better future, but today the Gao family seems left on the periphery of China's boom. Their plight's destabilizing potential seems obvious. How can the center hold its line?

Twelve years ago, Chang predicted that it wouldn't: Ever deepening economic and social conflicts would eventually spill over, taking the whole system down. His forecast, however, was off by a mile and serves as a reminder of how perilous it is to predict where such a rapidly changing country will end up. Chang was spectacularly and thoroughly wrong. But many other prognosticators, too, seemed to have underestimated the Chinese government's own self-awareness and ability to adapt. Last time around, the political system managed its economic and social problems in what in retrospect seems like the only possible way: by allowing and accommodating earth-shattering change.

The economy was transformed: markets opened to foreign competition and foreign companies; state-owned enterprises restructured; banks listed on public exchanges, subject to heretofore unimaginable public scrutiny; and workers given tremendous freedom to take and leave employment at will. The Chinese Communist Party (CCP) harnessed the country's demographic dividend, attracted foreign capital and technologies, accepted market principles, and encouraged relatively unfettered trade, turning a limp economy into the growth wunderkind of the developing world. These forces set the broad trajectories that blossomed into the Panda Boom. Once launched, competent Chinese technocrats only had to occasionally fiddle with macroeconomic dials to maintain course. The country seemed virtually invincible and weathered cyclical downturn after downturn.

Growth was so resilient that China could literally grow out of problems that would have derailed another country's course.

Social progress was substantial as well. Personal freedoms expanded: Relocation from country to town and city became more possible than ever before. Within cities, average Chinese could live where they chose, if they could afford it, work where they chose, and marry and divorce who they chose. While media censorship remained intense, it became much less heavy-handed and intrusive than a decade earlier. Non-CCP members are still prohibited from organizing political movements, but nevertheless have unprecedented latitude to influence public discourse, and indirectly, public policy, through the rough and tumble world of social media.

The CCP still sees deftly managed change as its way forward, at least according to official rhetoric. In his final report to the 18th Party Congress, outgoing President Hu Jintao's rejoinder to his successors was a warning: "We must unflaggingly hold high the great banner of socialism with Chinese characteristics, both avoiding the closed and rigid old path as well as the evil path of abandoning our national flag and changing the guard."[4] If it is to perpetuate its enormous success, the CCP must keep just light enough of a touch on the reins: not so tight as to cause stagnation and discontent, but not so loose that it loses control of the country. It's a tall order, but we wouldn't bet against their long record of success: The party-state has already survived longer, and brought the country it controls further and stronger, than its skeptics could have imagined.

Embracing change: the basecase

For two generations, Chinese leaders single-mindedly focused on growing the economy and maintaining social stability. The CCP struck an implicit bargain with the Chinese people: If they put their faith in the party's stewardship of economic development, they would see more money lining their pockets, a more prosperous and respected nation, and stability. It was a call to do away with revolutions and begin wealth accumulation. When compared to what these generations suffered through previously—poverty, mass starvation, political tumult, and constant instability—that bargain struck a chord and enjoyed broad buy-in from the Chinese public.

It all seemed so easy because what had set the growth machine in motion was a fundamental change in economic institutions. That was, in fact, the central purpose of Deng Xiaoping's reforms: He allowed market and competitive institutions to operate alongside state institutions, and market institutions forced the state sector to change its behavior too. One of Deng's lasting contributions had been, in the words of economists Daron Acemoglu and James Robinson, creating conditions that produced "inclusive economic institutions" in which the great majority of the Chinese public became invested and participated in the development and wealth accumulation of their nation.[5] That political breakthrough drastically altered existing economic institutional arrangements, becoming an indispensable ingredient in the so-called China miracle.

That grand bargain is now showing signs of wear. While not assured, it seems most likely that China's new leadership not only sees an urgent need to build reform momentum, but also that incremental reforms could be more destabilizing down the line than bolder initiatives. Stasis is no longer an option. Collective recognition is growing among policymakers and political elites that the only way to alleviate the country's daunting economic and social malaise, as well as to ensure the resilience of the party-state itself, is to once again embrace change. Consequently, a new round of reforms that could pay economic, political, and social dividends as great as those that have propelled China for the past 30 years seems to be peeking over the horizon.[6] If you pushed us for a number, we give this outcome a seven out of ten chance.

Growth without abundance

Let's recount briefly why dramatic change is not only necessary but also demands some urgency. The most obvious reason is that none of the factors that fed the Panda Boom could last indefinitely, least of all the deliberately subsidized and finite supply of resources needed to satisfy China's economic appetite. It has long been a concern that Chinese growth has come at the expense of environmental sustainability and natural resources. Any Beijinger who has recently looked out her window at the dismayingly dense pollution needs few reminders of the cost of growth.[7] Yet despite past prognostications of the coming resource crunch or environmental collapse that would hinder Chinese growth, China instead experienced a period of input-intensive hyper industrialization over the past decade. China now consumes nearly half of the world's coal and spits out 46% of its steel, 43% of its aluminum, and 59% of its cement.[8]

Yet that was only possible because the rest of the world started supplying China with the resources it could not provide on its own. China has all but in name given up on its sacrosanct goal of resource security in the face of the practical reality of sustaining its particular flavor of energy-intensive and inefficient growth. China now depends on foreigners to supply more than 50% of its oil, 60% of it soybeans, and nearly all of its iron ore.[9] The government has even tolerated importing millions of tons of coal in recent years, fully recognizing the irony of buying this resource, abundantly available domestically, from foreigners. When Chinese industry gets the occasional hiccup today, global commodity markets shudder.

Resource scarcity will become an overwhelming challenge for the Chinese government over the next decade. If the government does indeed embrace change, industry can become more efficient and less resource intensive through an orderly de-industrialization. Many industrialized nations have historically succeeded in de-industrialization, but the sheer scale of Chinese industry means that such a process will move gradually even if pursued earnestly. One factor that could delay meaningful de-industrialization in the short run is the new leadership's emphasis on accelerating urbanization to sustain domestically driven growth. Urbanizing another hundred million Chinese citizens over the next ten years will probably require another huge expansion of infrastructure—sustaining heavy industry and commodity demand in the process.

Even an aggressively reform-oriented government, however, may hesitate to touch the "third rail" of managing China's resource limitations: forcefully slowing the growth in Chinese consumption. For the past three decades, jittery policymakers unnerved by China's resource constraints could at least take some solace in the fact that Chinese people were too poor to consume heavily, allowing industry to do most of the energy and resource guzzling. Indeed, per capita consumption of natural resources remains much lower in China than in the United States. But that will likely change dramatically in the near future. The latent demand for cars and housing, status symbols for a ballooning middle (ownership) class, and the rise in food and meat consumption and luxuries afforded by rising disposable incomes, are unlikely to abate over the next decade. Each Chinese only needs to consume half as much as an American to shake global energy and food markets.

Without a genuine effort to embrace change, the government has few choices at its disposal, none of which will be appealing. It can dictate that industry make painful adjustments to become more efficient, as it has done for the past several years. But how could the government impose demand-side changes that involve restricting individual consumption? It seems hard to imagine a government demanding its citizens to spurn meat and return to riding bicycles, a particularly unconvincing appeal to the millions of Chinese who have only recently upgraded to eating meat regularly and ditched their bikes for mopeds or SUVs. However, this is also a government that has imposed a nationwide *diktat* on crude population control, a policy that, for its effectiveness, has left new problems in its wake. Its capacity to occasionally mobilize overwhelming resources to achieve a daunting policy objective has surprised foreign observers again and again. Beijing will also surely look to novel technologies as an eleventh-hour savior (for example, improving agricultural yields to unprecedented heights), but it is difficult to know how much they will really make a difference.

But even the most aggressive attempts to address China's resource limitations will find no silver bullet to entirely mitigate their impact over the next ten years. China needs a multiplicity of solutions and policy incentives. At the very least, the Chinese government at every level—from Beijing to townships—would have to fully acknowledge and commit to the need to transform the economy into an environmentally sustainable one, where the Growth Imperative ceases to always and everywhere trump environmental and resource costs.

A "New Deal" with Chinese characteristics

As if defending economic vitality simultaneously against growing resource scarcity and a demographic hangover isn't taxing enough, the government faces a new battlefront: deepening social cleavages. Foremost among these is the widening gap of income, wealth, and opportunity, threatening an important pillar of the bargain struck between the political class and the rest of the Chinese public, and by extension, social stability. This isn't simply the tensions between migrants and urbanites manifest in the Gao family's train journey. More importantly, inequality exacerbates the scarcity of social goods, fueling intense and socially corrosive competition. The middle class feels slighted and obstructed by this system and is more capable of contesting it than the rural farmers. The potential for bottom-up volatility is obvious.

A bold reform agenda will have to address the elephant in the room of China's economy: the huge amount of wealth and income accruing to a small slice of the elites, and stubbornly refusing to trickle down. In the early years of the post-1978 reform era, the economic pie was expanding fast enough that the uneven distribution of prosperity and opportunity could be overlooked, or at least rationalized away. In recent years, however, the political class or those elites with access to political power have noticeably sprinted far ahead of the rest. Magnifying the Chinese public's resentment is their belief that the elite nouveau riche won their fortunes through privileged access to the political system and their common condescension and wanton disregard of those "beneath" their status. That widespread resentment was crystallized in the famous Li Gang case in 2010. When a drunk driver was apprehended after running over two Chinese girls, the young man defied the police trying to arrest him, shouting "My father is Li Gang!" Li turned out to be the local police chief, and his son, under the influence of more than just alcohol, was drunk on power.[10]

It is little surprise that this story gripped the Chinese public's attention and became the dominant Internet meme of the year. Inequality and unrestrained privilege have become so fraught with political sensitivities that the government stopped publishing a Gini coefficient for years until 2012, when the state statistical bureau did an about-face and released its Gini estimate of 0.47. (Measured from 0 to 1, anything above 0.4 is generally considered highly unequal.)[11] Much of the inequality extends beyond what a single figure indicates. It affects not only the future livelihood of the Chinese middle class and the country's economic potential but also a growing scarcity of opportunity for large swathes of Chinese citizens. Part of the reform agenda will have to address inequality by strengthening the social safety net to unleash precautionary savings and transfer wealth from the state sector to households. It will also need to limit the dubious synergies of the political class and businesses so that average members of the middle class feel like they are getting a fair shake.

A proactive response will be required as well to nurse the country's demographic hangover. The growing realization that China is experiencing a speedier shift out of the youth bulge and toward a geriatric bulge has put social welfare into the spotlight like never before. The unsustainable healthcare system and its inadequacy for taking care of a burgeoning group of elderly dependents demand urgent attention. Not only are insurance coverage insufficient and costs exorbitant, the very act of visiting a hospital gives the average Chinese patient high blood pressure, knowing that she must fight her way to the front of a long line to receive service. On the other end, the doctors themselves, in addition to saving lives, now have to protect their own lives first. Repeated episodes of patient rampages, sometimes costing the lives of healthcare professionals, merely reinforce the broad sentiment that Chinese healthcare is deeply ill. Hospitals are supposed to be places where stab wounds find treatment, not where healthy individuals go to become victims of stabbings.

The government will have to engineer huge changes to the healthcare and pension systems very soon to prevent either an enormous unfunded public spending mandate or a rapid deterioration of its fiscal health over the next decade. Either way, they must weigh tough trade-offs between social spending priorities and investing in capital-intensive economic growth. In the near term, the government is flush with enough cash to raise healthcare and pension outlays for some time. But the scale of China's future needs virtually guarantee that government alone cannot shoulder the financial responsibilities indefinitely. Returning to the iron rice bowl of state company provision of all social welfare is unrealistic as well. Private savings, private industry, and the market will have to play a greater role in solving this monumental problem.

Inequality in the Chinese education system also demands a new solution. Like education in any other country, education in China arguably *should* count among the most important equalizers in a modern, developed society. Plenty of data show that completing higher education is strongly correlated with lifetime earnings potential and opportunities for professional and social advancement. When access to the education system becomes highly unequal, it affects future opportunities for upward mobility and lays the groundwork for intensifying extant inequality.

The most apparent, but also most politically daunting, front to attack this inequality is the systematic discrimination against migrants and rural residents in favor of the urban middle class. The *hukou* stands in the way of a proper education for migrant children, a barrier that urban Chinese are ambivalent about removing. With the supply of quality education already scarce, competition is exceedingly fierce even with rural children at a disadvantage. Chinese culture's emphasis on higher education makes its supply scarcity all the more a seller's market. Acceptance into a top-tier Chinese university such as Beijing University or Tsinghua University is exponentially more difficult than getting into a Harvard or Yale. Add to it local protectionism to preserve entry opportunities for registered residents and it becomes nearly impossible for students from outside of China's largest cities to secure a spot in these vaunted institutions.

The pressure on young test-takers has produced a generation of high strung and maladjusted young Chinese, many of whom retreat into the fictitious world of online gaming for temporary escape. And the wealthier tier of middle class and elites are voting by opting out of the system and sending their children to receive an education in places like the United States or England, often as early as high school. Opting out has become a hedge against the near impossibility of securing one of the precious few spots in top Chinese schools.

These choices also reflect a new generation of parents' realization that a Chinese university education may not adequately prepare their children for a 21st century professional life. Recent college graduates enter a job market short on positions for the growing influx of highly trained job seekers. Despite this, employers seem hard pressed to find college graduates qualified to competently perform in the real world where jobs are available. One solution is rather simple: increase the supply of colleges and universities by allowing private competition so that more seats and choices are available. Yet given the political dimension of higher education in China, it will be a hard sell.

Chinese governance 4.0

Economic restructuring and the social goods deficit are formidable enough quandaries. Over the next decade, both could be overshadowed by something more crucial: a deepening crisis of governance and credibility confronting the Chinese government. After nurturing a middle class's rise, the political system finds itself ill-equipped to handle the changing attitudes and demands of a wealthier and better educated citizenry.[12]

Unlike the economic institutions that changed dramatically to foster reforms, China's political institutions have remained basically static since Mao's death. The party left them so deliberately, to minimize unpredictable disturbances to the social order. Economic reforms were disruptive enough; the government needed no other distractions. But the same old political institutions no longer suffice in delivering the kind of governance that is now demanded of the system. The bulk of these demands reflect a post-growth search for what sort of country China ought to become.

In a way, it is actually very good news that China has become a victim of its own success. As the greatest beneficiaries of the three-decades-long bargain of growth for stability, the new Chinese middle class is well-off enough to aspire to more than just a preoccupation with GDP—growth is more than sufficient. Instead, they want the government to supply what remains relatively scarce: quality of life, open debate, transparent information, media freedom, and legal protections. At their core, a growing proportion of the Chinese public yearn for the sense of collective citizenship or unifying values that was eroded in the self-interested reform era.

This is probably the most formidable challenge for a reform agenda: Can the CCP find a way to share its authority in determining what's "best" or "good" for the country? It still claims to be the official and sole arbiter of social ethics and political morality. But the Chinese middle class, empowered by social media technologies that have created a pluralistic public sphere, increasingly disagrees. While the party and people fundamentally agree that China should be a strong and respected country, they increasingly part ways on what *strong* and *respected* actually mean, and how to realize those objectives.

The public's unexpected and sometimes ferocious criticisms lodged at the government's actions has caught the state flat-footed. For one, the ruling party remains uncomfortable with participatory policymaking, historically treating public opinion as something to bend rather than to bend to. In addition, the unremitting spotlight placed on the system's internal corruption in recent years has discredited one of the party's original justifications for its authority: Only the people are corruptible; the party, incorrigible. These revelations have chipped away at the CCP's brand in an era of information technology and when China is widely perceived as *the* rising power of consequence. The party may have little concern for how outsiders perceive it, but it cannot afford to become irrelevant to its own people.

If China pursues a new round of meaningful changes to tap the dividends of reform, the progressive elements within the political establishment would emerge victorious in the battle to shape China's future. After agreeing to this path, the new leadership would summon the political will to build a broad-based consensus for change, one both publicly popular and politically costly for vested interests to resist. Buoyed by a popular mandate, the execution of a reform agenda would prove relatively successful and unhindered.

With the agenda firmly in place, the results would once again astound over the next decade. The state sector's influence would likely wane dramatically. Even though they remain nominally state companies, they could come to dominate the Chinese economy less than do the large, politically connected *keiretsu* in Japan or *chaebols* in Korea. The private sector would flourish and lead an innovation drive, with the fruits of its labor protected by the rule of law. Fiscal and financial resources would be diverted to fund social welfare obligations, absorbing the savings glut that contributed to China's contentious trade surpluses. Many aspects of the economy would become liberalized—from energy pricing to interest rates and currency—facilitating an industrial and consumption rebalancing process that's beyond expectations. By 2022, China would be well on its way to becoming a high middle-income country, propelled by a formidable and competitive economy.

Baby steps

What if instead, the new leadership buys into the necessity of reforms, but pursues them in a more timid and piecemeal fashion, believing that incrementalism continues to be a less-risky proposition? Or if they are unable to forge an enduring and broad consensus for ambitious reforms, settling instead for numerous compromises that avoid offending any particular interest?

This more centrist approach, in some ways resembling the current status quo course, could well satisfy none but disappoint all. It would likely further polarize the reform debate both internally and publicly, making the execution of the reform agenda even more difficult. In the absence of a popular mandate for reform, the government would likely resort to mediating among powerful interests, producing small progress where possible, and delaying bold changes where it must. We see a roughly one in four chance of this outcome.

The economy would soon face substantial bottlenecks from the intensity of its resource constraints. Or unchecked growth in Chinese consumption, coupled with a sprawling heavy industry that refuses to fade away, could lead to undesirable consequences for China's sense of resource security and push up global prices from coal to corn.

Social inequality, too, far from being narrowed, could persist and widen, leading to a combustible mix of middle-class dissatisfaction and migrant-class discontent. Not only will Beijing have to manage a country in various stages of economic development, it will also have to accommodate a country in various states of social development. Without creating viable institutions to accommodate the middle class's priorities such as legal protection and educational attainment, it will be very difficult for the government to spend its way out of these thorny issues. Growing out of problems will no longer suffice.

The risk of reforms falling short seems highest in the political arena. Time and again in recent years the government has failed to meet new expectations for it, retreating into the old comforts of opacity only to be later forced to recant its mistakes. The 2010 deadly HSR crash in Wenzhou was one of those pivotal moments that magnified for the Chinese public precisely how easily the growth model can be derailed. Corruption among ministerial-level officials, secretive and opaque recovery efforts, and shoddy and unsafe construction—the scandal had all the mainstays of suboptimal governance that the Chinese middle class rejects more and more forcefully. If growth and high-tech flagship projects are to come at the expense of safety, how can the government remain credible on food safety or cleaning up rivers clogged with dead swine?[13] That was the question many Chinese asked and continue to ask.

The start of 2013 also provided stark reminders of how the scarcity of freedoms and ideology are leading to intensifying demands on the political system to adjust. The editors of a Guangzhou newspaper, usually viewed as powerless pawns in a tightly controlled media environment, stood up to a propaganda official who drastically altered their paper's editorial on the "Chinese dream" without informing the paper's editors. Although the Guangdong papers are generally considered more progressive than their competitors in other parts of China, the noteworthy support their protest received from Chinese netizens and other liberal Chinese media exceeded anything in recent memory and showed how many advocates for a more open society are now present in China. Far from bread and butter issues, or the perennially controversial land grabs, these were protests over values of freedom, not by extreme activists but by a broader slice representation of the middle class.

The irony of this episode was that the propaganda official's actions unintentionally captured the dissonance between the changes the Chinese public had hoped for and the state's resistance. The Guangdong newspaper cleverly co-opted the Chinese dream idea proposed by new President Xi Jinping and presented its version of a unifying ideology, including the rule of law and universal rights. Revitalizing China, in their view, requires a set of rights that have been in short supply. None of that sat particularly well with the local government, which clearly had a different idea of what the Chinese dream entails.[14]

That discrepancy, if left to grow, will increasingly become a source of tension and obstacle to institutional reforms over the next decade. If no broad consensus forms on what the proper changes to the political economy ought to be, whatever changes the state dictates will likely inflame fierce opposition from an ornery Chinese public, and particularly from the middle class. In many ways, China is undergoing a profound existential and practical internal debate over the role of the state vis-à-vis society and how to shape the future of the country.

Take, for example, venture capitalist Eric Li's contention that little to no institutional reform is necessary because the system is already resilient and innovative. Li has become the anti-Gordon Chang, an ardent proponent of how the Chinese system of governance will defy conventional wisdom and prove its long-term capability to fully address the country's accumulated sociopolitical ills. He made just such a case on the pages of a recent issue of *Foreign Affairs,* engaging MIT scholar Yasheng Huang in a debate over the future of Chinese governance. Li argues:

> Beijing will be able to meet the country's ills with dynamism and resilience, thanks to the CCP's adaptability, system of meritocracy, and legitimacy with the Chinese people. In the next decade, China will continue to rise, not fade. The country's leaders will consolidate the one party model and, in the process, challenge the West's conventional wisdom about political development and the inevitable march toward electoral democracy. In the capital of the Middle Kingdom, the world might witness the birth of a post-democratic future.[15]

Li's view is provocative, but he and a segment of the policy elite whose ideas he seems to espouse are dancing around the more fundamental issue. What confronts the Chinese leadership and the country writ large is not an immanent choice between full-fledged democratization and status quo single-party rule. In fact, public demand for Western-style democratic elections is negligible. Nor do many expect China to fade away economically, even as growth slows down a few notches.

The issue at hand is whether the party can maintain its mandate to govern and meet the changing demands of a changing public. Arguing against its ability to do so is the ample evidence that status quo inertia has grown much stronger over the past decade. Powerful interests, many of them with strong connections to the state, have proliferated and dug in their heels in opposition to reforms of the institutions that enrich them. If interest-driven politics is a defining feature of the American political system, China isn't so dissimilar in that regard, democracy or not.

Arguing the other side are a slew of official documents and speeches given by the new leadership that seem to contradict Li's overly sanguine assessment. An acute level of concern and vigilance appears to pervade the inner sanctum of the new leadership, fully aware of the ramifications of losing the confidence of the Chinese people. Indeed, the first 100 days of the new leadership marked a meticulously planned campaign to send a message of change and reform, as well as a meaningful anticorruption drive, under the banner of national revival and the Chinese dream, a seemingly appealing idea that has yet to be filled with specificity.

Another hint of the Chinese leadership's deep anxiety at this critical juncture—both in determining how it must govern a 21st century China and project an image as a global great power—is perhaps found in what some of the leaders and intellectuals have been reading: apparently, Alexis de Tocqueville's 1856 classic tome on the French Revolution. A 21st century CCP elite reflecting on the lessons of the French Revolution may be less obtuse than it seems at first. As China scholar Joseph Fewsmith writes:

> The interest in de Tocqueville's work revolves around what is sometimes called the "de Tocqueville paradox" (actually one of several in his work), namely that revolution rarely, if ever, occurs when social conditions are at their worst but rather breaks out when conditions improve, particularly when reform improves material conditions.[16]

How de Tocqueville's words apply to China today seem rather obvious to the Chinese ruling class and middle class alike. As material conditions have improved for the average Chinese, a burgeoning middle class is now demanding deeper reforms to improve sociopolitical conditions and defending an embryonic civil society. The existing political institutions, however, have lagged social developments. Further reforms risk catalyzing a process of change that could prove beyond the party-state's ability to control. Yet it is also clear that the new leadership under President Xi recognizes that, absent substantial improvements in governance and the creation of more credible institutions, even the more limited aims of their economic restructuring agenda will flounder, too.

If reform does progress in fits and starts it would postpone tackling the toughest of China's economic, financial, and institutional challenges. Accumulating problems would likely delay economic rebalancing and weigh down economic performance. If efforts to tackle the hardest reforms remain meek, China by 2022 would face an eventual reckoning that demands even more resources and political resolve at a time when growth has become constrained and another political transition looms.

What if the Chinese dream is deferred?

The possibility that the political establishment digs in its heels and refuses to meet the public's expectations for change and the urgent demands to adapt to 21st century governance and economic development cannot be ignored. A vocal segment of the Chinese political class remains gripped by fear of some new change sending the country sliding down a slippery slope into a tailspin. Instead of bending even a little, their overriding hostility to potentially destabilizing reforms could lead to paralysis and stasis. Highly unlikely, given China's recent history of transformation, we give it a one in twenty chance.

If this vocal group (*vocal minority* is probably a better descriptor, but of course there is no objective way to measure their influence) wins out, we fear the next decade will be a harrowing one for China, its government, and its people. The government's leadership and competence will likely be called into serious question by a public whose cynicism rises to an all-time high and whose patience eventually is exhausted. Without addressing the imbalances inherent in China's economic model, growth prospects could deteriorate drastically and exacerbate the vulnerabilities of the real estate market, or further expose the financial system to external shocks. If this occurs, the outside world can expect heightened social volatility and uncertainties from China, an outcome posing severe downside risks to global growth and development. By 2022, China may be left with a much weaker government and economically be on its way to becoming a poorer, more populous version of Japan.

For the past three-plus decades, China has been chasing an elusive modernity, however defined, incarnate in the latest iteration of the Chinese dream. That dream is both distinctly Chinese and universal. As astute students of history, China's leaders understand the weight of history on their nation's development. This is likely why the historical determinism inherent in Marxism appealed to Mao and successive generations of Chinese leaders. It is also likely why de Tocqueville resonates, particularly his observation that the French elite had "erroneously taken a country with a rich historical tradition for a blank sheet of paper, trying to draw the 'most beautiful blueprint'."

The leadership aspires to a goal both universal and quintessentially Chinese, but the recent history of Chinese success has been predominantly shaped by generally accepted, or dare we say *universal,* features shared by most modern societies: market forces, individual agency, social pluralism, and political accountability. Despite the best efforts of conservative and hawkish voices in the Chinese government to paint these elements as a poisonous Western cocktail foisted on China by imperialist agents, they aren't democratic or authoritarian prescriptions, Western or Eastern. They are simply what has proven to work effectively in lifting nations economically and in preserving their political systems' long-term viability. They are, in a word, modern.

China's amazing three decades of reform and opening are now history, and the reform dividends that era spawned have been realized. The country now stands at another significant moment in which it must decide, for the next generation, whether the realization of its future will be pushed forward by continuously adopting modern institutions or by allowing an obsession with historical uniqueness to overwhelm the imperative of becoming an enduring and dynamic global power. A resolution of the conflict over reform, in essence, will be the reconciliation of these disparate strains—that adopting economic and political reforms is not tantamount to westernization, nor is it incompatible with China's claim to unique historical and cultural circumstances.

Over the next decade, China will likely capture the top spot economically, putting it into a rarified global league. China will make history again. Yet the arrival of that achievement will likely be overshadowed by a set of sociopolitical complexities such as the country has never before confronted. How China's government, society, and citizens respond to these challenges will set the country and the world on a course that few can anticipate, for better or worse.

The world is not preventing China from becoming a truly exceptional great power. Only China can decide what kind of great power it wants to be. But that decision will have to come sooner rather than later because the Chinese public is growing impatient, and so is the world.

Endnotes

Introduction

1. See, for example, Niall Ferguson's contention that the world is shifting back to China and that Western dominance is over, http://online.wsj.com/article/SB10001424052748704104104575622531909154228.html.

2. Jacques, Martin, *When China Rules the World: The End of the Western World and the Birth of a New World Order,* Penguin Books, August 2012.

3. Adams et al., "On the Selection of Leading Economic Indicators for China," The Conference Board Working Papers 10-02 (July 2010), www.conference-board.org/publications/publicationdetail.cfm?publicationid=1802 and references cited therein.

Chapter 1

1. Liu, Xiaolin, "The End of Year Car Shortage," *China Economic Observer,* December 11, 2010, www.eeo.com.cn/industry/real_estate/2010/12/11/188721.shtml.

2. IBM, "IBM Global Commuter Pain Study Reveals Traffic Crisis in Key International Cities," www-03.ibm.com/press/us/en/pressrelease/32017.wss.

3. Ford, Peter, "China traffic jam enters day 11. A tale of deceit and criminality?" *The Christian Science Monitor,* August 24, 2010, www.csmonitor.com/World/Global-News/2010/0824/China-traffic-jam-enters-Day-11.-A-tale-of-deceit-and-criminality.

4. The measurement of inflation is controversial in China, and alternatives to the standard CPI measure suggest a whole-economy rate of inflation of 2% to 3% higher on average between 2000 and 2010 than the CPI measure. This higher measure still puts China on the low end of the range of inflation experienced by emerging market economies.

5. See, for example, the minutes to the 170th meeting of the Banco Central do Brasil Monetary Policy Committee, www4.bcb.gov.br/pec/gci/ingl/COPOM/COPOM20121025-170th%20Copom%20Minutes.pdf.

6. Adams, Bill, "Macroeconomic Implications of China Urban Housing Privatization, 1998-1999." *Journal of Contemporary China* 18-62 (2009), pp. 881-888.

7. Bank loans are funded by bank deposits. During the Panda Boom era, Chinese banks generated almost all of their income by loaning out deposited funds and profiting from the large difference between loan and deposit interest rates, as opposed to income from fee-based services. For additional background see Lardy, Nicholas, *Sustaining China's Economic Growth After the Global Financial Crisis*, Washington: Peterson Institute, 2012.

8. Martin Feldstein and Charles Hirioka demonstrated this phenomenon in "Domestic Saving and International Capital Flows," *The Economic Journal* 90 (June 1980): 314–329.

9. Bottelier, Pieter, and Fosler, Gail, "Can China's Growth Trajectory Be Sustained?" BI Norwegian School of Management Center for Monetary Economics Working Paper Series 6/07, http://www.bi.edu/cmeFiles/wp6.07.pdf.

10. Holz, Carsten A., "China's Reform Period Economic Growth: How Reliable Are Angus Maddison's Estimates?," *Review of Income and Wealth*, International Association for Research in Income and Wealth, 52-1 (2006), pages 85-119, and Wu, Harry X., "Accounting for China's Growth in 1952-2008: China's growth performance debate revisited with a newly constructed data set." RIETI Discussion Paper Series 11-E-003, January 2011, http://www.rieti.go.jp/jp/publications/dp/11e003.pdf.

11. "Mao Zedong Meets Nixon, February 21, 1972," U.S.C. U.S.-China Institute, http://china.usc.edu/ShowArticle.aspx?articleID=2248&Aspx AutoDetect CookieSupport=1.

12. Maddison, Angus, *Chinese Economic Performance in the Long Run*, Paris: OECD Development Centre, 1998: 32.

13. Dong, Zhen and Li, Yun, "City may grow beyond capacity within 3 years," *Shanghai Daily*, August 16, 2012, http://www.shanghaidaily.com/nsp/Metro/2012/08/16/City%2Bmay%2Bgrow%2Bbeyond%2Bcapacity%2Bwithin%2B3%2Byears/.

14. Brown, Lester, *Who Will Feed China? Wake-up Call for a Small Planet*, New York: Norton, 1995.

15. "State Grain Security Medium-Long Term Plan Draft (2008-2020), Full Text," Xinhua News Service, November 13, 2008, http://www.gov.cn/jrzg/2008-11/13/content_1148414.htm.

16. China's hypergrowth, peaking at 13% in 2007, even played a role in lowering Western interest rates during the first decade of the 21st century, supporting commodity prices. Huge Chinese central bank purchases of reserves (that is, of foreign governments' bonds) kept the yuan from

appreciating, inflated bond prices and, conversely, held down interest rates (when bond prices rise, interest rates fall). Quantitative easing in the advanced economies after the 2009 global financial crisis, in which the U.S. Federal Reserve, Bank of England, and Bank of Japan have monetized government debts, is partly to compensate for the shrinking demand for government debt from Chinese and other central banks as emerging market exchange rates become less undervalued.

17. Consequently, China's narrowing trade surplus after 2007 has as much to do with the changing value of Chinese exports and imports as with the change in the volumes of trade.

18. Maddison, p. 23, quoting S. Y. Teng and J. K. Fairbank et al. (eds.), *China's Response to the West: A Documentary Survey: 1839–1923*, Cambridge: Harvard University Press, 1954.

19. China has demonstrated itself to be a very weak price setter in several markets over the past several years, despite the fact that its demand is so huge, attempting unsuccessfully to use its market power to dictate prices of commodities ranging from iron ore to rare earths.

20. Economy, Elizabeth, *The River Runs Black*, Ithaca: Cornell University Press, 2010.

21. "River in Zhengzhou Turns Red," *China Daily*, July 11, 2012, http://www.chinadaily.com.cn/china/2012-07/11/content_15570845.htm.

22. "Environmental Standard for Surface Water," GB 3838-2002, Ministry of Environmental Protection, http://kjs.mep.gov.cn/hjbhbz/bzwb/shjbh/shjzlbz/200206/W020061027509896672057.pdf.

23. Ministry of Environmental Protection, "2011 Annual China Environmental Status Bulletin: Freshwater Environment," http://jcs.mep.gov.cn/hjzl/zkgb/2011zkgb/201206/t20120606_231040.htm.

24. Yin, Yueping, Zhang, Kaijun, and Li, Xiaochun, "Urbanization and Land Subsidence in China," IAEG2006 Paper number 31, www.iaeg.info/iaeg2006/PAPERS/IAEG_031.PDF.

25. "Water Plan to Take Effect by 2012," *China Daily*, June 11, 2012, http://www.chinadaily.com.cn/china/2012-06/11/content_15491752.htm.

Chapter 2

1. In the latest reconstruction of the Great Famine, Chinese author Yang Jisheng reveals that the number of those starved to death exceeded total casualties in World War I. See Yang, Jisheng, *Tombstone: The Great Chinese Famine, 1958-1962*, Farrar, Straus and Giroux, October 2012. Also see Dikotter, Frank, *Mao's Great Famine: The History of China's Most Devastating Catastrophe, 1958-1962*, Walker and Company, October 2011.

2. Palmer, James, "The Balinghou," *Aeon,* March 2013, www.aeonmagazine.com/living-together/james-palmer-chinese-youth/.

3. Patterson, Sky, "Obesity in China: Waistlines are Expanding Twice as Fast as GDP," *US-China Today,* University of Southern California, April 8, 2011, http://uschina.usc.edu/w_usci/showarticle.aspx?articleID=16595 &AspxAutoDetectCookieSupport=1.

4. Headey, Derek, and Fan, Shenggen, "Reflections on the Global Food Crisis: How Did It Happen? How Has It Hurt? And How Can We Prevent the Next One?" International Food Policy Research Institute, 2010, www.ifpri.org/sites/default/files/publications/rr165.pdf.

5. Thomas Malthus was an 18th century demographer and widely considered to be the pioneer theorist on the relationship between population growth and resource limitations. He authored "An Essay on the Principle of Population" in 1798.

6. Brown, Lester, *Who Will Feed China?: Wake-Up Call for a Small Planet,* W. W. Norton and Company, September 1995.

7. Fewsmith, Joseph, *Dilemmas of Reform in China: Political Conflict and Economic Debate,* M. E. Sharpe 1994.

8. Huang, Jikun, and Rozelle, Scott, "Agricultural Development and Nutrition: The Policies Behind China's Success," World Food Programme, November 2009, http://home.wfp.org/stellent/groups/public/documents/ newsroom/wfp213339.pdf. Also see Lin, Justin Yifu, "The Household Responsibility System in China's Agricultural Reform: A Theoretical and Empirical Study," *Economic Development and Cultural Change,* Vol. 36, No. 3., April 1988, The University of Chicago Press. Also see this Hexun series commemorating the 30th anniversary of HRS, http://news.hexun. com/2008/lccb1982/index.html.

9. Van den Berg, M. M. et al., "The Impact of Increasing Farm Size and Mechanization on Rural Income and Rice Production in Zhejiang Province, China," Agr Syst (2007), doi:10.1016/j.agsy.2006.11.010, http:// bsesrv214.bse.vt.edu/Grisso/Ethiopia/Books_Resources/Rice_Milling/ New/rice%20production%20in%20Zhejiang%20province.pdf.

10. Jin, Songqing, Huang, Jikun, and Rozelle, Scott, "The Production Performance of China's Transforming Agriculture," *Choices,* 4Q 2009 24(4), Agriculture and Applied Economics Association, http://ageconsearch. umn.edu/bitstream/93981/2/2009414.pdf.

11. Huang, Jikun, Rozelle, Scott, Hu, Rufia and Jin, Songqing, "The Creation and Spread of Technology and Total Factor Productivity in China: An Analysis of the Contribution of China's Research System and CG-supplied Genetic Material," A paper presented at the Workshop on the Impact of National and International Research Programs on Total Factor Productivity in Developing Countries, 1999 AAEA's Annual

Conference, Nashville, cited in Huang Jikun, Justin Yifu Lin, and Scott Rozelle, "What Will Make Chinese Agriculture More Productive?" Conference on Policy Reform in China, 18–20 November 1999, Stanford University.

12. "Chinese Academy of Sciences Report Says China Is a Century Behind the United States in Agriculture," *Beijing News*, May 14, 2012, http://news.xinhuanet.com/fortune/2012-05/14/c_111941276.htm.

13. Pan, Yaoguo, "China's Meat Production and Consumption Trends," October 7, 2010, www.chinareform.org.cn/economy/consume/forward/201010/t20101007_45452_2.htm. Also see Pan Yaoguo speech given at the Fifth World Meat Conference in Qingdao, Shandong, in September 2009, http://wenku.baidu.com/view/9648a0a0f524ccbff1218452.html.

14. Larsen, Janet, "Meat Consumption in China Now Double That in the United States," Earth Policy Institute, April 24, 2012, www.earth-policy.org/plan_b_updates/2012/update102.

15. Wines, Michael, "China Plans to Release Some of Its Pork Stockpile to Hold Down Prices," *New York Times*, July 15, 2011, www.nytimes.com/2011/07/16/world/asia/16china.html?_r=0.

16. Huang, Lin, and Rozelle, "What Will Make Chinese Agriculture More Productive," paper presented at a Conference on Policy Reform in China, Stanford University, November 1999.

17. Data from the U.S. Department of Agriculture, accessed at Earth Policy Institute, www.earth-policy.org/data_center/C24.

18. Data from the U.S. Department of Agriculture, accessed at Earth Policy Institute, www.earth-policy.org/datacenter/pdf/book_fpep_ch3_all.pdf.

19. Brown, Lester, "Growing Demand for Soybeans Threatens Amazon Rainforest," Earth Policy Institute, December 30, 2009, www.earth-policy.org/plan_b_updates/2009/update86.

20. Cui, Carolyn, "China Rice Imports Unsettle Market," *Wall Street Journal*, January 7, 2013, http://online.wsj.com/article/SB10001424127887323706704578228052284001608.html; also see USDA data, www.ers.usda.gov/publications/rcs-rice-outlook/rcs-12l.aspx.

21. Mohindru, Sameer and Shangguan, Zhoudong, "China's Cadmium Problem May Be Boost for Rice Exporters," *Wall Street Journal*, May 22, 2013, http://online.wsj.com/article/SB10001424127887323333610457849 8751887802128.html.

22. USDA Office of the Chief Economist, "USDA Agricultural Projections to 2021," February 2012, www.usda.gov/oce/commodity/projections/USDAAgriculturalProjections2021.pdf.

23. "China Floods Bring Steep Food Price Rises," *The Guardian*, June 19, 2011, www.guardian.co.uk/world/2011/jun/19/china-floods-food-price-rises.

24. Bradsher, Keith, "UN Food Agency Issues Warning on China Drought," *New York Times*, February 8, 2011, www.nytimes.com/2011/02/09/business/global/09food.html?pagewanted=all; also see "Drought Leaves 12 Million People Short of Drinking Water in SW China," *Xinhua*, September 8, 2011, http://news.xinhuanet.com/english2010/china/2011-09/08/c_131119041.htm.

25. Baculinao, Eric, "Chinese Expert: Drought Is a Warning Signal," *NBC News*, May 31, 2011, http://behindthewall.nbcnews.com/_news/2011/05/31/6755387-chinese-expert-drought-is-a-warning-signal?lite; also see Buckley, Chris, "China Drought Raises Question About Climate Change," *Reuters*, June 3, 2011, www.reuters.com/article/2011/06/03/us-china-drought-climate-idUSTRE7520KN20110603.

26. Woetzel, Jonathan et al., "Preparing for China's Urban Billion," McKinsey Global Institute, March 2009, www.circleofblue.org/waternews/wp-content/uploads/2010/11/China_urban_billion_full_report.pdf.

27. Larson, Christina, "Losing Arable Land, China Faces Stark Choice: Adapt or Go Hungry," *Science*, Vol. 339 no. 6120, February 2013, www.sciencemag.org/content/339/6120/644.full.

28. Gunders, Dana, "Wasted: How America is Losing Up to 40 Percent of Its Food From Farm to Fork to Landfill," National Resources Defense Council, August 2012, www.nrdc.org/food/files/wasted-food-IP.pdf.

29. Wines, Michael, "China Takes Loss to Get Ahead in the Business of Fresh Water," *New York Times*, October 25, 2011, www.nytimes.com/2011/10/26/world/asia/china-takes-loss-to-get-ahead-in-desalination-industry.html?pagewanted=all.

30. Backgrounder from the UN Food and Agriculture Organization, www.fao.org/nr/water/aquastat/countries_regions/china/index.stm.

31. Cowen, Tyler, *An Economist Gets Lunch: New Rules for Everyday Foodies*, Dutton Adult, April 2012.

32. "47 Detained for Selling Baby-Killer Milk," *China Daily*, May 10, 2004, www.chinadaily.com.cn/english/doc/2004-05/10/content_329449.htm

33. U.S. Food and Drug Administration, "Melamine Pet Food Recall of 2007," www.fda.gov/animalveterinary/safetyhealth/recallswithdrawals/ucm129575.htm.

34. Barboza, David, and Barrionuevo, Alexei, "Filler in Animal Feed is Open Secret in China," *New York Times*, April 30, 2007, www.nytimes.com/2007/04/30/business/worldbusiness/30food.html?pagewanted=all&_r=0.

35. Ramzy, Austin, and Yang, Lin, "Tainted-Baby-Milk Scandal in China," *Time,* September 16, 2008, www.time.com/time/world/article/ 0,8599,1841535,00.html.

36. "Two Executed Over Baby Formula Scandal," *China Daily,* November 25, 2009, www.chinadaily.com.cn/bizchina/2009-11/25/content_9046968. htm.

37. The food safety map, www.zccw.info.

38. Upton Sinclair's socialist polemic *The Jungle,* originally published in 1906, documented the abysmal food safety conditions in slaughterhouses. It failed to convert the U.S. public to socialism, but did convince them of the need for food safety regulation.

39. McDonald, Mark, "From Milk to Peas, a China Food-Safety Mess," *New York Times,* June 21, 2012, http://rendezvous.blogs.nytimes.com/ 2012/06/21/from-milk-to-peas-a-chinese-food-safety-mess/.

40. ChinaSmack, October 16, 2009, www.chinasmack.com/2009/pictures/ recycled-slop-swill-cooking-oil.html.

41. ChinaSmack, April 9, 2011, www.chinasmack.com/2011/pictures/blue-glowing-pork-meat-found-in-shanghai.html.

42. "Who Can Guarantee China's Pork Is Safe?," *China Daily,* April 6, 2011, www.chinadaily.com.cn/china/2011-04/06/content_12281515.htm.

43. Literally translated as "old one hundred names," it is a Chinese colloquialism that connotes the commoner or average folks as opposed to officials.

44. Ma, Damien, "Hu Jintao's Kennedy Moment," *The Atlantic Monthly* online, June 21, 2012, www.theatlantic.com/international/archive/2012/06/ hu-jintaos-kennedy-moment/258790/#.

45. "Astronauts' Food Special Provisions Base: Every Cow Has an ID," *QQ News,* June 14, 2012, http://news.qq.com/a/20120614/001480.htm.

46. "Astronauts' Special Food Supply Angers Netizens," Ministry of Tofu, June 18, 2012, www.ministryoftofu.com/2012/06/astronauts-special-food-supply-angers-chinese-netizens/.

47. Demick, Barbara, "In China, What You Eat Tells Who You Are," *Los Angeles Times,* September 16, 2011 http://articles.latimes.com/2011/ sep/16/world/la-fg-china-elite-farm-20110917.

48. Murphy, Colum, "China Cracks Down on Food Safety," *Wall Street Journal,* December 27, 2012, http://online.wsj.com/article/SB1000142412788 7323300404578205014086518522.html.

49. "Fast Food: Notes on a Scandal" *China Confidential,* January 24, 2013.

50. Langfitt, Frank, "Shanghai's Dead Pigs: Search for Answers Turns Up Denials," NPR, March 14, 2013, www.npr.org/blogs/thesalt/2013/03/14/ 174302750/shanghais-dead-pigs-search-for-answers-turns-up-denials.

51. Ausubel, Jesse H. et al., "Peak Farmland and the Prospect for Land Sparing," *Population and Development Review* 38 (2012), http://phe.rockefeller.edu/docs/PDR.SUPP%20Final%20Paper.pdf; also see Revkin, Andrew C., "Scientists Promise for People and Nature in 'Peak Farmland,'" *New York Times,* December 17, 2012, http://dotearth.blogs.nytimes.com/2012/12/17/scientists-see-promise-for-people-and-nature-in-peak-farmland/.

52. Clay, Jason W., "Agriculture from 2000-2050—The Business as Usual Scenario," draft paper, World Wildlife Foundation, http://dels.nas.edu/resources/static-assets/banr/AnimalProductionMaterials/ClayChapter3.pdf; also see Godfray, Charles et al., "Food Security: The Challenge of Feeding Nine Billion People," *Science,* Vol. 327 No. 5967, January 28, 2010, www.scientificamerican.com/article.cfm?id=civilization-food-shortages.

53. "Protect and Manage 'Heavenly Granaries' and Coordinated Push to Build the 'Four New Modernizations'," *People's Daily,* January 16, 2013, http://politics.people.com.cn/n/2013/0116/c1024-20212725.html.

54. "Possible Food Struggle Threatens China's Urbanization," *Global Times,* January 27, 2013, www.globaltimes.cn/content/758364.shtml.

Chapter 3

1. See the 1986 classic film *Labyrinth,* starring David Bowie and Jennifer Connelly.

2. China scholar Pieter Bottelier estimated at the time that 17 to 30 million workers were laid off, mostly migrant workers; "China's Economic Downturn: Employment is the Key Issue," *China Brief* 9:3, February 4, 2009, www.jamestown.org/single/?no_cache=1&tx_ttnews%5Btt_news%5D=34456.

3. Zhongnanhai is the Chinese leadership compound in central Beijing, akin to the White House or 10 Downing Street in London.

4. "Economic Downturn Leaves 26 Million Unemployed in China," *The Guardian,* February 2, 2009, www.telegraph.co.uk/news/worldnews/asia/china/4438965/Economic-downturn-leaves-26-million-unemployed-in-China.html.

5. Qiu, Quanlin, "Manufacturers Facing Labor Shortage," *China Daily,* February 24, 2010, www.chinadaily.com.cn/china/2010-02/24/content_9492229.htm.

6. For a digestible journalistic investigation into Chinese labor, see Harney, Alexandra, *The China Price: The True Cost of Chinese Competitive Advantage,* Penguin, January 2009.

7. "China's New Labor Contract Law: Overview and Recommended Action Steps for Employers." Troutman Sanders, www.troutmansanders.com/files/Publication/da0358e9-71d3-4370-82dc-5344756922ba/Presentation/PublicationAttachment/99cc8c35-65ae-4be2-b84e-63fec7baa708/

TS%20China%20New%20Labor%20Contract%20Law%20Overview.pdf.

8. Eunjung Cha, Ariana, "New Law Gives Chinese Workers Power, Gives Businesses Nightmares," *Washington Post,* April 14, 2008, http://articles.washingtonpost.com/2008-04-14/business/36781165_1_new-labor-contract-law-toy-factory-factory-owners; Mitchell, Tom and Dyer, Geoff, "Labor Law Set to Raise Costs in China," *Financial Times,* January 2, 2008, www.ft.com/intl/cms/s/0/86e24964-b8d4-11dc-893b-0000779fd2ac.html; Fong, Mei, "China's Rising Labor Costs Bode Well for Some Big Manufacturers," *Wall Street Journal,* January 25, 2008, http://online.wsj.com/article/SB120120382737914255.html.

9. Okudera, Atsushi, "Changing China: Chinese Companies Facing New Problem of High Turnover," *Asahi Shimbun,* September 19, 2011, http://ajw.asahi.com/article/asia/china/AJ2011091811081.

10. Lewis, W. Arthur, "Economic Development with Unlimited Supplies of Labour," *The Manchester School* Vol. 22, Issue 2, 1954.

11. For more reading on the household registration system, see, for example, Wu, Xiaogang and Treiman, Donald J., "Inequality and Equality under Chinese Socialism: The *Hukou* System and Intergenerational Occupational Mobility," *American Journal of Sociology*, Vol. 133, No. 2, September 2007; Chan, Kam Wing and Li, Zhang, "The *Hukou* System and Rural-Urban Migration in China: Processes and Changes," *The China Quarterly*, Vol. 160, December 1999; Liu, Zhiqiang, "Institution and Inequality: the Hukou System in China," *Journal of Comparative Economics*, Vol. 33, Issue 1, March 2005.

12. This chart makes the simplifying assumption that all workers in primary industry (agriculture, ranching, forestry, and so on) are rural workers.

13. "Report on the 2012 National Migrant Worker Measurement Survey," National Bureau of Statistics, May 27, 2013, www.stats.gov.cn/tjfx/jdfx/t20130527_402899251.htm.

14. "Chang Kai: 'We have Misinterpreted the New Generation of Migrant Workers'," Sohu.com, July 22, 2010, http://business.sohu.com/20100722/n273696052.shtml.

15. State Council Document 1, issued January 31, 2010, www.gov.cn/jrzg/2010-01/31/content_1524372.htm.

16. Tschang, Chi-Chu, "A Tough Year for China's Migrant Workers," *Bloomberg Businessweek,* February 4, 2009, www.businessweek.com/globalbiz/content/feb2009/gb2009024_357998.htm.

17. "Young Chinese Migrant Workers More Educated," *China Daily,* October 9, 2011, www.chinadaily.com.cn/china/2011-10/09/content_13857976.htm.

18. "Sun Zhigang's Brutal Killers Sentenced," *China Daily*, June 10, 2003, www.chinadaily.com.cn/en/doc/2003-06/10/content_168514.htm.

19. It remains to be seen how quickly or effectively this policy will be implemented. "State Council Notice Regarding Actively and Steadily Advancing Institutional Reforms of Household Registration Management," Guo Ban Fa 2011-9, February 23, 2012, www.gov.cn/zwgk/2012-02/23/content_2075082.htm.

20. Kahn, Joseph, "Rioting in China Over Label on College Diplomas," *New York Times*, June 22, 2006, www.nytimes.com/2006/06/22/world/asia/22china.html.

21. Si, Lian, ed., *Yi Zu: Daxue Biyesheng Jujucun Shi Ji*, Guilin: Guangxi Normal University Publishing House, 2009.

22. Junxiu, Wang, "What Does It Say that 69% of College Graduates Earn Lower Salaries Than Average Migrant Workers' Monthly Income?" Xinhua News Service, July 26, 2012, http://news.xinhuanet.com/politics/2012-07/26/c_123470308.htm.

23. "Industrial Enterprises Above Designated Size Realize 5.3 Percent Profit Growth in 2012," National Bureau of Statistics, www.stats.gov.cn/was40/gjtjj_nodate_detail.jsp?channelid=75004&record=49, and "National Economic Development Sees Progress Amid Stability in 2012," www.stats.gov.cn/was40/gjtjj_nodate_detail.jsp?channelid=75004&record=60.

24. Adams, Bill, "Commercial Banks and CIC: Where Did All the Forex Go?" *China Economic Quarterly* (Dragonomics), June 2008: 53–57.

25. See Figure 4.4 in *OECD Economic Surveys: China 2010*: 106, www.oecd.org/eco/economicsurveyofchina2010.htm.

26. Census International Division Projections, Mid-Year Population by Older Age Groups.

27. Studwell, Joe, *The China Dream: The Quest for the Last Great Untapped Market on Earth*, New York: Grove Press, 2003.

Chapter 4

1. Wang, Heyan, Wang Chen, Xu Chao, Lan Fang, "Series on Hospital Violence," *Caixin*, April 2012, http://topics.caixin.com/doctor_vs_patient/.

2. "Attacker of Beijing Tongren Hospital Doctor Receives 15-year sentence," NetEase, April 20, 2012, http://news.163.com/12/0420/22/7VILRLAB00011229.html.

3. "Female Doctor Killed While Working Overtime in Hengyang Hospital," *Caixin*, April 28, 2012. http://china.caixin.com/2012-04-28/100385528.html; also see http://magazine.caixin.com/2012-04-20/100382394.html.

4. Wang Jiana, Sun, Wei, Chi, Tie-Shuang, Wu Hui, and Wang, Lie, "Prevalence and Associated Factors of Depressive Symptoms among Chinese Doctors: A Cross-Sectional Survey," National Institutes of Health, www.ncbi.nlm.nih.gov/pubmed/20112108.

5. Chow, Gregory C., "An Economic Analysis of Healthcare in China," CEPS Working Paper No. 132, August 2006, http://www.princeton.edu/ceps/workingpapers/132chow.pdf.

6. Ibid.

7. Schumpeter, Joseph A., *Capitalism, Socialism, and Democracy*, Harper and Brothers, 1942.

8. See Gill, Bates, "China's Health Care and Pension Challenges," Testimony before the U.S.-China Security and Economic Review Commission, February 2006.

9. Ministry of Health statistics, accessed here: www.moh.gov.cn/publicfiles/business/htmlfiles/zwgkzt/ptjnj/200908/42635.htm.

10. World Development Indicators, World Bank, accessed here: databank.worldbank.org/data/views/reports/chart.aspx.

11. Loo, Daryl, "China Healthcare Spending May Hit $1 Trillion by 2020," *Bloomberg News*, August 29, 2012, www.businessweek.com/news/2012-08-29/china-health-care-spending-may-hit-1-trillion-by-2020.

12. Hu, Shanlian et al., "Reform of How Healthcare is Paid for in China: Challenges and Opportunities," World Health Organization, October 20, 2008, www.who.int/management/district/6.Financing.pdf.

13. Xiao, Yedong, "Policing Hospitals Won't Root Out Patient Disputes Problems," *People's Daily*, May 20, 2012, http://gs.people.com.cn/GB//n/2012/0520/c183343-17057875.html.

14. Yip, Winnie Chi-man et al., "Early Appraisal of China's Huge and Complex Health-care Reforms." *Lancet* 379, March 3, 2012: 833.

15. Li, Yongbin et al., "Overprescribing In China, Driven By Financial Incentives, Results in Very High Use of Antibiotics, Injections, and Corticosteroids," *Health Affairs* 31(5) (2012): 1075–1082.

16. Wang, Yonggai, "Striking at 'Hospital Disturbances' Should Move Forward from Critical Juncture," *People's Daily*, May 5, 2012, http://opinion.people.com.cn/GB/159301/17814435.html; also see "To Prevent Hospital Disturbances, Hospitals to Install Police Monitoring Stations," *Shanxi Evening Post*, May 5, 2012, http://politics.people.com.cn/GB/17815298.html.

17. Wang, Chen, "Who is the Real Victim?," *Caixin*, March 31, 2012, http://magazine.caixin.com/2012-03-31/100375232.html.

18. Xu, Yeshe, "Undercover: How Large Hospitals Let Scalpers Run Wild," *Xinhua*, August 11, 2005, http://news.xinhuanet.com/newscenter/ 2005-08/11/content_3337455.htm.

19. Wang, Yonggai, "Striking at 'Hospital Disturbances' Should Move Forward from Critical Juncture," *People's Daily*, May 5, 2012, http://opinion. people.com.cn/GB/159301/17814435.html.

20. Wang, Chen, "Who is the Real Victim?," *Caixin*, March 31, 2012, http:// magazine.caixin.com/2012-03-31/100375232.html?p0#page2.

21. Authors' conversation with Chinese journalist.

22. Ministry of Health notice, May 5, 2012, www.moh.gov.cn/publicfiles/ business/htmlfiles/mohylfwjgs/s7656/201204/54578.htm.

23. "Shameful Apology or Hospital Disturbances Too Ferocious?," Sina.com, May 5, 2012, http://news.sina.com.cn/o/2012-05-05/023524370147.shtml.

24. Barber, Sarah L., and Yao, Lan, "Health Insurance Systems in China: A briefing note," World Health Organization, www.who.int/healthsystems/ topics/financing/healthreport/37ChinaB_YFINAL.pdf.

25. Hu, Shanlian et al., "Reform of How Healthcare is Paid for in China: Challenges and Opportunities," World Health Organization, October 20, 2008, www.who.int/management/district/6.Financing.pdf.

26. Shan, Juan, "China Ramps up Healthcare Spending," *China Daily*, March 10, 2011, http://www.chinadaily.com.cn/bizchina/2011-03/10/ content_12151446.htm.

27. Ministry of Health press conference, January 2012, http://www.moh.gov. cn/publicfiles/business/htmlfiles/mohbgt/s3582/201201/53883.htm.

28. Yip, Winnie Chi-Man, "Early Appraisal of China's Huge and Complex Health-care Reforms," *Lancet* 379, March 3, 2012: 833.

29. Ibid.

30. Li, Xuena, "Four Injured in Shenzhen Pengcheng Hospital Stabbing," *Caixin*, September 3, 2012, http://china.caixin.com/2012-09-03/ 100432523.html.

31. Banister, Judith, Bloom, David E., and Rosenberg, Larry, "Population Aging and Economic Growth in China," March 2010, Program on the Global Demography of Aging, Harvard University, http://www.hsph. harvard.edu/pgda/WorkingPapers/2010/PGDA_WP_53.pdf.

32. Wang, Feng, "The Future of a Demographic Overachiever: Long-term Implications of the Demographic Transition in China," Brookings Institution, http://www.brookings.edu/~/media/research/files/articles/2011/3/ demographics%20china%20wang/03_demographics_china_wang.pdf.

33. Ibid.

34. "The Most Surprising Demographic Crisis," *The Economist,* May 5, 2011, www.economist.com/node/18651512.

35. Eberstadt, Nicholas, "The Demographic Future," *Foreign Affairs,* November/December 2010.

36. "Young Chinese Couples Face Pressure from '4-2-1' Family Structure," *People's Daily,* August 25, 2010, http://english.people.com.cn/90001 /90782/7117246.html.

37. Branigan, Tania, "China Faces 'Timebomb' of Ageing Population," *The Guardian,* March 20, 2012, www.guardian.co.uk/world/2012/mar/20/ china-next-generation-ageing-population.

38. French, Paul, *Fat China: How Expanding Waistlines Are Changing a Nation,* Anthem Press, July 2010.

39. Yang, Wenying et al., "Prevalence of Diabetes among Men and Women in China," *The New England Journal of Medicine,* March 25, 2010, www.nejm.org/doi/full/10.1056/NEJMoa0908292#t=articleBackground.

40. Burkitt, Laurie, "Study: China Getting Fatter, But Not Like US," *Wall Street Journal,* July 18, 2011, http://blogs.wsj.com/chinarealtime/2011/07/18/ study-china-getting-fatter-but-not-like-u-s/.

41. "China Faces Growing Gender Imbalance," BBC News, January 11, 2010, http://news.bbc.co.uk/2/hi/8451289.stm.

42. "China's Nursing Homes Falling Behind," *Xinhua,* January 18, 2012, http://news.xinhuanet.com/english/china/2012-01/18/c_131367103.htm.

43. Ministry of Human Resources and Social Security, "2011 Bulletin of Human Resources and Social Security Development," June 6, 2012, www.mohrss.gov.cn/SYrlzyhshbzb/zwgk/szrs/ndtjsj/tjgb/201206/ t20120605_69908.htm; also see "Wen Jiabao: Our Nation's Urban and Rural Old Age Insurance Participants Reach 790 Million; Enterprise Retirement Stipends Raised to 1,721 yuan per capita," *People's Daily,* March 5, 2013, http://lianghui.people.com.cn/2013npc/n/2013/0305/ c357862-20680117.html, and "Wen Jiabao: Speech at the Meeting Summarizing and Commending Work on a National New Socialist Countryside and Urban Resident Social Retirement Insurance," *Xinhua,* October 12, 2012, http://politics.people.com.cn/n/2012/1012/c1024-19248335. html.

44. Zuo, Xuejin, "Designing Fiscally Sustainable and Equitable Pension Systems in China," Shanghai Academy of Social Sciences Presentation to the IMF OAP/FAD Conference, Tokyo, January 9–10, 2013.

45. The demise of Shanghai Party Secretary Chen Liangyu was perhaps the biggest political struggle of the past decade before the latest crisis of Chongqing party boss Bo Xilai. It was widely believed that Chen's ouster was a ploy by former President Hu Jintao to get rid of a powerful political opponent.

46. "Shanghai Party Chief Sacked for Pension Scandal," *People's Daily*, September 25, 2006, http://english.people.com.cn/200609/25/eng20060925_306175.html; also see "Former Shanghai Party Chief Gets 18-year Term for Bribery," *Xinhua*, April 11, 2008, http://news.xinhuanet.com/english/2008-04/11/content_7959627.htm.

47. Ibid.

48. Authors' analysis of the U.S. Census Bureau International Database population projections.

49. Lan, Fang, "The Heavy Burden of Pensions," *Caixin*, September 3 cover series, http://magazine.caixin.com/2012-08-31/100431296_all.html#page2.

50. "Pension Fund Deficits Grew to 67.9 Bln Yuan in 2010," *Caixin*, December 23, 2011, http://english.caixin.com/2011-12-23/100342018.html.

51. Fauna, "Shanxi Coal Boss Spends 70 Million on Daughter's Wedding," ChinaSmack, March 26, 2012, http://www.chinasmack.com/2012/pictures/shanxi-coal-boss-spends-70-million-on-daughters-wedding.html.

52. Authors' conversation.

53. Lu, Rachel, "Women Declare Men of Average Income 'Underserving' of Marriage," January 9, 2012, *Tea Leaf Nation*, http://tealeafnation.com/2012/01/survey-says-no-money-no-honey/.

54. Wei, Shang-Jin, and Zhang, Xiaobo, "The Competitive Saving Motive: Evidence from Rising Sex Ratios and Savings Rates in China," National Bureau of Economic Research working paper, June 2009.

55. Larson, Christina, "The Startling Plight of China's Leftover Ladies," *Foreign Policy*, April 23, 2012, http://www.foreignpolicy.com/articles/2012/04/23/the_startling_plight_of_china_s_leftover_ladies.

56. Lim, Louisa, "Chinese Parents Play Matchmaker for Busy Children," National Public Radio, May 30, 2006, http://www.npr.org/templates/story/story.php?storyId=5438626.

57. Luo, Tianhao, "China Should Levy a 'Babe Tax'," February 17, 2011, *21st Century Business Herald*, http://news.21cbh.com/?c=print&id=221017.

Chapter 5

1. Robert H. Bates's *Markets and States in Tropical Africa: The Political Basis of Agricultural Policies*, University of California Press, 1981, provides a worthy introduction to this topic.

2. In *Battle Hymn of the Tiger Mother*, U.S.-born Amy Chua describes her attempts to pass on the brutally rigorous Chinese parental attitudes toward studying and education absorbed during her youth to her own children. Not surprisingly, her views stirred passions and captured the

zeitgeist in the United States, where higher education was getting much more competitive and in which the broader public viewed "Chinese" parenting as another way in which China would best the United States. See http://online.wsj.com/article/SB10001424052748704111504576059713528698754.html.

3. Elman, Benjamin A., *A Cultural History of Civil Examinations in Late Imperial China*, University of California Press, 2000.

4. "Male Student Learns of Mother's Death 12 Days After Completing Gaokao," *Sina Education Channel*, June 10, 2012, http://edu.sina.com.cn/gaokao/2012-06-10/1657342554.shtml.

5. "Hukou Regulation of the People's Republic of China," www.law-lib.com/law/law_view.asp?id=1338.

6. The *New York Times*'s Keith Bradsher dramatized the effect of this system on an individual Chinese student in his profile of college student Wu Caoying, "In China, Families Bet It All on College for Their Children," February 17, 2013, www.nytimes.com/2013/02/17/business/in-china-families-bet-it-all-on-a-child-in-college.html.

7. "2011 Roster of University Admission Cutoff Scores by Province and City," *People's Daily Education Channel*, June 27, 2011, http://edu.people.com.cn/GB/116076/15005780.html.

8. Ibid.

9. Chen, Liang et al., "Silent Revolution: Research Into the Social Background of Peking University and Suzhou University Students (1952-2002)," *China Social Science* 2012:1: 111.

10. Ibid.

11. China Statistical Yearbook 2012, Table 3-1.

12. See Chapter 3's description of the Sun Zhigang case.

13. See Chapter 6, "Housing: Home is where the wallet is" and sources cited therein.

14. "Ditching Gaokao, Students Choosing Elite Schools Abroad Rise Fourfold," *Sina Education Channel*, June 15, 2012, http://edu.sina.com.cn/a/2012-06-15/1719216355.shtml. See also "Beijing No. 4 High School: School Profile," www.bhsf.cn/news.php?id=4112.

15. "Outline of China's National Plan for Medium and Long-term Education Reform and Development (2010-2020)," English translation by Australian Education International (Australian Government), https://www.aei.gov.au/news/newsarchive/2010/documents/china_education_reform_pdf.pdf.

16. "Gaokao Reform Timetable Published to Promote Education Fairness," *China Daily*, December 31, 2012, http://english.sina.com/china/2012/1230/543472.html.

17. Jiang, Chengcheng, "In Beijing, Students in Limbo After Migrant Schools Closed," *Time*, September 14, 2011, www.time.com/time/world/article/0,8599,2093175,00.html.

Chapter 6

1. Chen, Shiyin, "China Is on 'Treadmill to Hell' as Property Prices Will Burst, Chanos Says," *Bloomberg News*, April 8, 2010, www.bloomberg.com/news/2010-04-08/china-is-on-treadmill-to-hell-as-property-prices-will-burst-chanos-says.html; and Dean, Jason, "Chinese Property: The Most Important Sector in the World," *Wall Street Journal*, March 16, 2011, http://blogs.wsj.com/chinarealtime/2011/03/16/chinese-property-the-most-important-sector-in-the-world/.

2. Adams, Bill, "Macroeconomic Implications of China Urban Housing Privatization, 1998-1999," *Journal of Contemporary China*, November, 2009: 881–888.

3. Ibid.

4. The authors gratefully acknowledge the insights of Atlantic Council Non-Resident Senior Fellow and China scholar Albert Keidel, cited in Adams: 887.

5. Estimates based on authors' analysis of Chinese national accounts data and the 2007 China Input-Output Table.

6. Adams, Bill, "Macroeconomic Implications of China Urban Housing Privatization, 1998-1999," *Journal of Contemporary China*, November, 2009: 881–888.

7. Authors' analysis of Chinese monthly data, based on National Bureau of Statistics figures.

8. Fan, Jiang, "Report: Nearly 90 pct of Chinese Families Own Houses," *People's Daily*, May 15, 2012, http://english.peopledaily.com.cn/90882/7817224.html.

9. Authors' analysis of data from the Fifth and Sixth Population Census long form survey results, Tables 4-1, 4-4, and 4-6, National Bureau of Statistics.

10. Adams, Bill, "Macroeconomic Implications of China Urban Housing Privatization, 1998-1999," *Journal of Contemporary China*, November, 2009: 881–888.

11. Sanderson, Henry and Zhou, Xin, "Chinese Anger Over Pollution Becomes Main Cause of Social Unrest," *Bloomberg News*, March 6, 2013, www.bloomberg.com/news/2013-03-06/pollution-passes-land-grievances-as-main-spark-of-china-protests.html.

12. Arora, Raksha, "Homeownership Soars in China," Gallup, March 1, 2005, www.gallup.com/poll/15082/homeownership-soars-china.aspx.

13. China Merchants Bank and Bain & Company, "2011 China Private Wealth Report," www.bain.com/Images/2011_China_wealth_management_report.pdf, page 16, and authors' calculations.

14. "Hurun Rich List 2012," Hurun, www.hurun.net/.

15. A major fiscal reform in 1994 essentially centralized tax revenue and budgets, which are then redistributed back to the provinces through transfer mechanisms. Provincial coffers dwindled, and local authorities had to find other avenues for revenue. For more on local finances, see Wong, Christine, "Some Suggestions for Improving China's Municipal Finance for the 21st Century," The Paulson Institute, December 2012, http://cache.cantos.com/mp4/websites/paulsoninstitute/Some-Suggestions-for-Improving-Chinas-Municipal_Finance-en.pdf.

16. While credible estimates usually cite these ranges, calculating the average home price as percentage of the typical income is not trivial given the challenges of measuring both quantities. See Orlik, Tom, and Fung, Esther, "Hope for Home Buyers in China," *Wall Street Journal*, January 16, 2013, http://online.wsj.com/article/SB10001424127887324235 10457824204333846897 4.html; see also Wu, Yixue, "Making Homes Affordable," *Xinhua*, April 15, 2012, http://news.xinhuanet.com/english/china/2012-04/15/c_131527666.htm; and see Figure 9 of Ahuja et al., "Are House Prices Rising Too Fast in China?" IMF Working Paper No. 10/274, www.imf.org/external/pubs/cat/longres.cfm?sk=24404.0.

17. Zhu, Pei, "Prices of Newly Constructed Homes in Shenzhen Rise 2.03% MoM; Average Price 26,221 yuan/sqm," *Soufun Net*, April 4, 2013, http://news.sz.soufun.com/2013-04-02/9833130.htm.

18. "Per Capita Income of Urban Residents in Our City Rose 10.8% Year Over Year Between January and December," Beijing Municipal Statistical Bureau, January 22, 2013, www.bjstats.gov.cn/sjjd/jjxs/201301/t20130121_242330.htm.

19. If both housing prices and salaries rise 10% per year, and workers earn a steady 5% return on savings, it would take 11 years for someone saving 90% of his income to accumulate a down payment equivalent to 20 times his salary.

20. Arora, Raksha, "Homeownership Soars in China," Gallup, March 1, 2005, www.gallup.com/poll/15082/homeownership-soars-china.aspx.

21. For example, see Tania Branigan's profile of a laid-off Shenzhen worker's trip home to her village in Jiangxi, "Unemployment Forces Chinese Migrants Back to the Countryside," *The Guardian*, May 17, 2009, www.guardian.co.uk/world/2009/may/17/china-crossroads-migrants-tania-branigan.

22. Galbraith, John Kenneth, *The Essential Galbraith*, Boston & New York: Houghton Mifflin Company, 2001: 308.

23. Xin, Zhou, "Li Keqiang Urges More Urbanization to Support China's Growth," *Bloomberg News,* November 21, 2012, www.bloomberg.com/news/2012-11-21/li-keqiang-urges-deeper-urbanization-to-support-china-s-growth.html.

24. "The Next Big Question for China: Rural Land Reform," AmCham China, August 8, 2012, http://www.amchamchina.org/article/10028; and Landesa, "Summary of 2011 17-Province Survey's Findings," April 26, 2012, http://www.landesa.org/wp-content/uploads/Landesa_China_Survey_Report_2011.pdf.

25. Huang, Xiaohu, "Explaining Land Finance," Ministry of Land and Natural Resources, www.mlr.gov.cn/wskt/glkx/tdgl/201110/t20111008_981766.htm.

26. "China to Build More Affordable Houses Next Year: Minister," *Xinhua,* http://www.chinadaily.com.cn/china/2012cpc/2012-11/12/content_15919353.htm.

27. National Bureau of Statistics, "2012 Statistical Report on National Economic and Social Development of the People's Republic of China" (Chinese), www.stats.gov.cn/tjgb/ndtjgb/qgndtjgb/t20130221_402874525.htm; see also "China Targets 7 Million Low-Income Houses in 2012: Minister," *Xinhua,* December 23, 2011, http://news.xinhuanet.com/english/china/2011-12/23/c_131324101.htm.

28. Dafeng Real Estate Network, "Two Trillion in Land Use Right Fees For Three Hundred Cities in 2012" (Chinese), January 10, 2013, www.dafcw.com/InfoView/2437.html.

29. Rabinovitch, Simon, "China's Officials Forced to Sell Luxury Cars," *Financial Times,* June 25, 2012, www.ft.com/intl/cms/s/0/02ba4b9c-beb9-11e1-8ccd-00144feabdc0.html#axzz2Nl7c0WdB.

30. "State Council Notice on Continuing to Properly and Effectively Manage Propery Market Adjustments," State Council, March 1, 2013, Document #17, www.gov.cn/zwgk/2013-03/01/content_2342885.htm.

31. This is a specific example of the more general role of local government officials in lobbying for loose macroeconomic policies described by political scientist Victor Shih in his book *Factions and Finance in China: Elite Conflict and Inflation.*

32. Xie, Andy, "Fear Empty Flats in China's Property Bubble," *Caixin,* August 8, 2010, http://english.caixin.com/2010-08-03/100166589.html.

33. "Shanghai's Property Tax Last Year Covered 37,000 Housing Units, Taxes Totaled 2.46 Billion Yuan," *Sina Shanghai Channel,* February 21, 2013, http://sh.sina.com.cn/news/economy/2013-02-21/083235052.html.

34. Xing, Yun, "Price Threshhold Raised for Real Estate Tax Collection on High-End Housing in Chonqing," *Caixin,* January 11, 2013, http://economy.caixin.com/2013-01-11/100481676.html.

35. "State Council Notice on Continuing to Properly and Effectively Manage Property Market Adjustments," State Council, March 1, 2013, Document #17, www.gov.cn/zwgk/2013-03/01/content_2342885.htm.

36. "Guangdong Officials Face Investigation over Property," *Xinhua,* January 12, 2013, www.china.org.cn/china/2013-01/12/content_27665096.htm.

37. Tan, Lin, "'Lu Feng', 'Property Boss', Two Identities! Owns 192 Units?," *Southern Metropolitan Post,* http://epaper.oeeee.com/A/html/2013-02/05/content_1805986.htm.

38. "Is China's Property Tax Going Crazy?" NTD, December 4, 2012, www.en.ntd.tv/chinablog/is-chinas-property-tax-going-crazy/."

39. Sina Weibo poll as of December 3, 2012, sourced from NTD China Blog, http://en.ntd.tv/reference/chinablog/is-chinas-property-tax-going-crazy/screen-shot-2012-12-03-at-7-20-53-pm/.

40. "Web China: Property Tax TV Show Stirs Online Debate," Sina.com, original source *Xinhua,* www.english.sina.com/2012/0907/504390.html.

41. Sanderson, Henry, "China Auditor Finds Irregularities in $1.7 Trillion Local Government Debt," *Bloomberg News,* June 27, 2011, www.bloomberg.com/news/2011-06-27/china-audit-office-warns-of-risk-on-1-7-trillion-of-local-government-debt.html.

Chapter 7

1. "2011 National Civil Service Examination Questions and Answers," Baidu, http://wenku.baidu.com/view/b927208b6529647d2728522b.html.

2. CCTV English, http://english.cntv.cn/20121009/105443.shtml.

3. Mao Zedong thought is derived from Marxism-Leninism. Its essential features included a focus on agrarian revolt against the bourgeoisie (that is, the monied urban class), constant revolutions to achieve socialist egalitarianism, and contradictions within society. Deng Xiaoping theory marked a dramatic departure from Mao, instead adopting market economics, depoliticizing economic development, and emphasizing pragmatism. The Three Represents concept was essentially a rebranding effort to firmly ensconce the Chinese Communist Party (CCP) as the establishment, elite governing party, not a revolutionary party. Scientific outlook on development emphasized rational and sustainable development, invoking the Confucian idea of harmony to address ostensible social and economic imbalances.

4. Ching, Frank, "China's Fluid Ideology," *The Diplomat,* August 4, 2011, http://thediplomat.com/2011/08/04/china%E2%80%99s-fluid-ideology/.

5. Pye, Lucian W., "Social Science Theories in Search of Chinese Realities," *China Quarterly* 132, December 1992.

6. "China's First Aircraft Carrier Commissioned," *Xinhua,* September 25, 2012, http://news.xinhuanet.com/english/china/2012-09/25/c_131871538. htm.

7. Spence, Jonathan D., *The Search for a Modern China,* W. W. Norton, 1990.

8. Callahan, William A., "National Insecurities: Humiliation, Salvation, and Chinese Nationalism," *Alternatives* 29 (2004), www.humiliationstudies. org/documents/CallahanChina.pdf; also see "The Century of Humiliation Atlas," www.mutantpalm.org/2007/05/21/century-of-humiliation-atlas.html.

9. Japan's encroachment on China during the Century of Humiliation continues to dominate Sino-Japanese relations to this day, echoing in recent tensions over the Senkaku/Diaoyu Island dispute between China and Japan. For example, see Manning, Robert A., "Behind Sino-Japanese Tensions," *The National Interest,* November 13, 2012, http://nationalinterest.org/commentary/asias-morass-its-not-about-the-rocks-7725; also see Barme, Geremie R., "Mirrors of History: On a Sino-Japanese Moment and Some Antecedents," *The Asia-Pacific Journal,* www.japanfocus.org/-Geremie-Barme/1713.

10. Ibid; also see Wasserstrom, Jeffrey N., "Chinese Students and Anti-Japanese Protests, Past and Present," *World Policy Journal* XXII(2), Summer 2005, www.worldpolicy.org/journal/articles/wpj05-2/wasserstrom.html.

11. Lawrence, Alan (ed.), *China Since 1919: Revolution and Reform: A Source Book,* Routledge, 2004.

12. Chen, Duxiu, *Call to Youth,* 1915. Also see Chen's *Our Final Awakening,* 1916, excerpts at http://afe.easia.columbia.edu/ps/china/chen_duxiu_final_awakening.pdf.

13. Full translation of Lu Xun's *A Madman's Diary* at www.marxists.org/archive/lu-xun/1918/04/x01.htm. Also see Lovell, Julia (translator), *The Real Story of Ah-Q and Other Tales of China: The Complete Fiction of Lu Xun,* Penguin Classics, 2009. Also see Wasserstrom, Jeffrey, "China's Orwell," *Time,* December 7, 2009, www.time.com/time/magazine/article/0,9171,1943086,00.html.

14. For further reading on this period, see Spence, Jonathan D., *The Gate of Heavenly Peace,* Penguin Books, 1982.

15. The Qin emperor was the ruthless ruler who united China in 221 B.C. See "Mao Zedong: To Solve China's Problems Requires Marx and Qin Emperor," QQ news, December 27, 2011, http://news.qq.com/a/20111227/000376.htm.

16. For further reading on China's move toward reforms, see Kissinger, Henry, *On China*, Penguin Books, 2012.

17. For further reading on Deng Xiaoping, see Vogel, Ezra, *Deng Xiaoping and the Transformation of China*, Harvard University Press, 2011.

18. Bao, Tong, "A Pivotal Moment for China," translated by Radio Free Asia, www.rfa.org/english/news/china/thirdplenum-12272008165259.html.

19. Schram, Stuart, "'Economics in command?' Ideology and Policy Since the Third Plenum 1978-84." *China Quarterly* 99, September 1984.

20. "Deng Xiaoping's Black Cat/White Cat Theory Galvanizes 30 Years of Rapid Development," Sina.com, http://news.sina.com.cn/c/2008-12-12/040416831808.shtml.

21. Wasserstrom, Jeffrey N., and Perry, Elizabeth J. (eds.), *Popular Protest and Political Culture in Modern China*, 2nd edition, Westview Press, 1994.

22. "Three Represents," *People's Daily*, June 23, 2006, http://english.cpc.people.com.cn/66739/4521344.html.

23. "Heirs of Mao's Comrades Rise as New Capitalist Nobility," *Bloomberg Businessweek*, December 26, 2012, www.bloomberg.com/news/2012-12-26/immortals-beget-china-capitalism-from-citic-to-godfather-of-golf.html; also see *Wall Street Journal*, "Defying Mao, Rich Chinese Crash the Communist Party," December 26, 2012, http://online.wsj.com/article/SB10001424127887323723104578187360101389762.html; also see *New York Times*, "Billions of Hidden Riches for Family of Chinese Leader," October 25, 2012, www.nytimes.com/2012/10/26/business/global/family-of-wen-jiabao-holds-a-hidden-fortune-in-china.html?pagewanted=all.

24. "Gov't Still Refuses to Release Gini Coefficient," *Caixin*, January 18, 2012, http://english.caixin.com/2012-01-18/100349814.html.

25. "Map: US Ranks Near Bottom on Income Inequality," *The Atlantic Monthly* online, www.theatlantic.com/international/archive/2011/09/map-us-ranks-near-bottom-on-income-inequality/245315/#; also see *Reuters* series "The Unequal State of America," December 2012, www.reuters.com/subjects/income-inequality.

26. Herbert Kitschelt uses the terms *clientelistic, charismatic,* and *programmatic* to describe these sources of political loyalty. See Kitschelt, Herbert, "Linkages between Citizens and Politicians in Democratic Polities," *Comparative Political Studies* 33(6-7), September 2000.

27. Fewsmith, Joseph, "Promoting the Scientific Development Concept," *China Leadership Monitor* 11, http://media.hoover.org/sites/default/files/documents/clm11_jf.pdf; also see "Hu Jintao Proposes Scientific Outlook on Development for Tackling China's Immediate Woes,

Challenges," *Xinhua*, October 15, 2007, http://news.xinhuanet.com/english/2007-10/15/content_6883135.htm.

28. "Decision of the 17th CCP Congress on Revisions to the CCP Prospectus," *People's Daily*, October 21, 2007, http://cpc.people.com.cn/GB/104019/104101/6410786.html.

29. Lewis, John W., and Litai, Xue, "Social Change and Political Reform in China: Meeting the Challenge of Success," *China Quarterly*, 2003, http://iis-db.stanford.edu/pubs/20615/Lewis-Xue-poli_reform.pdf.

30. Ma, Damien, "Hu Jintao's Kennedy Moment," *The Atlantic Monthly* online, June 21, 2012, www.theatlantic.com/international/archive/2012/06/hu-jintaos-kennedy-moment/258790/.

31. "Significant Achievements under Scientific Development," *People's Daily*, November 4, 2012, http://cpc.people.com.cn/18/n/2012/1104/c350837-19490004.html.

32. Branigan, Tania, "China Needs Political Reform to Avert 'Historic Tragedy', says Wen Jiabao," *The Guardian*, March 14, 2012, www.guardian.co.uk/world/2012/mar/14/china-political-reform-wen-jiabao.

33. Gong, Fangbin, "Political System Reforms Need Support from New Political Outlook," *People's Daily*, October 8, 2010, http://theory.people.com.cn/n/2012/1008/c49152-19192764.html.

34. For brief explanations of Confucius's life and philosophy, see the Stanford Encyclopedia of Philosophy, http://plato.stanford.edu/entries/confucius/#ConPol.

35. Dotson, John, "The Confucian Revival in the Propaganda Narratives of the Chinese Government," United States-China Economic and Security Review Commission research report, accessed here, www.uscc.gov/researchpapers/2011/Confucian_Revival_Paper.pdf.

36. "Confucius Makes a Comeback," *The Economist*, May 17, 2007, www.economist.com/node/9202957.

37. "Confucius Statue Shows Up in China's Tiananmen Square," *Huffington Post*, January 14, 2011, www.huffingtonpost.com/2011/01/14/confucius-statue-tiananmen-square_n_809038.html.

38. Bell, Daniel, "The Chinese Confucian Party?" *The Globe and Mail*, February 19, 2010, www.theglobeandmail.com/commentary/the-chinese-confucian-party/article1365495/?page=all; also see Bell, Daniel, "The Confucian Party," *New York Times*, May 11, 2009, www.nytimes.com/2009/05/12/opinion/12iht-edbell.html.

39. Jacobs, Andrew, "Confucian Statue Vanishes Near Tiananmen Square," *New York Times*, April 22, 2011, www.nytimes.com/2011/04/23/world/asia/23confucius.html.

40. Chinese photographer tracking down all the remaining Mao statues and iconic sculptures across China, see http://vimeo.com/35243527.

41. Ministry of Tofu, www.ministryoftofu.com/2011/04/picture-of-the-day-come-and-go-of-confucius/.

42. "Mao Still Stands," *China Daily,* January 18, 2010, www.chinadaily.com.cn/life/2010-01/18/content_9334837.htm; also see documenting Mao nostalgia across China at Ministry of Tofu, www.ministryoftofu.com/2012/02/world-press-photo-winner-the-return-of-the-native-mao-zedong-remembered/.

43. Ma, Damien, "Avatar Backlash in China," *Forbes,* February 3, 2010, www.forbes.com/2010/02/03/avatar-james-cameron-china-beijing-opinions-contributors-damien-ma.html.

44. "Rectification of Statues," *The Economist,* January 20, 2011, www.economist.com/blogs/asiaview/2011/01/china%E2%80%99s_confucius_institutes.

45. "Confucius Institute: Promoting Language, Culture, and Friendliness," *Xinhua,* October 2, 2006, http://news.xinhuanet.com/english/2006-10/02/content_5521722.htm.

46. "316 Confucius Institutes Established Worldwide," *Xinhua,* July 13, 2010, http://news.xinhuanet.com/english2010/culture/2010-07/13/c_13398209.htm.

47. *Hexie* (or "harmonized") is often invoked by Chinese netizens when mocking the web censorship system.

48. The jingoistic and deliberately pro-China tone of the paper is often likened to China's Fox News. Although state-owned, the paper should not always be interpreted as representing official views. Often it deliberately takes a stance far removed from official Chinese government positions.

49. "2010 Nobel Peace Prize a Disgrace," *Global Times,* October 9, 2010, www.globaltimes.cn/opinion/editorial/2010-10/580091.html.

50. Wong, Edward, "For Putin, a Peace Prize for a Decision to Go to War," *New York Times,* November 15, 2011, www.nytimes.com/2011/11/16/world/asia/chinas-confucius-prize-awarded-to-vladimir-putin.html.

51. Schell, Orville, "China's Post-Olympic Challenge," *Project Syndicate,* August 25, 2008, www.project-syndicate.org/commentary/china-s-post-olympic-challenge.

Chapter 8

1. Gansberg, Martin, "Thirty-Eight Who Saw Murder Didn't Call the Police," *New York Times,* March 27, 1964, www2.southeastern.edu/Academics/Faculty/scraig/gansberg.html.

2. "China's Hit and Run Scandal: Yue Yue Dies," *AFP*, October 21, 2011, www.theage.com.au/world/chinas-hitrun-scandal-yue-yue-dies-20111021-1mbpc.html.

3. "Chinese Toddler Yue Yue Dies But Morality Debate Lives On," *Christian Science Monitor*, October 21, 2011, www.csmonitor.com/World/Latest-News-Wires/2011/1021/Chinese-toddler-Yue-Yue-dies-but-morality-debate-lives-on.

4. MacFarquhar, Roderick and Schoenhals, Michael, *Mao's Last Revolution*, Harvard University Press, 2006.

5. Putnam, Robert, *Bowling Alone: The Collapse and Revival of American Community*, Simon & Schuster, 2000.

6. Osnos, Evan, "Meet Dr. Freud," *New Yorker*, January 20, 2011, www.capachina.org/zips/Meet%20Dr.%20Freud%20-%20The%20New%20Yorker.pdf.

7. Hu, Angang, "China Must Measure Happiness," *China Dialogue*, February 24, 2011, www.chinadialogue.net/article/show/single/en/4130--China-must-measure-happiness-.

8. Easterlin, Richard A. et al., "China's Life Satisfaction, 1990-2010," National Academy of Sciences, April 6, 2012, www.pnas.org/content/early/2012/05/09/1205672109.full.pdf. Easterlin's methodology and survey findings have been debated in academia.

9. Demick, Barbara, "China Checks Its Own Mood," *Los Angeles Times*, May 16, 2011, http://articles.latimes.com/2011/may/16/world/la-fg-china-happiness-20110516.

10. CCTV segment, accessed at www.ministryoftofu.com/2012/10/chinese-nonsensical-answers-to-are-you-happy-baffles-cctv-and-amuses-netizens/.

11. Inglehart, Ronald, World Values Survey, www.worldvaluessurvey.org/wvs/articles/folder_published/article_base_56.

12. Inglehart, Ronald et al., appendix to "Social Change, Freedom, and Rising Happiness," *Journal of Personality and Social Psychology*, www.worldvaluessurvey.org/wvs/articles/folder_published/article_base_106.

13. Friedman, Thomas L., "Justice Goes Global," *New York Times*, June 14, 2011, www.nytimes.com/2011/06/15/opinion/15friedman.html.

14. Fallows, James, "The Most Important Film I've Seen in Years: 'Last Train Home,'" *The Atlantic Monthly* online, July 1, 2012, www.theatlantic.com/international/archive/2012/07/the-most-important-film-ive-seen-in-years-last-train-home/259265/.

15. "China's Migrant Population Reaches 211 Million," *People's Daily*, June 29, 2010, http://english.peopledaily.com.cn/90001/90776/90882/7044776.html.

16. "I Fought for 18 Years to Have a Cup of Coffee with You," ChinaHush, http://www.chinahush.com/2011/10/25/i-fought-for-18-years-to-have-a-cup-of-coffee-with-you/?utm_source=feedburner&utm_medium=feed&utm_campaign=Feed%3A+ChinaHush+%28ChinaHush%29.

17. A *veil of ignorance* essentially stipulates that "... no one knows his place in society, his class position or social status; nor does he know his fortune in the distribution of natural assets and abilities, his intelligence and strength, and the like." Rawls, John, *A Theory of Justice,* Harvard University Press, 1971.

18. Cheng, Tiejun, and Selden, Mark, "The Origins and Social Consequences of China's *Hukou* System," *The China Quarterly* 139, September 1994.

19. Branigan, Tania, "Millions of Rural Chinese Migrants Denied Education for Their Children," *The Guardian*, March 14, 2010, www.guardian.co.uk/world/2010/mar/15/china-migrant-workers-children-education.

20. Lei Feng was supposedly an exemplary soldier who was morally upright and selfless, the kind of everyday proletariat role model that the CCP relied on in the 1950s during its agitprop and cult of personality propaganda campaigns, see www.globaltimes.cn/NEWS/tabid/99/ID/697218/When-Lei-Feng-meets-non-believers.aspx.

21. Davis, Bob, "In Guangdong, 'Happiness' Is Indexed," *Wall Street Journal*, July 27, 2012, http://online.wsj.com/article/SB10000872396390444330904577537510151380468.html.

22. Page, Jeremy, "Guangdong's Recipe for Happiness: Fewer People, More Sex," *Wall Street Journal*, November 11, 2011, http://blogs.wsj.com/chinarealtime/2011/11/11/guangdongs-recipe-for-happiness-fewer-people-more-sex/.

23. Jacobs, Andrew, "Residents Vote in Chinese Village at Center of Protest," *New York Times,* February 1, 2012, www.nytimes.com/2012/02/02/world/asia/residents-vote-in-chinese-village-at-center-of-protest.html.

24. Bandurski, David, "Inside the Southern Weekly Incident," China Media Project, January 7, 2013, http://cmp.hku.hk/2013/01/07/30402/.

25. The excerpt is taken from Bo Yibo's memoir. Bo is considered one of the "eight immortals" in the CCP who fought with Mao and is the father of the now disgraced Bo Xilai. *China Heritage Quarterly*, translation by Qiang Zhai, www.chinaheritagequarterly.org/features.php?searchterm=018_1959preventingpeace.inc&issue=018.

26. Fukuyama, Francis, *The End of History and the Last Man,* Avon Books 1992.

27. Deng's quote is generally translated as "If you open the window for fresh air, you have to expect some flies to blow in."

28. Waxman, Sharon, "White House Gets China to Open Market to U.S. Movies," *Reuters*, February 18, 2012, www.reuters.com/article/2012/02/18/idUS420251887620120218.

29. Rovnick, Naomi, "Behind the Boom in Chinese Students at US Colleges," *Quartz*, November 13, 2012, www.nationaljournal.com/thenextamerica/education/behind-the-boom-in-chinese-students-at-u-s-colleges-20121113.

30. "The Debate over Universal Values," *The Economist*, September 30, 2010, www.economist.com/node/17150224.

31. Osnos, Evan, "A Collage of Chinese Values," Letters from China, *New Yorker*, March 21, 2012, www.newyorker.com/online/blogs/evanosnos/2012/03/a-collage-of-chinese-values.html.

32. Ding, Sean, and Wu, Jingjing, "Universal Values in China: A Domestic Debate," China Elections and Governance, http://chinaelectionsblog.net/?p=13298.

33. "From the Painful Wenchuan Quake Emerges a New China," *Southern Weekend*, May 22, 2008, www.infzm.com/content/12439.

34. Interview with Sima Nan, "Universal Values Is a Fairy Tale," *Ifeng News*, June 16, 2008, http://news.ifeng.com/opinion/200806/0616_23_598761.shtml.

35. "How to Understand the So-Called Universal Values," *People's Daily*, September 10, 2010, www.chinanews.com/gn/news/2008/09-10/1377451.shtml.

36. "Theoretical and Practical Questions Regarding Clearly Setting the 'Four Major Boundaries,'" *Qiushi (Seeking Truth)*, August 16, 2010, www.qstheory.cn/zz/zztj/201008/t20100816_42820.htm.

37. Yan, Xuetong, "Sharing Chinese Values with the World," *Xinhua*, May 11, 2012, www.china.org.cn/opinion/2012-05/11/content_25361798.htm.

38. Yan, Xuetong, "The Sources of Chinese Conduct," *Project Syndicate*, March 28, 2011, www.project-syndicate.org/commentary/the-sources-of-chinese-conduct.

39. Yan, Xuetong, "How China Can Defeat America," *New York Times*, November 20, 2011, www.nytimes.com/2011/11/21/opinion/how-china-can-defeat-america.html?pagewanted=all&_r=0.

40. Kissinger, Henry, *On China*, Penguin Books, 2012.

41. Pei, Minxin, "The Loneliest Superpower," *Foreign Policy*, March 20, 2012, www.foreignpolicy.com/articles/2012/03/20/the_loneliest_superpower?page=0,1.

42. Giridharadas, Anand, *Chinese Dreams: An Essay*, Amazon Digital Services, January 17, 2011.

43. Ma, Damien, "What It Means to be a Rising Public Intellectual in China," *The Atlantic Monthly* online, February 28, 2012 www.theatlantic.com/international/archive/2012/02/what-it-means-to-be-a-rising-public-intellectual-in-china/253610/.

44. *Reuters* series on US inequality, www.reuters.com/subjects/income-inequality/washington.

45. Ibid. Founder of Chengwei Capital in Shanghai, Li is on the board of the Keck Center at Claremont Mckenna College, is a fellow at the Aspen Institute, has funded Francis Fukuyama's Governance Project at Stanford University, and is a regular contributor to the *Huffington Post*. He also founded the Equinox (Chunqiu) Institute, a research shop that is focused on researching Chinese values; he reportedly serves as an adviser to the Carnegie Endowment, and he founded the Dulwich College system in China.

46. Delong, J. Bradford, and Cohen, Stephen S., *The End of Influence: What happens when other countries have the money*, Basic Books 2010.

47. Chinese commentary and fascination with U.S. school buses, see ChinaSmack, www.chinasmack.com/2012/pictures/american-school-bus-fawned-over-at-beijing-bus-exhibition.html.

48. Wong, Edward, "Signals of a More Open Economy in China," *New York Times*, December 9, 2012, www.nytimes.com/2012/12/10/world/asia/chinese-leaders-visit-to-shenzhen-hints-at-reform.html?pagewanted=2&ref=edwardwong.

Chapter 9

1. Ministry of Tofu, April 18, 2012. www.ministryoftofu.com/2012/04/dog-owners-irate-tearful-over-harbins-crackdown-on-large-dogs/.

2. Ibid.

3. Pew Global Attitudes Project, "Growing Concerns in China about Inequality, Corruption," October 16, 2012, www.pewglobal.org/files/2012/10/Pew-Global-Attitudes-China-Report-FINAL-October-10-2012.pdf.

4. Gallup, June 8, 2012, www.gallup.com/poll/155102/Majority-Chinese-Prioritize-Environment-Economy.aspx.

5. "Pew Global Attitudes Project 2012 Spring Survey Topline Results," www.pewglobal.org/files/2012/10/Pew-Global-Attitudes-China-Report-FINAL-TOPLINE-October-10-2012.pdf.

6. Graham-Harrison, Emma, "China's Water Pollution Level Higher than Estimated in 2007," *Washington Post*, February 10, 2010, www.washingtonpost.com/wp-dyn/content/article/2010/02/09/AR2010020903572.html.

7. Sample, Ian, "Yangtze River Dolphin Driven to Extinction," *The Guardian* August 7, 2007, www.guardian.co.uk/environment/2007/aug/08/endangeredspecies.conservation.

8. Liu, Melinda, "Where Poor Is a Poor Excuse," *The Daily Beast*, June 28, 2008, www.thedailybeast.com/newsweek/2008/06/28/where-poor-is-a-poor-excuse.html.

9. Ma, Damien, "Why China Wants to Slow Down Its Own Economy," *The Atlantic Monthly* online, March 13, 2012, www.theatlantic.com/international/archive/2012/03/why-china-wants-to-slow-down-its-own-economy/254374/.

10. Dan, Guangnai, "Assessment of 2009 Mass Incidents," *Southern Weekend*, May 2011, www.infzm.com/content/41159/0.

11. Xu, Kai and Chen, Xiaoshu, "The Bill for Public Security," *Caijing*, May 8, 2011, http://misc.caijing.com.cn/chargeFullNews.jsp?id=110712639&time=2011-05-08&cl=106&page=1#.

12. Buckley, Chris, "China's Domestic Security Spending Rises to $111 Billion," *Reuters*, March 5, 2012, www.reuters.com/article/2012/03/05/us-china-parliament-security-idUSTRE82403J20120305.

13. O'Brien, Kevin J., "Rightful Resistance," *World Politics* 49(1), October 1996.

14. Mackinnon, Mark, "The Flash Cars of Beijing's Poorly Paid Public Servants," *The Globe and Mail*, May 24, 2012, www.theglobeandmail.com/news/world/world-view/in-photos-the-flash-cars-of-beijings-poorly-paid-public-servants/article4204318/#gallery_1752=0.

15. Xu, Kai and Li, Weiao, "The Stability Maintenance Machine," *Caijing*, June 6, 2011, www.caijing.com.cn/2011-06-06/110738832.html. Translation at Duihua Foundation, www.duihuahrjournal.org/2011/06/translation-machinery-of-stability.html.

16. Godement, Francois, "Control at the Grassroots: China's new toolbox," European Council on Foreign Relations, June 2012, http://ecfr.eu/page/-/China_Analysis_Control_at_the_Grassroots_June2012.pdf.

17. Freeman, Will, "The Accuracy of China's 'Mass Incidents'," *Financial Times*, March 2, 2010, www.ft.com/intl/cms/s/0/9ee6fa64-25b5-11df-9bd3-00144feab49a.html#axzz1yjMR16nu.

18. Feng, Shu, "A National Conundrum," *Global Times*, February 10, 2012, http://english.peopledaily.com.cn/90882/7725198.html.

19. Xu, Kai and Chen, Xiaoshu, "The Bill for Public Security," *Caijing*, May 8, 2011, http://misc.caijing.com.cn/chargeFullNews.jsp?id=110712639&time=2011-05-08&cl=106&page=1#.

20. Sun, Liping, "How to Get Officials to Declare Property and Assets," September 28, 2011, www.chinareform.net/con_special.php?id=278.

21. Yu, Jianrong, "The Unbearable Cost," *Caixin,* January 19, 2011, http://english.caixin.com/2011-01-19/100218601.html.

22. Sun, Liping, "Society Is Speeding Toward Defeat," *People's Daily,* February 27, 2011, http://news.ifeng.com/history/zhongguoxiandaishi/special/daodededixian/detail_2011_02/27/4877743_0.shtml.

23. Lee, Mark and Cao, Belinda, "Sina Offers Web TV Service to Win China Social Networkers," *Bloomberg News*, July 12, 2012, www.bloomberg.com/news/2012-07-12/sina-offers-web-tv-service-to-win-china-social-networkers.html.

24. "Statistical Report on China's Internet Development," China Internet Network Information Center (CNNIC), July 2012, www.cnnic.org.cn/hlwfzyj/hlwxzbg/hlwtjbg/201207/t20120723_32497.htm. Full report at www.cnnic.cn/hlwfzyj/hlwxzbg/hlwtjbg/201207/P020120723477451202474.pdf.

25. Epstein, Gady, "China's Internet: A Giant Cage," *The Economist,* April 6, 2013, www.economist.com/news/special-report/21574628-internet-was-expected-help-democratise-china-instead-it-has-enabled.

26. Gladney, Dru, "China's Ethnic Tinderbox," *BBC*, July 9 2009, http://news.bbc.co.uk/2/hi/8141867.stm.

27. "China Restores Internet to Xinjiang," *The Guardian*, May 14, 2010, www.guardian.co.uk/world/2010/may/14/china-restores-internet-access-xinjiang.

28. Shanghaiist, February 24, 2011, http://shanghaiist.com/2011/02/24/video-jon-huntsman-jasmine-revolution.php.

29. Ma, Damien, "2011: When Chinese Social Media Found Its Legs," *The Atlantic Monthly* online, December 18, 2011, www.theatlantic.com/international/archive/2011/12/2011-when-chinese-social-media-found-its-legs/250083/.

30. Cao, Haili, Yu, Ning, Liang, Dongmei, and Bi, Aifang, "Where is High Speed Rail Headed?" *Caixin,* March 28, 2011, http://magazine.caing.com/2011/cwcs443/index.html; also see Ma, Damien, "China's Long, Bumpy Road to High-Speed Rail," *The Atlantic Monthly* online, March 30, 2011, www.theatlantic.com/international/archive/2011/03/chinas-long-bumpy-road-to-high-speed-rail/73192/.

31. Osnos, Evan, "Boss Rail," *New Yorker,* October 22, 2012, www.newyorker.com/reporting/2012/10/22/121022fa_fact_osnos.

32. "High-Speed Rail's Illusory Indigenous Innovation," *Caixin,* July 2, 2012, http://magazine.caixin.com/2012-06-29/100405438.html.

33. "China's Medium and Long Term Railway Network Plan (2008 revisions)," *Xinhua*, November 27, 2011, http://news.xinhuanet.com/newscenter/2008-11/27/content_10422275_1.htm.

34. See, for example, Friedman, Tom, "Their Moon Shot and Ours," *New York Times*, September 25, 2010, www.nytimes.com/2010/09/26/opinion/26friedman.html.

35. Wang, Chen, "Liu Zhijun Admits to Taking 64.6 Mln Yuan in Bribes," *Caixin*, June 10, 2013, http://english.caixin.com/2013-06-10/100540244.html.

36. "Editorial: Letter to Yiyi—When You've Grown Up," *Economic Observer*, August 1, 2011, www.eeo.com.cn/ens/2011/0801/207710.shtml.

37. "Han Han: The Derailed Country," translated by Charlie Custer, *ChinaGeeks*, July 28, 2011, http://chinageeks.org/2011/07/han-han-the-derailed-country/.

38. Shanghaiist, "Even CCTV is Turning Up the Heat on the Ministry of Railways," July 28, 2011, http://shanghaiist.com/2011/07/28/watch_cctv_news_anchor_qin_fang_una.php; also see video of Qiu Qiming, anchor of popular CCTV news show *24 Hours,* comments on the rail crash, www.youtube.com/watch?v=xqjMEQjhKQs.

39. "Beijing Reaches Annual 'Blue Sky Days' Target," *Xinhua,* December 18, 2011, www.china.org.cn/environment/2011-12/18/content_24184374.htm.

40. Zhang, Chi-chi, "US Embassy: Beijing Air Quality is 'Crazy Bad'," *Associated Press*, November 19, 2010, http://wwwwww.msnbc.msn.com/id/40273827/ns/world_news-world_environment/t/us-embassy-beijing-air-quality-crazy-bad/#.UAyhWDFSTtI.

41. Shen, Feifei, "China Calls on Foreign Embassies to Halt Pollution Data," *Bloomberg News*, June 6, 2012, www.businessweek.com/news/2012-06-05/china-calls-on-foreign-embassies-to-halt-pollution-data.

42. Li, Long, "When Will the Time be Ripe to Raise Air Pollution Standards?" *Guangzhou Daily*, November 3, 2011, http://news.ifeng.com/opinion/politics/detail_2011_11/03/10381328_0.shtml.

43. "China's Environmental Mass Incidents Average 29% Growth Per Year, Less Than 1% of Cases Resolved Through Administrative Means," *Caijing,* October 27, 2012, http://politics.caijing.com.cn/2012-10-27/112233970.html.

44. Tao, Anthony, "Information Emerges About Yesterday's Shifang Protest," Beijing Cream, July 3, 2012, http://beijingcream.com/2012/07/information-emerges-about-yesterdays-shifang-protest-plus-videos/.

45. Han, Han, "The Liberation of Shifang," translation by *China Digital Times*, July 3, 2012, http://chinadigitaltimes.net/2012/07/han-han-the-release-shifang/.

46. Jacobs, Andrew, "Protests Against Expansion of China Chemical Plant Turn Violent," *New York Times,* October 27, 2012, www.nytimes.com/2012/10/28/world/asia/protests-against-expansion-of-china-chemical-plant-turn-violent.html?_r=0

47. Lu, Rachel, "NIMBY Protest Watch: Tear Gas Used in Ningbo," *Tea Leaf Nation*, October 27, 2012, http://tealeafnation.com/2012/10/nimby-protest-watch-tear-gas-used-in-ningbo/.

48. "Weibo Blocks Photo Uploading in Ningbo," *China Digital Times*, October 27, 2012, http://chinadigitaltimes.net/2012/10/weibo-blocks-photo-uploading-in-ningbo/

49. Yandle, Bruce, Vijayaraghavan, Maya, and Battarai, Madhusudan, "The Environmental Kuznets Curve: A Primer," PERC Research Study 02-1, May 2002; also see Stern, David I., "The Environmental Kuznets Curve," International Society for Ecological Economics, June 2003.

50. Magistad, Mary Kay, "How Weibo is Changing China," *Yale-Global* Online, August 9, 2012, http://yaleglobal.yale.edu/content/how-weibo-changing-china.

51. "Michael Anti: Behind the Great Firewall of China," TEDGlobal, June 2012, www.ted.com/talks/michael_anti_behind_the_great_firewall_of_china.html.

52. Mckenzie, Hamish, "The *New Yorker*'s Evan Osnos on How Sina Weibo Changes Lives in China," interview in *Pando Daily*, July 16, 2012, http://pandodaily.com/2012/07/16/the-new-yorkers-evan-osnos-on-how-sina-weibo-changes-lives-in-china/.

Conclusion

1. Chang, Gordon, *The Coming Collapse of China*, Random House, 2001.

2. Liu, Melinda, "Inside China's High-Speed Rail Triumph," *The Daily Beast,* January 5, 2013, www.thedailybeast.com/articles/2013/01/05/inside-china-s-high-speed-rail-triumph.html.

3. "Returning Home After Four Years, a Migrant Family Bites the Bullet and Takes the Bullet Train for the Children," *QQ News*, January 22, 2013, http://news.qq.com/a/20130122/000323.htm#p=1.

4. "Quick Take on the 18th Party Congress: Returning to the Rigid and Closed Old Path or Walking Down the Path of Crooked Ideology are Both Dead Ends," *People's Daily*, November 8, 2012, http://opinion.people.com.cn/n/2012/1108/c1003-19527410.html.

5. Acemoglu, Daron, and Robinson, James, *Why Nations Fail: The Origins of Power, Prosperity, and Poverty,* Crown Business, 2012.

6. Garnaut, John, "China Plans Revolution to Head Off Fiscal Crisis," *The Age,* May 13, 2013, http://www.theage.com.au/business/china/china-plans-revolution-to-head-off-fiscal-crisis-20130512-2jg5n.html?utm.

7. "Li Keqiang Reportedly Insisted on Making PM2.5 Data Transparent: Maintaining Opacity is Lying to Ourselves," *Caijing,* January 21, 2013, http://politics.caijing.com.cn/2013-01-21/112448566.html.

8. US Geological Service Mineral Commodity Summaries for Aluminum and Cement, http://minerals.er.usgs.gov/minerals/pubs/commodity/aluminum/mcs-2013-alumi.pdf and http://minerals.usgs.gov/minerals/pubs/commodity/cement/mcs-2012-cemen.pdf; also see World Steel Association 2012 Statistical Release, www.worldsteel.org/media-centre/press-releases/2012/12-2012-crude-steel.html.

9. Shaolong, Shi, "Grain Imports Not Excessive, but Caution Needed Over Side Effects," *Global Times,* February 7, 2013, www.globaltimes.cn/content/760817.shtml.

10. Wines, Michael, "China's Censors Misfire in Abuse-of-Power Case," *New York Times,* November 17, 2010, www.nytimes.com/2010/11/18/world/asia/18li.html?pagewanted=all&_r=0.

11. "NBS: China's Gini Coefficient Drops for Fourth Consecutive Year to 0.474 in 2012," *Caijing,* January 18, 2013, http://english.caijing.com.cn/2013-01-18/112445259.html.

12. "Li Keqiang Proposes for First Time of Assessing Performance Based on Transforming Government's Function," *Caijing,* January 25, 2013, http://politics.caijing.com.cn/2013-01-25/112463759.html.

13. Davison, Nicola, "River of Blood: The Dead Pigs Rotting in China's Water Supply," *The Guardian,* March 29, 2013, http://www.guardian.co.uk/world/2013/mar/29/dead-pigs-china-water-supply.

14. Liu, Shengjun, "The Chinese Dream," *Caixin,* January 31, 2013, http://english.caixin.com/2013-01-31/100488402.html.

15. Li, Eric X., "The Life of the Party," www.foreignaffairs.com/articles/138476/eric-x-li/the-life-of-the-party; also see Huang, Yasheng, "Democratize or Die," www.foreignaffairs.com/articles/138477/yasheng-huang/democratize-or-die, *Foreign Affairs,* January/February 2013.

16. Fewsmith, Joseph, "De Tocqueville in Beijing," *China Leadership Monitor,* 2012 No. 39, www.hoover.org/publications/china-leadership-monitor/article/129501.

Index

Guangdong model, 224
Guangdong Province,
  happiness, 224
gutter oil, 69

H

Han Chinese, riots, 252-253
Han dynasty, Confucianism, 200
Han Han, 258
Hanban, 205
happiness, 215-219
  Guangdong Province, 224
  prioritizing with economic
    progress, 223
Harbin (Heilongjiang Province),
  237-239
hard capital, 213
harmonious society, 242
Harmonious Society campaign, 201
Harmony Express, 256
He Daxing, 121
healthcare, 102-103, 275
  communes, 104
  demand for, 110-111
  diabetes, 121
  doctors, 109, 111
  drugs, 108-109
  hospital violence, 101-102
  hospitals, 108-109
  household responsibility
    system, 105
  obesity, 121
  public perception of, 115
  reforming, 112-117
  rural China, 104, 116
  scalping, 110-111
  spending, 106-108
    since reform, 113
  urban China, 104
hexie, 309
high inflation, 20
high schools, 138-139

higher education, 90-91
high-speed rail (HSR), 255-260, 268
  7.23 incident, 257-260
  crashes, 257-260
  Harmony Express, 256
  Liu Zhijun, 256-258
history, beginning of a young
  nation-state, 182-185
home ownership, urban middle
  class, 156-157
hospital incidents, 111, 116
hospital violence, 101-102, 116
hospitals, 108-109
  drugs, 108-109
house slave (fangu), 169
household registration system, 81
household responsibility system, 30,
  54, 105
housing, 151-153. *See also* real
estate
  affordable housing
    future of, 167-169
    marriage, 162
  down payments, 162
  empty units, 171
  jobs, 157-159
  marriage, 162-165
  monetary policy, 169-170
  overview, 173-175
  Panda Boom, 153-156
  privatization of, 154-155
  property taxes, 170-172
  social scarcity, 8
  subsidies, 154
    parents' role in, 164
HSR. *See* high-speed rail (HSR)
Hu doctrine, 195-198
  Confucianism, 205
  harmonious society, 242
Hu Jintao, 69, 193, 195-198
  final report, 270
  green GDP, 243
  Panda Boom, 243